Response to Intervention

RTI and CSI

Continuous School Improvement

USING DATA, VISION, AND LEADERSHIP
TO DESIGN, IMPLEMENT, AND EVALUATE
A SCHOOLWIDE PREVENTION SYSTEM

BY

VICTORIA L. BERNHARDT, Ph.D.
AND CONNIE L. HÉBERT, M.S.

EYE ON EDUCATION
6 Depot Way West
Larchmont, NY 10538
(914) 833-0551
(914) 833-0761 Fax
www.eyeoneducation.com

Library of Congress Cataloging–in–Publication Data

Bernhardt, Victoria L.
    Response to intervention (RtI) and continuous school improvement (CSI):
using data, vision, and leadership to design, implement, and evaluate a schoolwide
prevention system / by Victoria L. Bernhardt and Connie L. Hébert.
        p. cm.
Includes bibliographical references and index.
    ISBN 978-1-59667-174-4
    1. Continuous school improvement--United States. 2. Learning disabilities--United
States--Diagnosis. 3. Inclusive education--United States--Handbooks, manuals, etc.
I. Hébert, Connie L. II. Title.
    LB1029.R4B47 2010
    371.2'070973--dc22
                                2010041785

10 9 8 7 6 5 4 3

ALSO AVAILABLE FROM EYE ON EDUCATION

DATA, DATA EVERYWHERE
Bringing All the Data Together for Continuous School Improvement
Victoria L. Bernhardt

FROM QUESTIONS TO ACTIONS
Using Questionnaire Data For Continuous School Improvement
Victoria L. Bernhardt and Bradley J. Geise

TRANSLATING DATA INTO INFORMATION TO IMPROVE TEACHING AND LEARNING
Victoria L. Bernhardt

USING DATA TO IMPROVE STUDENT LEARNING IN SCHOOL DISTRICTS
(With CD-Rom)
Victoria L. Bernhardt

USING DATA TO IMPROVE STUDENT LEARNING IN HIGH SCHOOLS
(With CD-Rom)
Victoria L. Bernhardt

USING DATA TO IMPROVE STUDENT LEARNING IN MIDDLE SCHOOLS
(With CD-Rom)
Victoria L. Bernhardt

USING DATA TO IMPROVE STUDENT LEARNING IN ELEMENTARY SCHOOLS
(With CD-Rom)
Victoria L. Bernhardt

DATA ANALYSIS FOR CONTINUOUS SCHOOL IMPROVEMENT
Second Edition
Victoria L. Bernhardt

THE SCHOOL PORTFOLIO TOOLKIT
A Planning, Implementation, and Evaluation Guide for
Continuous School Improvement (With CD-Rom)
Victoria L. Bernhardt

THE SCHOOL PORTFOLIO
A Comprehensive Framework for School Improvement, Second Edition
Victoria L. Bernhardt

ACKNOWLEDGEMENTS

If we are truly judged by the company we keep, we are two extremely lucky individuals. We are honored to know so many wonderful people who are willing to assist us in creating a product that will help schools better meet the learning needs of their students, and of which we are proud.

We are indebted to the many colleagues, friends, and family who encouraged us along the way by reading the manuscript and offering extremely helpful comments. We are grateful for the continuous support and editing from Joy Rose. Although her official school days ended several years ago, her desire and passion to contribute to education has never ended. Even when she was traveling in another country, there was not a day in the last year or so that we did not get a response to a request we had for her. Thank you so very much, Joy, for all you do for us, every day. And thank you Aurora Ahson, Kerry Barger, Sharon Draggoo, Robert Geise, Bradley Geise, Steve Johnson, Jeff Keller, Glen Kusko, Marfel Kusko, Susan Porter, Lori Rice, and Patsy Schutz (California); Phyllis Unebasmi (Hawaii); Louise Stearns (Illinois); Kathy Miller (Michigan); Cindy Presnell and Carol Reimann (Missouri); Joe Petrosino (New Jersey); and Sowmya Kumar and Michael Webb (Texas) for reviewing an extremely rough draft of the book early on. You gave us the information and motivation we needed to keep going. A speical thank you to Kathy Miller and Susan Porter, who read at least one more version of the book later on, and gave us the courage to call it done, with suggested improvements. We wish we could express how much all of you help keep us going.

A special thank you to Dr. Donald Deshler, University of Kansas, and the National Center for RtI, for the review of the RtI Continuums when we needed it most.

We thank, with all our hearts, the Marylin Avenue Elementary School staff in Livermore, California, who willingly shared their data and experiences to enable us to write a book that is based in reality and offers teaching and learning suggestions with integrity and fidelity. Thank you, Marylin Avenue Staff.

Jeff Keller, Principal	Sue Carling	Anna MacIntire
Lori Rice, Secretary	Sharon Draggoo	Therese Maldonado
Teachers:	Erin Eddy	Lori Olsen
Sharon Abri	Gretchen Fajardo	Wendy Otvos
Auora Ahsan	Erika Johnston	Christina Pomykal
Debbie Anderson	Gina Juarez	Anne Rosendin
Kimberly Anderson	Amy Kass	Allison Rossen
Jan Achtold	Noah King	Laura Schuler
Kerry Barger	Eric Kishi	Karen Woodward
Casie Benjamin	Marfel Kusko	Diana Wooten
Pat Bieler	Michael Levy	Debbie Zimmerman
Candice Bolar	Donielle Machi	

We are very thankful to the *Education for the Future* staff—Lynn Swaim, Brad Geise, Patsy Schutz, Sally Withuhn, and Jessica Jackson—who offer encouragement and support for all that we do, all year long. These are some of the folk who keep the work going, while we balance our real jobs with study, research, and writing.

Lynn Swaim did a phenomenal job keeping the drafts and many, many edits of this book ordered and converted into a lovely layout. Lynn's work makes it easy for the authors to keep going while working full time on other projects. We could not have done this book in the timeframe we had without Lynn.

Brad Geise, Brian Curtis, and the staff at MC^2 did a wonderful job on the cover.

A huge thanks to our publisher, affectionately known as *Cousin Bob,* Mr. Robert Sickles, and his staff, for assisting us in getting the product quickly through the production line. We are grateful for all you do to support the creation and marketing of all *Education for the Future* books.

Special Thanks from Vickie:

Special thank you to my husband, Jim Richmond, for not only reading (parts of) the manuscript and giving us ideas to make it better, but for putting up with the ongoing writing process by letting me off the hook from indoor work and outdoor chores in the forest.

A huge thank you to Connie L. Hébert for her knowledge of the subject area, passion to help schools, patience, gentle persistence, and good humor. Connie amazes me with all she can get done in her life in a week's time.

Special Thanks from Connie:

I give thanks for the blessings of a supportive family. To my husband, Joel and two children, Calvin and Aléthia, for the countless hours of adjustment to not having mom around, allowing me the opportunity to travel and do the work this book required, and especially for the unending support in pursuing my own business and maintaining my career; permitting the use of personal stories that illustrate so well the journey of becoming educated in our public schools; and finally, letting me block out chunks of time for uninterrupted writing.

A final thank you to Dr. Victoria Bernhardt who had the vision for this book, the experience, knowledge, and skills to make it happen; and the perseverance and energy to keep us both going, overcoming unforeseen obstacles to completing the book within our timeline.

And thank you, readers and educators, for your interest, hard work, and skills in providing an education for students that will help them become whatever they want to become in the future.

Vickie Bernhardt and Connie Hébert

ABOUT THE AUTHORS

VICTORIA L. BERNHARDT

Victoria L. Bernhardt, Ph.D., is Executive Director of the *Education for the Future Initiative*, a not-for-profit organization in Chico, California, whose mission is to build the capacity of all learning organizations at all levels to gather, analyze, and use data to continuously improve learning for all students. She is also a Professor (currently on leave) in the College of Communication and Education, at California State University, Chico. Dr. Bernhardt is the author, or co-author, of the following books:

♦ *From Questions to Actions: Using Questionnaire Data for Continuous School Improvement* (2009), with Bradley J. Geise.

♦ *Data, Data Everywhere: Bringing All the Data Together for Continuous School Improvement* (2009).

♦ *Translating Data into Information to Improve Teaching and Learning* (2007).

♦ A four-book collection of using data to improve student learning—*Using Data to Improve Student Learning in Elementary Schools (2003); Using Data to Improve Student Learning in Middle Schools (2004); Using Data to Improve Student Learning in High Schools (2005);* and *Using Data to Improve Student Learning across School Districts (2006).*

♦ *Data Analysis for Comprehensive Schoolwide Improvement* (First Edition, 1998; Second Edition, 2004).

♦ *The School Portfolio Toolkit: A Planning, Implementation, and Evaluation Guide for Continuous School Improvement,* and CD-Rom (2002).

♦ *The School Portfolio: A Comprehensive Framework for School Improvement* (First Edition, 1994; Second Edition, 1999).

Dr. Bernhardt is passionate about her mission of helping all educators continuously improve student learning in their classrooms, their schools, their districts, and states by gathering, analyzing, and using actual data—as opposed to using hunches and "gut-level" feelings. She has made numerous presentations at professional conferences and conducts workshops on the school portfolio, data analysis, data warehousing, and school improvement at local, state, regional, national, and international levels.

Dr. Bernhardt can be reached at:

Victoria L. Bernhardt, Ph.D.
Executive Director
Education for the Future Initiative
400 West First Street, Chico, CA 95929-0230
Tel: 530-898-4482 ~ Fax: 530-898-4484
e-mail: vbernhardt@csuchico.edu
website: *http://eff.csuchico.edu*

CONNIE L. HÉBERT

Connie L. Hébert, M.S. Ed., is the Director of the Southeast Missouri State University Autism Center for Diagnosis and Treatment. Connie has years of experience supporting individuals with Autism Spectrum Disorders across the lifespan through professional development and consultation provided for a variety of public and private educators and service providers, as well as support and training for families and community members. She has a diverse background regarding various methodologies and approaches used to address the needs of individuals with Autism, particularly those used in educational settings.

An experienced educator and consultant in the field of special education, Connie also works as an independent consultant from her personal business, *here2help, LLC,* to provide services to school districts in many areas, including the development of Response to Intervention systems.

Her experience includes special education teacher for students with cognitive disabilities, learning disabilities, emotional disturbance, autism, and multiple disabilities. Connie served as a classroom consultant in Central Pennsylvania providing supports to teachers for behavior assessment and intervention, and implementing strategies for working with students with Autism Spectrum Disorders.

Following relocation to Southeast Missouri, Connie became a systems-level Special Education Improvement Consultant in the southeast region of Missouri. In 2005, she was named Missouri Staff Developer of the Year. In March 2009, Connie was appointed to one of the two seats designated for Higher Education on the Missouri Governor's Commission on Autism Spectrum Disorders.

Connie believes her career has been blessed with opportunity to learn about effective supports and systems level data analysis from skilled experts in the field and national speakers and consultants, including Dr. Bernhardt. She has worked with systems level data analysis for continuous improvement since 2003, including working as an Associate with *Education for the Future* at the annual Summer Data Analysis and School Improvement Institutes. Schools that work with Connie find her approach to be student focused while remaining sensitive to the responsibilities of teaching in today's classroom. She is enthusiastic about supporting schools in the use of proven practices for meeting the expectations of federal and state legislation or other mandates as they relate to school improvement.

Connie can be reached at:

Connie L. Hébert
Independent Consultant
here2help, LLC
Cape Girardeau, MO
Tel: 573-450-6997
e-mail: connie.here2help@gmail.com

CONTENTS

PREFACE

The focus of these two authors' work is to improve teaching and learning for teachers and all students. In this book, *Response to Intervention (RTI) and Continuous School Improvement (CSI): Using Data, Vision, and Leadership to Design, Implement, and Evaluate a Schoolwide Prevention System,* we share what we have learned about getting all staff working together to create, implement, and evaluate a schoolwide prevention system by committing to a vision that will allow staff to restructure the school day—using comprehensive data analysis and leadership structures to guide their efforts. A real example is shown, and a framework for schools to use is provided.

Interacting with teachers and other school leaders attempting to continuously improve schoolwide and to implement *Response to Intervention* (RtI) systems is a weekly, if not daily, occurrence. Victoria works with schools and school districts around the country to establish comprehensive data analysis and continuous school improvement structures; Connie works with schools and school districts, in multiple states, to assist them with their RtI and school improvement needs.

As we work with schools on continuous improvement, we watch staffs struggle with creating structures to implement the concepts of RtI. In worse case scenarios, we listen as staffs discuss accepting a current structure they think might "meet the requirement," adding an After-School Program "to solve that requirement issue"; and we hear some teachers bemoan the fact that incorporating research-based strategies that would support a quality RtI system, as well as support their students' learning needs, "is just not possible to do in the structure of our day." It seems like a dream to many of these teachers to think that the entire staff would and could collaborate to study and implement the same effective principles.

Victoria and Connie help school staffs work through these issues and improve what they are doing for each student, in every classroom, throughout the school and school district, by starting with a solid continuous school improvement model that features the ongoing use of data and a shared vision.

The authors invite all educators to join in these efforts to improve instruction for all students.

Sincerely,

Victoria L. Bernhardt, Ph.D.
Executive Director
Education for the Future Initiative
400 West First Street, Chico, CA 95929-0230
Tel: 530-898-4482 ~ Fax: 530-898-4484
e-mail: vbernhardt@csuchico.edu
website: *http://eff.csuchico.edu*

Connie L. Hébert
Independent Consultant
here2help, LLC
Cape Girardeau, MO
Tel: 573-450-6997
e-mail: connie.here2help@gmail.com

Chapter 1

RtI AND CSI: RESPONSE TO INTERVENTION AND CONTINUOUS SCHOOL IMPROVEMENT

Until you get continuous school improvement right,
you cannot get RtI right. If you do continuous
school improvement right, you will have a good
start toward an effective RtI system.
If you do RtI right, you will be engaged in a
continuous school improvement process.

Victoria L. Bernhardt and Connie L. Hébert

Attend any school staff meeting in the United States these days and you are likely to hear the topic *Response to Intervention* (RtI) being discussed. RtI refers to a comprehensive and deliberate multi-level instruction and assessment system designed by schools to address the learning needs of *all* students. RtI encourages early intervention to prevent student failure and to ensure academic success and positive behavior, while reducing the likelihood that students are wrongly identified for special education services. RtI is defined by the National Center on Response to Intervention as follows:

> *Response to intervention integrates assessment and intervention within a multi-level prevention system to maximize student achievement and to reduce behavioral problems. With RtI, schools use data to identify students at risk for poor learning outcomes, monitor student progress, provide evidence-based interventions and adjust the intensity and nature of those interventions depending on a student's responsiveness, and identify students with learning disabilities or other disabilities. (www.rti4success.org)*

Significant redesign of general education and special education is required for a school or school district to implement RtI and to improve the learning of "all" students. Adding a program or intervention, here or there, will not provide the improvement which schools desire or require to meet the learning needs of "all" students.

Significant redesign of general education and special education is required for a school or school district to implement RtI and to improve the learning of *all* students. Adding a program or intervention, here or there, will not provide the improvement which schools desire or require to meet the learning needs of *all* students.

Continuous School Improvement (CSI) is the process of improving an organization on an ongoing basis. CSI involves—

♦ using data to understand where the school is now,

♦ clarifying where the school wants to go,

♦ understanding how the school is getting its current results,

♦ determining how the school will get to where it wants to go,

♦ implementing the processes to take the school where it wants to go,

♦ evaluating the parts and the whole, on an ongoing basis, to know if the parts are effective and aligned to where the school wants to go, and

♦ improving the parts and the whole on an ongoing basis.

RtI requires a paradigm shift for all staff members that CSI can provide.

As a method for schools to rethink regular and special education and to avoid piece-meal change, CSI processes facilitate the design, implementation, and evaluation of Response to Intervention systems.

School staffs that start RtI at the whole school level using a CSI framework understand what their students know and do not know, and make agreements and commitments to get all students on grade level, with direct, intense intervention, even when that means moving some students more than one grade level in one year.

School staffs that start RtI at the whole school level using a CSI framework understand what their students know and do not know, and make agreements and commitments to get all students on grade level, with direct, intense intervention, even when that means moving some students more than one grade level in one year. When schools establish RtI systems through CSI processes, staffs get the system and commitments in place before specific strategies.

Schools that start RtI at the individual student level assess the students and then think about interventions, sometimes coming to dead ends when they realize they cannot possibly do all the interventions they deem necessary.

PURPOSES OF THIS BOOK

The purposes of *Response to Intervention (RtI) and Continuous School Improvement (CSI): Using Data, Vision, and Leadership to Design, Implement, and Evaluate a Schoolwide Prevention System*, also known as *RtI and CSI*, are fourfold. These purposes are to:

When schools establish RtI systems through CSI processes, staffs get the system and commitments in place before specific strategies.

1. Describe a CSI framework that will allow the schoolwide redesign of regular and special education to implement a schoolwide prevention system.

2. Explain how to design, implement, and evaluate CSI and RtI systems.

3. Share a case study illustrating how one school used a CSI framework to establish its RtI system. The case study is included so schools can see what an RtI system looks like, and to provide a model to guide their work. (This is a real school with *real* results—not *perfect* results.)

4. Provide tools to get schools started on designing, implementing, and evaluating their CSI and RtI systems.

INTENDED AUDIENCE

The intended audiences for this book are:

1. School and school district administrators and teachers working to integrate general education and special education to continuously improve their learning organizations and implement robust RtI systems.

2. College professors and students learning about CSI and RtI implementation in schools.

3. School staff book study groups. This book can help staffs start, troubleshoot, and evaluate their own efforts for CSI and RtI implementation.

4. District administrator book study groups. This book can help district administrators think about CSI and RtI implementation from the perspective of the schools, and help them create a framework in which all their schools can thrive.

5. Leadership training programs that are teaching about the impact strong leadership has on the implementation of CSI and RtI in schools.

Intended audiences for this book are:
- *School and school district administrators and teachers*
- *College professors and students*
- *School staff book study groups*
- *District administrator book study groups*
- *Leadership training programs*

STRUCTURE OF THIS BOOK

RtI and CSI is a guidebook for using Continuous School Improvement to develop a Response to Intervention system that will ensure student success.

Chapter 2 reviews the concept and intent of ***Response to Intervention (RtI)*** and addresses the common components in implementing a comprehensive, responsive, evidence and research-based instruction and assessment system. This chapter shows why CSI is necessary for the creation of an RtI system.

Chapter 3, the concept and intent of ***Continuous School Improvement (CSI),*** provides a framework for reviewing where the school is now, for creating and implementing a shared vision, and for measuring the impact the vision and implementation strategies have on student achievement. A solid CSI foundation is the logical way to redesign general and special education to improve the learning of all students.

Chapter 4, ***From Reactive to Proactive,*** provides RtI Continuums that illustrate how critical elements of the school system evolve when schools move from loosely-connected general education and special education systems to integrated, data-informed, collaborative multi-level prevention systems. Schools can determine where they are right now on the continuums, as well as establish what they need to do to move toward an effective RtI system that is implemented with integrity and fidelity.

Chapter 5, ***Designing and Implementing an RtI system with Continuous School Improvement: The CSI Part,*** describes how to use the CSI framework to establish staff readiness for creating the specifics of an RtI system. The data and details of an actual school that has done this work are shown as an example.

Chapter 6, ***Designing and Implementing an RtI system with Continuous School Improvement: The RtI Part,*** describes the elements that must be a part of any RtI system. Our example demonstrates what it looks like when the specifics of a schoolwide RtI system are implemented in a continuously improving school.

Chapter 7, ***Evaluating CSI and RtI,*** provides suggestions for using data to evaluate CSI and RtI to know if your processes and interventions are making the differences you want to see in every classroom, in every grade level, and in every subject area. An evaluation of our example school's first year RtI implementation in English Language Arts is shown.

Chapter 8, ***Summary and Conclusions,*** pulls together concepts from the seven previous chapters to provide guidance and logical considerations for getting started with designing, implementing, and evaluating an RtI system, using continuous school improvement. In addition, intended and unintended changes in the school that might result with CSI and RtI implementation are discussed.

Example School

In our experiences working with schools, we have found that school staffs do a better job of implementing new concepts when they have comprehensive examples and activities to follow. We use a real example and provide activities in the appendices to guide your school's work with these concepts.

Marylin Avenue Elementary School in Livermore, California, started with a solid CSI framework and ensured that every teacher understood what and how she/he would teach each essential standard, and what each teacher would do when students were not proficient. We use this school because we have a complete example, with longitudinal data, that shows how Marylin Avenue used the CSI framework to evaluate and improve its RtI system along the way, and shows how the teaching and support staff knew if what they were doing was making a difference and why. The example includes Marylin Avenue's first year of implementing RtI that ended with mixed results. A summary of the evaluation of the system, shown in Chapter 7, analyzes these results, which helps us all learn more about implementing CSI and RtI. Even though the example is an elementary school, the concepts can also be used at the middle school, high school, and school district levels. It is the CSI plan that generates RtI, not the school level.

Appendices

The appendices include the following:

Appendix A: *The Education for the Future Continuous Improvement Continuums Activity* provides the instructions for recommended use of the *Education for the Future School Continuous Improvement Continuums*, a self-assessment tool for staffs to use to understand where their schools are with respect to CSI. A full set of school and school district continuums are included.

Appendix B: *Marylin Avenue Data Profile* has two purposes: 1) to show what it looks like when a school does a comprehensive job of presenting its schoolwide data, and 2) to provide a model for schools to use to create their own data profile. A subset of Marilyn Avenue's actual data is shown.

Appendix C: *What we saw in the Marylin Avenue Data Profile* makes available a summary of what the authors and Marylin Avenue staff saw in their data. This appendix illustrates how we would like schools to analyze their comprehensive data.

Appendix D: *Analyzing Data for Continuous School Improvement Planning Activity* provides the "process protocol" or facilitation guide for engaging staff in the analysis of multiple measures of data.

Appendix E: *Creating a Shared Vision Activity* is a guide for facilitating the creation of a shared vision, including the handouts to use with staff.

Appendix F: *Problem-Solving Cycle Activity* shows how to get all staff involved in thinking through a "problem" with data, before determining a solution.

Appendix G: *Developing a Continuous School Improvement Plan Activity* provides the steps in creating a CSI plan with staff.

Appendix H: *Evaluating a Program or Process Activity* provides an outline for evaluating the impact of school programs and processes.

Appendix I: *Flowcharting School Processes Activity* shows how to create flowcharts to support the implementation, evaluation, and improvement of school processes.

Written in a conversational style, *RtI and CSI* is firmly based on research and practice. The **References and Resources** section lists some of the many references and resources used to write this book. The authors strongly recommend them for deeper reading.

Study Questions at the end of each chapter are designed to engage individuals in the content of the chapter and to promote conversations about chapter content that will lead to the application of new ideas throughout the school. Team study questions are intended to encourage action and guide the conversations of Professional Learning Communities, design teams, learning teams, leadership teams, and/or entire school staffs to implement these concepts. This book can be read twice: once to study the concepts and get an overview, and the second time to set up your CSI plan and RtI system.

BOOK STUDY QUESTIONS

♦ Will you read this book for the example and opportunity to compare your school's RtI system to that of another school, or will you read this book to begin creating, implementing, and evaluating an RtI system as a part of your CSI efforts?

TEAM STUDY QUESTIONS

♦ Does your school currently have a Response to Intervention system in place?

♦ As you begin this journey, think about what your school does to help students who are not proficient. What does your school do to accelerate students who are proficient? How successful are these efforts? How do you measure the success of these efforts?

Chapter 2

RESPONSE TO INTERVENTION (RtI)

The purpose of RtI is not to prevent special education. Rather, its twin aims are to prevent serious, long-term negative consequences associated with exiting school without adequate academic competence and to identify children with disabilities. So, RtI is very ambitious in intent and scope. Doing RtI right is not for the faint of heart. It will require commitment, energy, teamwork, and smarts. But the potential payoff of doing it right is large.

Dr. Doug Fuchs and Dr. Lynn Fuchs
(Responsiveness to Intervention, 2009)

The framework for RtI includes a multi-level prevention system designed to address the learning needs of *all* students with intervention provided as *each* student demonstrates a need. RtI seeks to prevent school failure through coherent, evidence-based instruction for all students and frequent on-going assessment and progress monitoring to inform instruction. Increasingly intensive levels of evidence-based interventions are provided for students who demonstrate they are at risk for poor learning outcomes. Students who do not show a response to intensive interventions may be in need of special education.

RtI includes a multi-level prevention system designed to address the learning needs of all students with intervention provided as each student demonstrates a need.

RtI is a system for—

♦ Screening all students using valid, reliable, accurate measures to determine who may be at risk for poor learning outcomes.

♦ Providing multiple levels of evidence-based instruction and intervention to meet the specific needs of students.

RtI is a system for—

♦ Screening all students using valid, reliable, accurate measures to determine who may be at risk for poor learning outcomes.

♦ Providing multiple levels of evidence-based instruction and intervention to meet the specific needs of students.

♦ Progress monitoring within each intervention level to assist in determining the effectiveness of instruction and interventions.

♦ Analyzing and utilizing data from multiple sources to inform decisions for designing systems of instruction and support.

♦ Progress monitoring within each intervention level to assist in determining the effectiveness of instruction and interventions.

♦ Analyzing and utilizing data from multiple sources to inform decisions for designing systems of instruction and support.

Figure 2.1 is the National Center on Response to Intervention's representation of these components that reflects the interrelated, dynamic nature of the essential elements—*all* centered on data-informed decisions for improved student outcomes and reflecting culturally sensitive and evidence-based practices. (Retrieved from *www.rti4success.org,* September 23, 2010.)

Figure 2.1
THE SYSTEM OF RESPONSIVE INTERVENTIONS

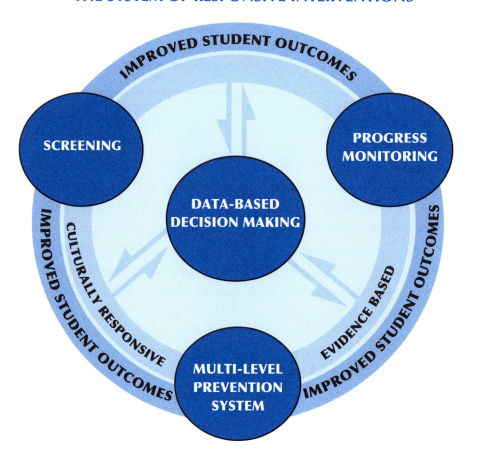

Conceptually, the structure for RtI has been around for some time and is being implemented in many places very effectively. Schools engaged in CSI efforts have in place many structures and processes that support implementation of these components, including multiple levels of support and assessments that inform instruction, and the analysis and utilization of data from multiple sources to inform decisions. For these schools, the work involves creating the connections among special education eligibility determinations and documenting the activities that demonstrate Response to Intervention for *each* student while maintaining a multi-level system of supports for *all* students.

Figure 2.2 illustrates the multi-level prevention system associated with RtI as a three-level triangle or pyramid graphic. The pyramid graphic shows dotted lines with the secondary and tertiary preventions being nested inside the primary prevention pyramid because all students are always a part of primary level instruction.

(*Note:* The term *tier* is often used in schools; however, the National Center on Response to Intervention uses the term *level* to avoid any misconceptions that students are literally moved someplace else—such as pulled out of the classroom.)

Figure 2.2
MULTI-LEVEL PREVENTION SYSTEM

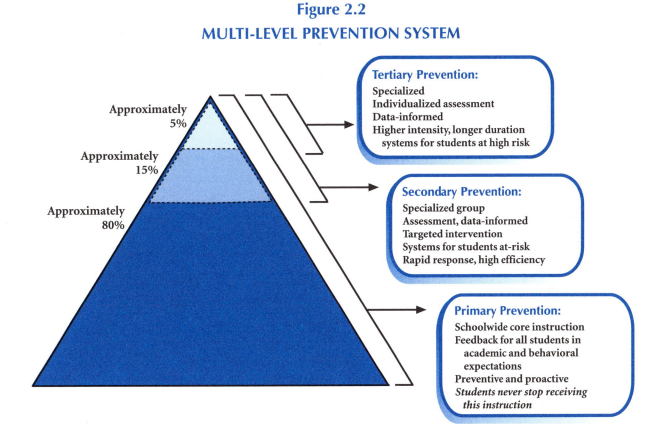

When teachers provide well-articulated, standards-based, aligned curriculum that is delivered with evidence-based, differentiated, and targeted instruction to match the characteristics of the learners, the needs of approximately 80% of students will be met at the primary level.

The theory that underlies the three-level RtI structure is this: When teachers provide well-articulated, standards-based, aligned curriculum that is delivered with evidence-based, differentiated, and targeted instruction to match the characteristics of the learners, the needs of approximately 80% of students will be met at the *primary* level.

Once *primary* level strategies are in place and delivered with *integrity* and *fidelity* (i.e., completely implemented as they were designed) within and among grade levels, staff can identify students for whom this is not enough. When the *primary* level is effective, 20% or fewer students should need *secondary* level interventions.

Students who need *secondary* level interventions are provided with supports targeted to specific areas in which they demonstrate a risk for failure. The *secondary* intervention level builds on primary instruction and is mostly delivered in small groups within the general education classroom by the classroom teacher with support from resource or instructional specialists.

The secondary intervention level builds on primary instruction and is mostly delivered in small groups within the general education classroom by the classroom teacher with support from resource or instructional specialists.

For students who demonstrate significant risk of failure or students who do not make sufficient progress with instruction and support provided at the *primary* and *secondary* levels, a *tertiary* level of intervention is provided that is more targeted and intensive. At the *tertiary* level, intensive, evidence-based interventions are provided to individual students or to very small groups, often delivered by a specialist or special education teacher. Typically, 5% or fewer of the student population require this level of intensive intervention.

When students demonstrate insufficient progress after receiving all levels of intensive intervention, the school can consider referral for evaluation of eligibility as a child with a disability.

At the tertiary level, intensive, evidence-based interventions are provided to individual students or to very small groups, often delivered by a specialist or special education teacher.

RtI structures at some schools have four or more levels. The more levels, the more complex the implementation is likely to become. What matters most are the types and intensities of interventions used within the levels. The interventions must become more focused and powerful, directly targeting the deficit area, and are informed by assessment data as students move up the levels.

RtI is not simply a set of interventions but a systematic model within general and special education of preventive and supplementary instructional services for students who are at risk for school failure.

CORE PRINCIPLES OF RtI

The National State Directors of Special Education and The Council of Administrators of Special Educators (2006) identify the core principles of RtI as follows:

♦ The educational system can effectively teach all children.

♦ Early intervention is critical to preventing problems from getting out of control.

♦ The implementation of a multi-level service delivery model is necessary.

♦ A problem solving model should be used to make decisions between levels.

♦ Research-based interventions should be implemented to the extent possible.

♦ Progress monitoring must be implemented to inform instruction.

♦ Data should drive decision making.

♦ Assessments are used in RtI for three different purposes: (1) screening applied to all children to identify those who are not making progress at expected rates; (2) diagnostics to determine what children can and cannot do in important academic and behavioral domains; and (3) progress monitoring to determine if academic or behavioral interventions are producing desired effects.

> ### Core Principles of RtI
>
> The National State Directors of Special Education and The Council of Administrators of Special Educators (2006) identify the core principles of RtI as follows:
>
> ♦ The educational system can effectively teach all children.
>
> ♦ Early intervention is critical to preventing problems from getting out of control.
>
> ♦ The implementation of a multi-level service delivery model is necessary.
>
> ♦ A problem-solving model should be used to make decisions between levels.
>
> ♦ Research-based interventions should be implemented to the extent possible.
>
> ♦ Progress monitoring must be implemented to inform instruction.
>
> ♦ Data should drive decision making.
>
> ♦ Assessments are used in RtI for three different purposes: (1) screening applied to all children to identify those who are not making progress at expected rates; (2) diagnostics to determine what children can and cannot do in important academic and behavioral domains; and (3) progress monitoring to determine if academic or behavioral interventions are producing desired effects.

THE INTENT OF RtI

The intent of RtI is to make our systems, our schools, and our classrooms more responsive to the demonstrated instructional needs of students, and to match those demonstrated needs with evidence-based, effective, instructional interventions to prevent failure.

Some staff view RtI as a way to delay special education identification—or as an obstacle to that inevitable outcome. The determination for eligibility and need of special education services too often becomes the focus for development and implementation of RtI systems. Helping staff understand RtI as a preventive system may help this focus move from an inaccurate belief of the way to get students into special education to a much more accurate belief of designing processes and supports to ensure successful performance for each student—the way we do business.

The intent of RtI is to make our systems, our schools, and our classrooms more responsive to the demonstrated instructional needs of students, and to match those demonstrated needs with evidence-based, effective, instructional intervention to prevent failure.

As a multi-level prevention system with assessments for screening and progress monitoring to inform instruction and intervention at each level, RtI serves the multiple purposes of support and prevention, as well as identification for special education services. It includes supports designed to address the learning needs of all students while being responsive to unique characteristics of learners with targeted interventions provided as *each* student demonstrates a need.

Through early detection of risk for poor academic or behavioral outcomes, students receive needed instruction or intensive intervention and, therefore, experience success without the need for special services.

Through early detection of risk for poor academic or behavioral outcomes, students receive needed instruction or intensive intervention and, therefore, experience success without the need for special services. When students do not respond sufficiently to this culturally sensitive, evidence-based instruction and intervention, they may be referred for determination of eligibility as a student with a specific learning disability or other disability.

THE COMPONENTS OF RtI

Many complex issues must be considered when designing and implementing an RtI system. Which assessments will be used for screening and progress monitoring, level and type of interventions, location and delivery of intervention sessions, frequency and duration of intervention sessions, and the difficulty of teaching multiple interventions are just a few of the logistics to consider.

In addition to designing and delivering research-based instruction and interventions at each level, schools must have—

RtI Components

Schools must have—

- *Screening* and *progress monitoring assessments* that are brief, reliable, valid, accurate predictors of risk, and sensitive to small amounts of growth.
- *Universal strategies* for achieving academic outcomes and meeting social/behavioral expectations.
- *Evidence-based interventions* at multiple levels and of varying type, number, length, duration, and intensities.
- *Cut points* or entry and exit criteria for movement between intervention levels.
- *Referral processes and documentation* necessary to support the evaluation of students who do not respond to interventions as expected.

- *Screening and progress monitoring assessments* that are brief, reliable, valid, accurate predictors of risk, and sensitive to small amounts of growth.
- *Universal strategies* for achieving academic outcomes and meeting social/behavioral expectations.
- *Evidence-based interventions* at multiple levels and of varying type, number, length, duration, and intensities.
- *Cut points* or entry and exit criteria for movement between intervention levels.
- *Referral processes and documentation* necessary to support the evaluation of students who do not respond to interventions as expected.

Districts that invest the time and energy to do RtI right find it extremely beneficial for student learning. Developing and sustaining such a preventive, supportive, and corrective system requires investment of energy and resources; but the power of creating such a system rejuvenates the passion that will increase energy and desire for staff to engage in these change efforts. There is a balance required between addressing the needs of *all* students through the primary level designed for this purpose and addressing the needs of *each* student through effective differentiated and targeted instruction, and intervention strategies at secondary and tertiary levels.

FIDELITY OF IMPLEMENTATION

In an RtI model, fidelity is important at both the school level (e.g., implementation of the system) and the teacher level (e.g., implementation of instruction). Although fidelity of implementation is critical to an intervention's successful outcome, the practical challenges associated with achieving high levels of fidelity are well documented. Factors that reduce fidelity of implementation include the following:

♦ *Complexity.* The more complex the intervention, the lower the fidelity because of the level of implementation difficulty. (This factor includes time needed for instruction in the intervention.)

♦ *Materials and resources required.* If new or substantial resources are required, they need to be readily accessible.

♦ *Perceived and actual effectiveness (credibility).* Even with a solid research base, if teachers believe the approach will not be effective, or if it is inconsistent with their teaching style, they will not implement it well.

♦ *Interventionists.* The number, expertise, and motivation of individuals who deliver the intervention are factors in the level of fidelity of implementation.

(Johnson, Mellard, Fuchs, and McKnight, 2006)

There is a balance required between addressing the needs of all students through the primary level designed for this purpose and addressing the needs of each student through effective differentiated and targeted instruction, and intervention strategies at secondary and tertiary levels.

Factors that reduce fidelity of implementation include the following:
♦ Complexity.
♦ Materials and resources required.
♦ Perceived and actual effectiveness (credibility).
♦ Interventionists.

THE RELATIONSHIP OF RtI TO SPECIAL EDUCATION

RtI provides an alternative or additional means of gathering information to be used when classifying students for special education, but this is not the purpose or focus of the RtI system.

RtI provides an alternative or additional means of gathering information to be used when classifying students for special education, but this is not the purpose or focus of the RtI system. When a student is identified as having difficulties in school, a team provides interventions of increasing intensity to help the child catch up with the rest of her/his peers. After interventions have been tried and proven ineffective, the child may then be referred for additional special education services. Opponents of RtI say this is a way to allow some school districts to avoid or delay identifying students as needing special education. Proponents of RtI claim that RtI is a way to ensure each student is afforded the opportunity to learn. When interventions work, fewer children, particularly minority children, are referred for special education. The RtI model acts as a safeguard, insuring that a child is not given a label of a disability inappropriately.

The effort behind designing, implementing, and evaluating an RtI system that will lead to the large payoff is not easy to initiate and sustain. While educators in schools that experience this payoff report they would not go back to the way they did things before, many readily admit they are working harder (and smarter) than before. RtI can reinstate the passion that brought educators to the field to begin with—and with passion comes energy.

BOOK STUDY QUESTIONS

- What are the essential elements of an RtI system?
- What is the intent of RtI?
- What are the components of RtI?

TEAM STUDY QUESTIONS

- What is the intent of your school's RtI system?
- What are some common misperceptions about RtI at your school? Who holds these misperceptions or beliefs? How can you clarify the intent?
- Which components or features of RtI are working in your school? Which are not? Do you know what needs to be done to improve or establish these components?

Chapter 3

CONTINUOUS SCHOOL IMPROVEMENT (CSI)

---

*Continuously improving schools clarify whom they have
as students, understand where the learning organization is right
now on all measures, consider processes, as well as results,
create visions that will make a difference for whom they have
as students, help everyone get on the same page with
understanding how to achieve a vision, and know if what
the learning organization is doing is making a difference.*

Victoria L. Bernhardt

When staff design RtI systems consistent with continuous school improvement, they begin with—

♦ a comprehensive review of all their data to answer the question, *Where are we now?*

♦ the creation of a shared vision to answer the question, *Where do we want to be?*

♦ a study of contributing causes of undesirable results to answer the question, *How did we get to where we are now?*

♦ the development of structures required to get all staff implementing the vision to answer the question, *How are we going to get to where we want to be?* and

♦ formative and summative evaluation structures to answer the question, *Is what we are doing making a difference?*

By answering these key questions, staffs learn how to improve student learning in every grade level, in every subject area, and with every student group. By doing this work, staff is set up to redesign the school day, if necessary, in order to establish a multi-level prevention system. By doing this work, these staffs have also completed a comprehensive needs assessment and have set themselves up for comprehensive evaluation.

A CONTINUOUS SCHOOL IMPROVEMENT FRAMEWORK

Figure 3.1 displays a framework for continuous school improvement that can help schools design, implement, and evaluate their RtI systems. As the figure shows, for a school to create a learning organization that will make a difference for all students and all teachers, staffs must answer five essential and logical questions.

- Where are we now?
- Where do we want to be?
- How did we get to where we are?
- How are we going to get to where we want to be?
- Is what we are doing making a difference?

These questions are detailed on the pages that follow the figure, along with why it is important to consider the questions and their answers.

Figure 3.1
CONTINUOUS SCHOOL IMPROVEMENT FRAMEWORK

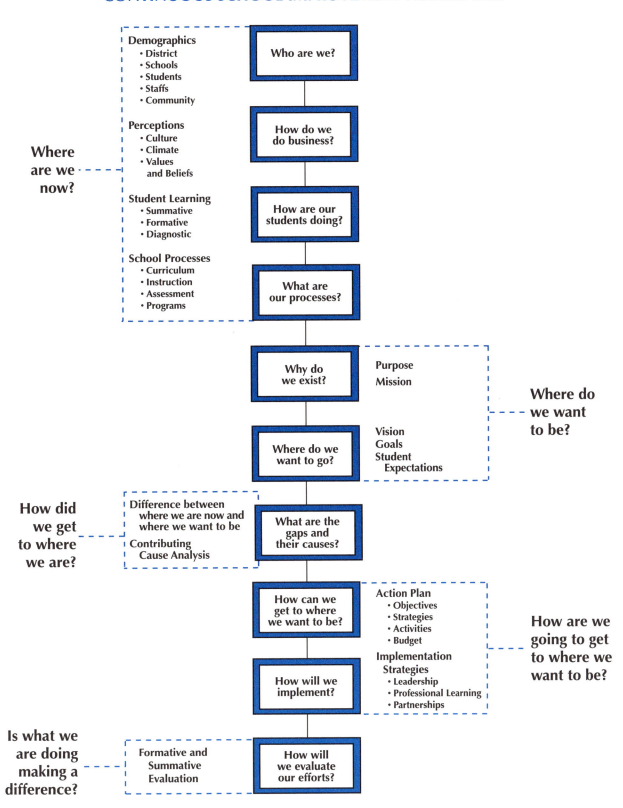

© Education for the Future Initiative, Chico, CA *(http://eff.csuchico.edu)*

Where Are We Now?

Knowing where a school is now is the part of planning for continuous school improvement that requires a comprehensive and honest look at all the school's data—not just student learning results. Figure 3.2 shows the categories of data that are used to answer four sub-questions of *Where are we now?*

- ◆ *Who are we?* answered through demographic data.

- ◆ *How do we do business?* mostly answered through perceptions and organizational assessments.

- ◆ *How are our students doing?* answered through formative and summative student learning results.

- ◆ *What are our processes?* answered through listing programs and processes, and their intents.

Figure 3.2
MULTIPLE MEASURES OF DATA

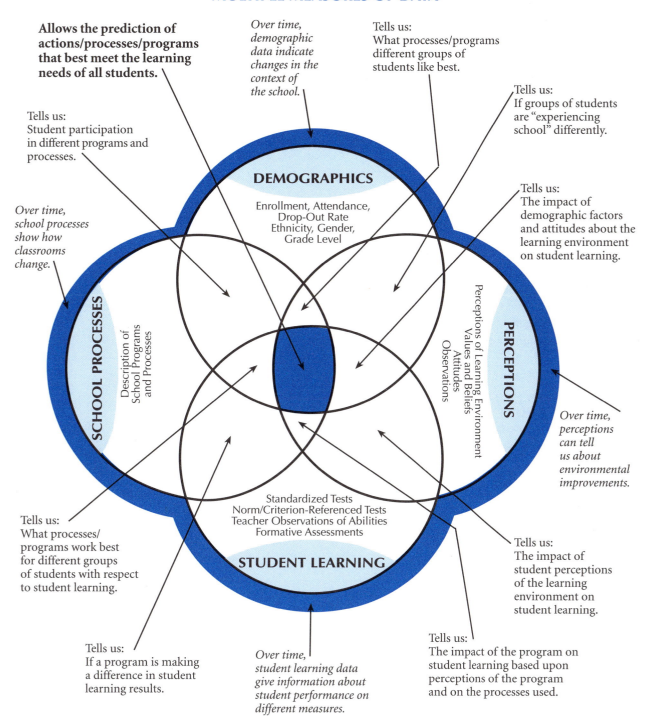

Allows the prediction of actions/processes/programs that best meet the learning needs of all students.

Over time, demographic data indicate changes in the context of the school.

Tells us:
What processes/programs different groups of students like best.

Tells us:
Student participation in different programs and processes.

Tells us:
If groups of students are "experiencing school" differently.

Over time, school processes show how classrooms change.

Tells us:
The impact of demographic factors and attitudes about the learning environment on student learning.

DEMOGRAPHICS

Enrollment, Attendance, Drop-Out Rate Ethnicity, Gender, Grade Level

SCHOOL PROCESSES

Description of School Programs and Processes

Perceptions of Learning Environment Values and Beliefs Attitudes Observations

PERCEPTIONS

Over time, perceptions can tell us about environmental improvements.

Standardized Tests
Norm/Criterion-Referenced Tests
Teacher Observations of Abilities
Formative Assessments

STUDENT LEARNING

Tells us:
What processes/ programs work best for different groups of students with respect to student learning.

Tells us:
The impact of student perceptions of the learning environment on student learning.

Tells us:
If a program is making a difference in student learning results.

Over time, student learning data give information about student performance on different measures.

Tells us:
The impact of the program on student learning based upon perceptions of the program and on the processes used.

© Education for the Future, Chico, CA *(http://eff.csuchico.edu)*

Who Are We?

Demographic data are important because they provide the context of the school, and answer the continuous school improvement questions, "Who are we?"

Demographic data are important because they provide the context of the school, and answer the continuous school improvement question, *Who are we?* Demographic data include enrollment in the school, by grade level, gender, ethnicity, language proficiency, indicators of poverty, etc. Demographic data also include behavior (e.g., office referrals, suspensions, expulsions), drop-out/graduation rates, students identified for special needs/exceptionalities, program enrollment, and staff demographics. Three years of demographic data can show a trend. Five years will give an even better idea of how your data are changing, and will assist with the prediction of how your population might change in the future.

Demographic data show how the student population has changed over time, which can give staffs an idea of what they need to study to better meet the needs of the students they have. Demographic data also show leadership philosophy of the school, through indicators of which and how students are disciplined, identified for special education, advanced placement, gifted programs, etc.

Questions to answer with longitudinal demographic data include:

♦ How has our student population changed over time? How will our population change in the near future? Do we, as staff, have the professional development, instructional methodologies, and materials in place to teach whom we have as students now and in the future?

♦ Do we know the who, what, when, where, and why of our behavior and attendance data? What do we need to do differently to ensure the behavior and attendance we want to see with our students?

♦ Does the program enrollment for each of our programs represent the overall enrollment of the school? (For example, does the percentage of students, by gender and ethnicity, assigned to gifted classes or special education, correspond to the overall percentage of students, by gender and ethnicity, in the school?) If not, why not?

DEMOGRAPHIC DATA TO GATHER

♦ **Number of schools, administrators, students, and teachers.**
♦ **Class sizes: student-teacher ratio.**
♦ **Student living situation, family structure, and size.**
♦ **Preschool attendance.**
♦ **Student gender, ethnicity, free/reduced lunch status, language fluency.**
♦ **Student/teacher attendance.**
♦ **Student mobility, retention, dropout rate.**
♦ **Safety/crime data.**
♦ **Teacher years of experience, degrees, ethnicity, gender, languages spoken, turnover, retirement projections.**

Enrollment in:
♦ **Title I/schoolwide.**
♦ **Extracurricular activities.**
♦ **After-school programs/summer school.**
♦ **Gifted, AP classes.**
♦ **Tutoring/peer-mentoring.**
♦ **Community support services.**
♦ **Counseling opportunities.**
♦ **Special education.**
♦ **Interventions.**

How Do We Do Business?

Perceptions data are important because they can tell us what students, staff, and parents are thinking about the learning organization, and answer the continuous school improvement question, *How do we do business?* The question is answered through assessing the school's culture, climate, and organizational processes. Staff values and beliefs, most often assessed through questionnaires and/or determined during visioning processes, tell a staff if team building or specific professional learning is necessary, and what is possible to implement. Perceptions can also show where the deep changes are happening in the school with respect to staff values and beliefs.

Student and parent questionnaires can add different perspectives to the information generated from staff data. Students can report what it takes for them to learn and how they are being taught and treated. Parent perceptions can help staff know what parents need to become more involved in their child's learning.

A schoolwide self-assessment can provide an overview of where the staff believes the school is on the measures that make a difference for school improvement. These assessments often surprise administrators who may think all staff members are thinking about school in the same way. If a school staff does not know how it does business, in reality, it could be creating plans and structures that might never be implemented or might not lead to the desired outcomes.

Questions to answer with perceptions data that will assist with continuous school improvement include:

- How does our student population perceive the learning environment?
  Do they feel like they belong, that they are safe, that they are cared for, that they have fun learning? Do they feel challenged by the work they are being asked to do?

- How do parents perceive the learning environment? Do they feel welcome in the school? Do they know how to help their child(ren) learn at home? Do they feel the school is a good school and that it has a good public image?

- How does staff perceive the learning environment? Do staff members feel it is challenging, safe, and welcoming to students, staff, and parents? Do staff members feel there is a shared vision in place, that everyone knows what her/his job is in the school, and that staff collaborate to make learning consistent across grade levels?

> *Perceptions data are important because they can tell us what students, staff, and parents are thinking about the learning organization, and answer the continuous school improvement question, "How do we do business?"*

PERCEPTIONS DATA TO GATHER

- Students' perceptions of the learning organization.
- Staff perceptions of the learning organization.
- Parents' perceptions of the learning organization.
- Community perceptions of the learning organization.
- Alumni perceptions of learning experiences.
- Perceptions of program implementation.

How Are Our Students Doing?

The next data question, *How are our students doing?*, requires a synthesis of student learning data in all subject areas, disaggregated by all student groups, by grade levels, by following the same groups of students (cohorts) over time, as well as looking at individual student growth. Student learning data show if schools are meeting the needs of all students and uncover strengths and areas for improvement. If students are not proficient, teachers need to know what the students know and what they do not know. If students are not proficient, teachers also need to know how many, and by how much, students must improve. Looking at student learning across grade levels also reveals if a school has instructional coherence.

Student learning data show if schools are meeting the needs of all students and uncover strengths and areas for improvement.

Student learning data include diagnostic assessments, classroom assessments, formative assessments, state/provincial assessments, and grades. In a perfect scenario, we would be clear and agree on what we want students to know and be able to do by the end of the year, course, or lesson. We would use diagnostic assessments to discover what students know and do not know as we begin to plan instruction for the students. We would then assess on a regular basis to understand what students are learning and which students need extra support, and adjust instruction to meet student needs. Then we would assess to know if the students learned what we wanted them to learn.

STUDENT LEARNING DATA TO GATHER
+ **Diagnostic assessments.**
+ **Formative assessments.**
+ **Summative assessments.**
+ **Classroom assessments.**

Questions to answer with student learning data to assist with continuous school improvement include:

+ Are teachers teaching to the standards?

+ Is student learning increasing over time, for the school, by grade level and subject area, and for each student?

+ Which subject areas are students strongest in, and in which subject areas do they need more support?

+ Is there instructional coherence? Does each grade level build on previous grade levels and prepare students for the future?

What Are Our Processes?

School processes data are important because they tell us about the way we work, about how we get the results we are getting, set us up to know what is working and what is not working, and answer the continuous school improvement question, *What are our processes?*.

School processes include curriculum, instruction and assessment strategies, leadership, and programs. These are the elements of our organizations over which we have almost complete control, but we tend to measure these elements the least. Answering the question, *What Are Our Processes?*, calls for a complete accounting and evaluation of all programs and processes operating throughout the learning organization.

Questions to answer with school process data to assist with continuous school improvement include:

School processes data are important because they tell us about the way we work, about how we get the results we are getting, set us up to know what is working and what is not working, and answer the continuous school improvement question, "What are our processes?"

♦ What is the intent of each program that we operate? Whom is each program intending to serve, and whom is it serving?

♦ How will we know if each program is successful? What are the results?

♦ To what degree are the programs being implemented?

♦ How is our school doing with respect to continuous school improvement, as measured by a self-assessment tool, like the *Education for the Future Continuous Improvement Continuums?* What does the school need to do to improve? (See Appendix A for the *Education for the Future Continuous Improvement Continuums Activity*, with a complete set of the school and district *Continuous Improvement Continuums*.)

> **SCHOOL PROCESS DATA TO GATHER**
> ♦ Curriculum.
> ♦ Programs.
> ♦ Instructional strategies.
> ♦ Assessment strategies.
> ♦ Interventions.
> ♦ Multi-level prevention system.
> ♦ Response to intervention (RtI).
> ♦ All other classroom practices.
> ♦ Implementation integrity and fidelity.
> ♦ Self-assessment.

Looking Across the Multiple Measures of Data

Figure 3.2 shows the categories of data that are important to gather and analyze in schools for continuous school improvement. The graphic also indicates that intersecting these types of data will answer deeper questions.

Looking across all types of data is important for seeing the linkages in the data results. There might be issues that show up in demographics, perceptions, and school processes that can help explain how a school is getting the results it is getting in student learning, that could be an easy fix. Looking across all data can help improve all content areas at the same time.

Where Do We Want to Be?

A school defines its destination through its mission, vision, goals, and objectives—aligned with the district's vision, goals, and standards (i.e., student grade level expectations), which, in turn, are aligned with the state vision, goals, and standards. The school's vision, goals, and standards must also reflect the core values and beliefs of the staff, merged from personal values and beliefs. Creating a vision from core values and beliefs ensures a vision to which all staff members can commit. Without a vision to which all staff members commit, a school's collective efforts have no target.

FROM VALUES AND BELIEFS TO ACTION

Figure 3.3 shows that *Random Acts of Improvement* result when there is no specific target. Strong leadership inspires a shared vision and ensures its implementation. A strong leader also encourages and models the analysis and use of data. A continuous school improvement process can ensure that all professional development is focused on implementing the vision, that all staff members understand their roles in implementing the vision and helping students learn, and that there is evaluation to know how to improve on an ongoing basis to reach school goals. A vision which is shared and to which all staff are committed is the key to getting *Focused Acts of Improvement* (Figure 3.4).

Figure 3.3
RANDOM ACTS OF IMPROVEMENT

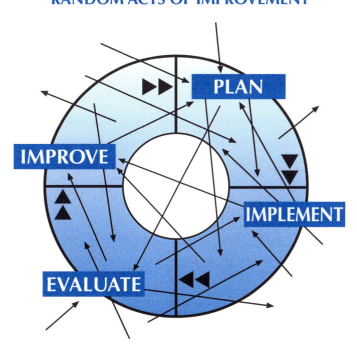

Figure 3.4
FOCUSED ACTS OF IMPROVEMENT

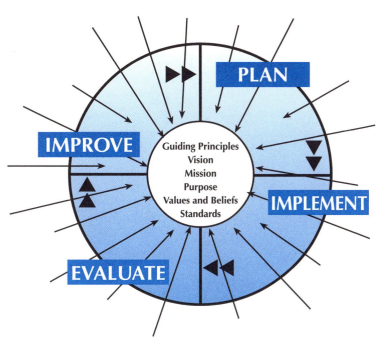

How Did We Get to Where We Are?

Gaps are determined by synthesizing the differences between the results the school is getting with its current processes and the results the school wants to get. Contributing cause analyses, along with comprehensive data analysis, help schools understand how they are getting their current results, and what it will take to eliminate the gaps.

It is particularly important to know how the school is getting its current results in all areas of student learning, so processes that are not achieving the school's desired results are not repeated, and so new strategies and structures can make a difference.

It is particularly important to know how the school is getting its current results in all areas of student learning, so processes that are not achieving the school's desired results are not repeated, and so new strategies and structures can make a difference.

Many schools begin their school improvement plans by looking at the gaps between where they are now and where they want to be, with respect to student learning results only. While these data provide valuable information, starting here does not give schools a complete picture. By starting and ending with the gaps, schools miss the opportunities to improve, innovate, and rethink their systems. The *Education for the Future Problem-Solving Cycle Activity,* described in Chapter 5 and shown in Appendix F, is a great way to engage staff in understanding how they are getting the results they are getting.

Figure 3.5 repeats the framework for continuous school improvement (previously seen in Figure 3.1), pointing out where schools too often begin and end their school improvement efforts.

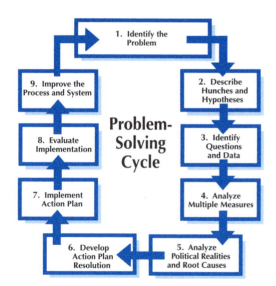

Figure 3.5

CONTINUOUS SCHOOL IMPROVEMENT FRAMEWORK

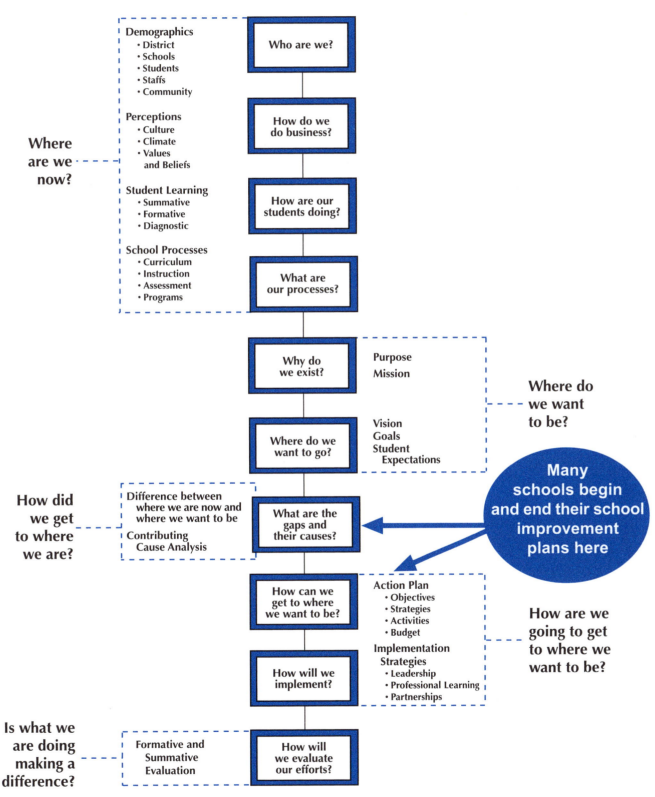

How Are We Going to Get to Where We Want to Be?

The answer to *How are we going to get to where we want to be?* is key to unlocking how the vision will be implemented and how gaps will be eliminated. An action plan, consisting of goals, objectives, strategies, activities, measurement of strategies and activities, person(s) responsible, due dates, timelines, and required resources, needs to be developed to implement and achieve the vision and goals and to eliminate the contributing causes of the gaps.

Leadership structures, professional learning, structured collaboration to share data and professional learning experiences, and parent/community involvement are key elements for ensuring implementation of the shared vision. Action plans must include how and when decisions will be made, identify professional learning and collaboration required to gain new skills and knowledge, and clarify how working with partners will help with achieving the vision.

Marylin Avenue Elementary Continuous School Improvement (CSI) Plan

Goal 1: All students will exhibit their best effort for themselves, their families and the community, including a demonstration of respect for their peers and for property.

Goal 2: Create an environment where every student, family, staff member, and community member will be excited to be at Marylin Avenue School; and be flexible in order to accomodate the educational needs of all.

Strategies and Activities	Person(s) Responsible	Measurement	Expenditures	Estimated Cost
Alignment of instruction with content standards: All grade levels have identified essential standards for all curricular areas. Each essential standard has been unwrapped (in order to feature needed prerequisite skills and concepts), vertically aligned, mapped, and paced for all curricular areas.	Whole Staff / Ongoing	Essential standards are documented for all curricular areas for all grade levels. Grade-level teams agree on the standards. Cross-grade-level teams agree on the standards.		
I. Improvement of instructional strategies and materials: 1. All teachers will use the unwrapped essential standards to target instruction. A. Learning objectives will be based on assessment data. B. Learning objectives will be clearly stated. C. Students will understand the importance of the learning objective.adjust instruction as needed.	Teachers / Ongoing	Classroom observations that describe what instruction and the classroom would look like if RtI implemented will also determine if teachers are: • using the unwrapped essential standards to target instruction • creating clear learning objectives to teach the		

Note: Please see Chapter 5 for the complete example of a school plan.

Is What We Are Doing Making a Difference?

Formative evaluation and reflective learning are required to assess the effectiveness of all school programs and processes, the alignment of all parts of the system to the vision, and to determine if what a school is doing is making a difference for students on an on-going basis. Summative evaluations, i.e., at the end of the year, allow reflection on all the parts of the system, and the alignment of the parts to the whole, and to assess if the school made a difference as expected.

Evaluation must be both formative—as it looks at the success of the various parts of the plan—and summative, as it looks at the plan as a whole and at the end of each phase.

BOOK STUDY QUESTIONS

♦ Consider Figure 3.1, the *Continuous School Improvement Framework.* How do the various parts of the framework align with each other?

♦ Why is it important to look at a school's data before creating a vision?

♦ Why is it important to identify all programs and processes?

♦ Why is it important to know how a school is getting its results before creating a plan?

TEAM STUDY QUESTIONS

♦ Can you list all the programs and processes in your school? Do you understand the components of every program and process?

♦ Who is responsible for developing the Continuous School Improvement Plan for your school?

♦ As you review the *Continuous School Improvement Framework* (Figure 3.1), what components are missing from your school's continuous school improvement efforts?

♦ What data do you have? What data do you need?

♦ Does your school have a shared vision?

♦ Does your school have leadership and professional learning structures in place to implement the vision and plan?

Chapter 4

FROM REACTIVE TO PROACTIVE

If we knew what it would look like, sound like, and feel like
when we are doing what we are supposed to be doing,
we could do it! We need that clarity so all teachers, staff,
and administrators understand where we are going,
and what we need to do in the classroom—in the same way.
We have been working very hard; unfortunately, we do not know
what we "looked" like when we started because we were not
measuring ourselves. That is important now, because we do not
know if we are making progress. If we are still close to where we
were when we started, we need to rethink everything we are doing
or get out of the business; if we are closer to getting to where
we want to be, we need to figure out how to keep going.
We need a tool to know where we were when we started,
where we are right now, and where we want to be ultimately.
This tool needs to provide direction about why we are not
getting the results we want, and what we need to do next.

Heard from teachers in many restructuring schools when
asked why they were not implementing the vision.

About two decades ago, *Education for the Future* started working intensively with a number of schools to rethink the way they do business to ensure all students' learning. After doing the hard work of gathering and analyzing data, creating a shared vision, a continuous school improvement plan, and structures to implement the vision, we were sometimes dismayed to see that the vision was not implemented in every classroom. After teachers were asked why they were not implementing their vision, we heard the explanation above. *The Education for the Future Continuous Improvement Continuums* were created in response to these comments. (Referenced in Bernhardt,

2002-2010, and downloadable from the *Education for the Future* website: *http://eff.csuchico.edu/html/ download_center.html;* also see Appendix A.) These continuums have since been used effectively in thousands of schools—all over the world. As self assessments, the continuums help staffs see what all staff members are thinking about where the school is with respect to using data, creating and implementing a shared vision, a continuous school improvement plan, leadership, professional learning, partnerships, and how they will continuously improve and evaluate. After determining next steps, staffs implement the next steps. The next assessments typically show the staff coming together on their thoughts of where the school is. The results reveal that when you get all staff on the same page, with respect to where staff thinks the school is, you can move them all forward together. Administrators often find they are thinking in different ways from the staff about where the school is on major school improvement topics. While it may be discouraging in the short term, the self-assessment provides powerful information about how to get all staff on the same page and moving forward together. Once staff get on the same page and together agree on what has to happen to move forward, they make progress.

THE RtI CONTINUUMS

Because of the successful use of the *Education for the Future Continuous Improvement Continuums* and the clarity they provide staffs, the authors created RtI Continuums to show how the elements of effective RtI implementation evolve in most schools. Schools can identify the elements that must be addressed to move an entire school from a reactive system (Level 1) where general education and special education work separately most of the time, or perhaps all of the time, to a proactive system (Level 5) where general education and special education work together for the benefit of each student's learning.

How to Use the RtI Continuums

The RtI continuums, shown as Figure 4.1, are categorized as follows—

♦ Curriculum/Instruction/Assessment/Behavior

♦ Collaboration

♦ Referral Procedures

♦ Data Analysis and Use

♦ Professional Learning

♦ Leadership

As a school moves from reactive to proactive, the elements of the system become more blended and interdependent. It is difficult to perform at Levels 4 or 5 in one category without all the categories being simultaneously and effectively implemented.

Figure 4.1
RtI CONTINUUMS

CURRICULUM ~ INSTRUCTION ~ ASSESSMENT ~ BEHAVIOR

RESPONSE TO INTERVENTION (RtI)	One	Two	Three	Four	Five
	From a focus on teaching textbooks to a focus on student learning.				
	Curriculum is driven primarily by teacher preference and not aligned to the state/local standards.	Curriculum is driven primarily by textbooks.	Curriculum is aligned vertically and horizontally to state/local standards. Teachers embed evidence-based teaching practices in a multi-level system of support within the integrated general education and special education curriculum.	Curriculum is vertically and horizontally aligned with state/local standards. Evidence-based quality instruction is adjusted according to students' needs and their responses to instruction and interventions.	The aligned curriculum is implemented in every classroom and leads to a continuum of teaching and learning, allowing all students to meet and exceed state/local standards, and for teachers to help students prevent failure.
	From just teaching to teaching with impact.				
	Teaching occurs in isolation, without consideration to adjusting instruction to meet the needs of all students. All students are expected to learn in the same way. Many students with Individualized Education Programs (IEPs) are removed from the general education setting for specialized instruction.	Students with IEPs are included in the general education setting where special educators may assist with implementation of accommodations. Some students with IEPs, who need additional instruction, learn in special education classrooms.	Staffs agree on and are committed to a shared vision regarding curriculum, instruction, and assessments across and between grade levels. Multi-level systems of support and prevention are embedded within the general education curriculum and setting. Most students with IEPs fully participate in the general education setting.	General educators and special educators develop a common understanding in reference to instruction and assessment responsibilities within collaborative structures that include a well defined multi-level system of teaching and learning.	Evidence-based teaching practices and learning strategies are implemented with integrity and fidelity to meet the needs of all students. Implementation of interventions is continually monitored and evaluated to ensure fidelity and integrity.

Note: From Response to Intervention (RtI) and Continuous School Improvement (CSI): Using Data, Vision, and Leadership to Design, Implement, and Evaluate a Schoolwide Prevention System, by Victoria L. Bernhardt and Connie L. Hébert, 2011, Larchmont, NY: Eye On Education.

Figure 4.1 (Continued)
RtI CONTINUUMS

CURRICULUM ~ INSTRUCTION ~ ASSESSMENT ~ BEHAVIOR

	One	Two	Three	Four	Five
RESPONSE TO INTERVENTION (RtI)			*From assessment of learning to assessment for learning.*		
	Assessments are given at the end of units or when the teacher feels so inclined.	Assessments, usually aligned to textbooks, may include informal as well as formal approaches. Some results are used by some staff to inform and design instruction.	Common formative assessments, aligned to the standards, are used to monitor student learning in every subject area, and to adjust and improve instruction so all students can become proficient.	Common formative assessments inform curricular and standards alignment. Common formative assessments are used with ongoing progress monitoring to assign students to intervention groups and ensure each student's success.	All student outcome data are openly discussed and analyzed. These data are used to make instructional decisions. Students who receive additional instructional support receive ongoing monitoring of progress using curriculum-based measures.
			From responding to behavior to developing behavioral competence.		
	Behavioral issues are addressed via office referrals. There is no differentiation of disciplinary action or intervention.	Some teachers have proactive approaches to discipline. Behavioral interventions are sometimes used in addition to, or in place of, traditional disciplinary action. Most behavior issues are referred to the office.	Behavioral issues are viewed primarily as instructional issues. Staffs agree on how behavior should be handled within a multi-level preventive system. Severe incidents are dealt with by the office.	The multi-level prevention system includes targeted, evidence-based behavioral interventions. Expectations and strategies are taught consistently for students to improve their own behavior to support learning.	Social and behavioral expectations are clearly defined, agreed upon, monitored, and enforced. Students demonstrate social and behavioral competence. Behavior issues do not exist, only instructional concerns.

Note: From Response to Intervention (RtI) and Continuous School Improvement (CSI): Using Data, Vision, and Leadership to Design, Implement, and Evaluate a Schoolwide Prevention System, by Victoria L. Bernhardt and Connie L. Hébert, 2011, Larchmont, NY: Eye On Education.

Figure 4.1 *(Continued)*
RtI CONTINUUMS

COLLABORATION

	One	Two	Three	Four	Five
RESPONSE TO INTERVENTION (RtI)			*From teaching in isolation to learning communities.*		
	Teaching occurs in isolation. "Yours" and "mine" mentality exists regarding students identified with special needs. Learning problems are based on opinion rather than data.	Teachers independently engage in problem solving to design interventions for at-risk students. General educators and special educators may share information regarding accommodations for students either as they are being considered for evaluation or based on expectations outlined in IEPs.	Staffs are committed to a shared vision that includes collaborative structures to implement the vision. Collaboration includes structures such as formal teams, peer coaching, protected meeting and planning times.	All teachers collaborate to implement an RtI system that includes universal screenings and common formative assessments across all subject areas including behavioral/social expectations. Collaborative decision making occurs for student assignment to intervention levels as well as for adjustments to curriculum and instruction. Collaborative structures, implemented with integrity and fidelity, allow teachers to support each other for increased student achievement and attainment of the shared vision.	All staffs are engaged in collaborative structures to ensure and maintain student success. Collaborative structures are utilized to implement a continuum of learning for all students. No student falls through the cracks. The RtI system ensures student success and identifies needed adjustments to address the unique characteristics of the learners.
			From separate practices and environments to a collaborative system.		
	General educators attend IEP meetings because they are required to, but are not sure how to contribute. Special educators are unclear how to include general educators in the IEP process.	Special educators may assist general educators with implementation of pre-referral strategies for students who struggle, but these are often not documented until a referral is made. When students are identified, general educators are involved in the IEP based on knowledge of the general curriculum and need for identifying accommodations.	Roles and responsibilities are defined for special education and general education and both are committed to the implementation of the shared vision. General educators participate fully in the special education process: from referral, evaluation, and eligibility determination, to IEP development, implementation, progress monitoring, annual review, and re-evaluation.	General and special education teachers agree upon and share instructional and assessment responsibilities through protected, job embedded collaborative time. Coaching and feedback support integrity and fidelity of implementation. Staffs collaborate, using common formative assessment data, to determine intervention level based on established entry and exit criteria of a multi-level prevention system.	Responsibility for steps in the special education process is blended among general and special education personnel. The process is intertwined in the RtI system, creating reliance on documentation from instructional data to help all students learn.

Note: From *Response to Intervention (RtI) and Continuous School Improvement (CSI): Using Data, Vision, and Leadership to Design, Implement, and Evaluate a Schoolwide Prevention System*, by Victoria L. Bernhardt and Connie L. Hébert, 2011, Larchmont, NY: Eye On Education.

Figure 4.1 (Continued)
RtI CONTINUUMS

REFERRAL PROCEDURES

	One	Two	Three	Four	Five
			From learning disabilities to learning differences.		
RESPONSE TO INTERVENTION (RtI)	Students exhibiting learning and/or behavior problems are promptly referred to special education for evaluation. Referrals from parents most often lead to evaluation without additional consideration.	Classroom interventions or pre-referral strategies may occur before referral for consideration of special education evaluation; however, referrals from parents usually lead to immediate evaluation.	Teachers strive to identify at-risk students for early prevention and pre-referral strategies. Pre-referral teams monitor interventions prior to referral for consideration of special services. Referrals from parents are reviewed and may be redirected to the multi-level RtI system.	Referrals made outside of the RtI system, including referrals from parents, are directed to the appropriate team for documentation of interventions. Clear and helpful documentation procedures exist to determine intervention effectiveness. This information is used for special education referral and eligibility determinations.	Progress monitoring consistently informs staff of students' needs and their responses to interventions. From this information, teachers determine if interventions should continue or if students need to be referred for consideration of evaluation for special education services. Students with disabilities are not seen as qualitatively different from non-disabled students.
			From compliance to best practices.		
	Learner characteristics associated with poverty, limited English proficiency, and learning styles are mistaken for learning disabilities, resulting in a high number of students referred for special education evaluation, while the percent determined eligible is often low because no significant discrepancy exists. Referrals for special education are reviewed by administrators for processing.	Referrals are processed by the appropriate team of professionals who determine if an evaluation is needed. Pre-referral teams may assist with interventions, but there is no multi-level system of prevention for monitoring implementation and student responsiveness. The ratio of students referred for evaluation and those found eligible improves as some referrals are addressed through pre-referral strategies. The time it takes to refer a student is unnecessarily extended.	Staff discusses and uses common formative assessment data (screening, benchmark, and progress monitoring) informally to determine appropriate intervention level and referral for consideration of special education evaluation. Referrals for special education are processed by the appropriate team of professionals, and pre-referral data are considered in determining need for evaluation. RtI data are used to assist in determination of eligibility for specific learning disability or other disabilities because consistent procedures are in place.	Assignment to appropriate levels of intervention results in decreased referrals for special services. Accurate referrals for special education evaluation are made, evidenced by marginal differences in the number of referrals for consideration of evaluation, the number of students evaluated, and the number of students found eligible. Referrals made through the RtI system are increasingly accurate and accepted due to intervention integrity, fidelity, and effectiveness, as well as sufficient documentation.	RtI system is fluid between and among special and general education environments, students, and staff. Components of an RtI system, such as multi-level instruction and intervention, instructional coherence, ongoing formative assessments, including progress monitoring, and collaboration for informed decision making are embedded in daily practices and processes and have become "the way we do business."

Note: From *Response to Intervention (RtI) and Continuous School Improvement (CSI): Using Data, Vision, and Leadership to Design, Implement, and Evaluate a Schoolwide Prevention System*, by Victoria L. Bernhardt and Connie L. Hébert, 2011, Larchmont, NY: Eye On Education.

**Figure 4.1 (*Continued*)
RtI CONTINUUMS**

DATA ANALYSIS AND USE

	One	Two	Three	Four	Five
			From limited data collection to comprehensive schoolwide data utilization.		
RESPONSE TO INTERVENTION (RtI)	Data or information about student performance and student learning needs are not collected in any systematic way.	Some teachers collect some student learning data, other than grades and state testing results. There is no specifically appointed time, designated personnel, or responsibilities for data collection and review.	Expectations regarding data collection and analysis are communicated to all staff. Student feedback, acquired through perceptions data, classroom performance, analysis of behavior, and achievement data are used to determine support strategies and interventions.	All elements of the school organization are improved on the basis of comprehensive data analyses including: analysis of contributing causes of undesirable results and analysis of process effectiveness. Roles and responsibilities include data collection, analysis, and use.	Data and information gathered, analyzed, utilized, and shared with stakeholders are accurate and comprehensive, reflecting all programs and processes in the school. Time and personnel are designated and protected for continually monitoring schoolwide data.
			From reactive problem solving to proactive decision making.		
	Data are not used to determine what needs to change at the school or classroom levels. Problems are solved reactively with short-term results.	Change is limited to areas of the school where individual teachers see a need, with decisions being made one student or group at a time. Schools analyze or review little data other than annual performance data, and this is to identify lowest performing students, to provide tutoring to the "bubble kids," or to look at specific areas of weakness of all students.	Schoolwide data are used to assess instructional coherence and to determine areas for improvement. Staff discuss and use assessment data informally for determining flexible groups and assigning students to intervention groups. Progress monitoring of student performance is part of intervention implementation, and is used to make decisions regarding intervention effectiveness, and the need for referral for consideration for special education evaluation.	Student performance data are available and accessible for staff in a meaningful format for interpretation, discussion, and decision making in all academic and behavioral/social areas. Continuous analysis of student achievement and instructional strategies are rigorously reinforced within each classroom and across learning levels to ensure a continuum of learning for students and to prevent student failure.	Data inform decisions and include multiple measures to ensure all aspects of the school organization are improved to support teachers' efforts and students' success. Information is analyzed and used to assist with identification and implementation of strategies matched to student need, to prevent student failure, to predict student success, and to address system congruence.

Note: From Response to Intervention (RtI) and Continuous School Improvement (CSI): Using Data, Vision, and Leadership to Design, Implement, and Evaluate a Schoolwide Prevention System, by Victoria L. Bernhardt and Connie L. Hébert, 2011, Larchmont, NY: Eye On Education.

Figure 4.1 *(Continued)*
RtI CONTINUUMS

PROFESSIONAL LEARNING

RESPONSE TO INTERVENTION (RtI)

One	Two	Three	Four	Five
From professional development events to professional learning experiences.				
Professional development for general and special educators is held separately as the same topics are not perceived as relevant to both groups. Outcomes for professional development are not measured.	Teachers seek professional development, including book studies, for personal professional growth or topics that apply to their students or school. Professional development is evaluated by assessing participants' views of presenter's knowledge, skills, and relevance of content to them.	Professional development includes staffwide professional learning, shared learning experiences, shared readings, and peer coaching and feedback structures to support integrity and fidelity of implementation strategies. Professional development and learning is monitored and evaluated for implementation, and includes content related to implementing the schoolwide vision and its multi-level prevention system.	Professional learning includes job-embedded structures, allowing teachers to have ongoing conversations about student learning data and to acquire training to teach students based on the demographic and learning profile of the school. Professional learning is linked with the shared vision, comprehensive data analysis, and contributing cause analyses. Professional learning is evaluated to determine follow-through and to inform future needs.	Effective job-embedded professional learning, based on the evaluation of staff and student needs, leads to the achievement of student learning standards, and helps all staff implement the vision and RtI system. Varied and targeted collaborative professional learning opportunities exist. The professional learning strategies focus on implementing strategies that lead to increased student achievement at each instructional and intervention level.

Note: From Response to Intervention (RtI) and Continuous School Improvement (CSI): Using Data, Vision, and Leadership to Design, Implement, and Evaluate a Schoolwide Prevention System, by Victoria L. Bernhardt and Connie L. Hébert, 2011, Larchmont, NY: Eye On Education.

Figure 4.1 *(Continued)*
RtI CONTINUUMS

LEADERSHIP

From management to leadership.

	One	Two	Three	Four	Five
RESPONSE TO INTERVENTION (RtI)	Decisions are reactive to requirements with little knowledge of continuous improvement. Administrators serve as evaluators of personnel and programs with limited input from staff, parents, students, or other data sources. Responsibilities for scheduling professional development, curriculum selection or development, and other decisions are made by administration.	Administrators are supportive of efforts to improve, such as teaming and collaboration. Staff discussions guide decision-making; however, improvement efforts are focused on solving individual problems. Data are analyzed by the administrator; results are shared with teachers, and directives are given for improvement.	All staff, including administration, engage in professional learning. Leadership teams are established to inform decisions and to implement the vision. Roles and responsibilities of all staff members and leadership teams are identified. The shared vision and expectations are implemented by all.	Leadership participates in proactive, data informed, and preventive decision making. Administration and teaching staff are informed regarding evidence-based practices and share professional learning experiences. Time and resources are allocated and protected for instruction, collaboration, planning, and interventions, which are implemented with integrity and fidelity.	The vision is vigorously supported and implemented with consistent communication regarding implementation expectations and outcomes. Leadership protects and honors allocated time and resources for collaboration, professional learning, and interventions. Comprehensive data analysis informs decisions and allows leadership to accurately predict the professional needs of colleagues for continuous improvement and the achievement of student learning standards.

Note: From *Response to Intervention (RtI) and Continuous School Improvement (CSI): Using Data, Vision, and Leadership to Design, Implement, and Evaluate a Schoolwide Prevention System*, by Victoria L. Bernhardt and Connie L. Hébert, 2011, Larchmont, NY: Eye On Education.

For each category of the RtI Continuum, the move from 1 to 5 does not reflect equal intervals. A school at a 1 level is reactive and has neither started a CSI process nor the implementation of an RtI system. While it is relatively easy for a school to become a 2, moving further up the continuums requires considerable commitment and effort. To become a 3, a school needs to have systems in place to implement a CSI process and an RtI system that is responsive to student learning. From Level 3 on, the elements build on each other. At Level 4, all the elements in Level 3 need to be in place; and at Level 5, all the elements in Levels 3 and 4 should be in place. Moving to the proactive levels of 4 and 5 requires a school to have a responsive system in place where the work of prevention becomes systemic—the way business is done. A summary of the continuums follow.

CURRICULUM, INSTRUCTION, ASSESSMENT, BEHAVIOR

This category might easily be considered the heart and soul of teaching and learning. This continuum is the largest of the six because the interdependence of the elements becomes apparent once staff initiates the work of RtI and CSI. How well the curriculum is designed, aligned, and articulated has a direct impact on how instruction is delivered. Assessment is critical for informing instructional design and curriculum implementation. The influence of a student's social and behavioral competence in terms of being a self-motivated learner plays a critical role in the ultimate success of this system.

From a Focus on Teaching Textbooks to a Focus on Student Learning

When schools allow curriculum to be driven by teacher preferences or allow the textbook to serve as the primary guide for instruction, they are denying their students the opportunity to thrive in a proactive system.

When schools allow curriculum to be driven by teacher preferences or allow the textbook to serve as the primary guide for instruction, they are denying their students the opportunity to thrive in a proactive system.

Level 1: Teachers teach to the materials they prefer or focus on content coverage rather than teaching for student learning.

Level 2: Teachers teach primarily what is in the textbook.

Level 3: The curriculum becomes aligned with learning standards within and across grade levels, and content areas.

Level 4: The aligned curriculum is adjusted based on demonstrated needs of students, and responsiveness to interventions.

Level 5: Every classroom provides a continuum of learning that allows all students to meet or exceed established standards.

From Just Teaching to Teaching with Impact

For instruction, moving across the continuum is contingent on a well-defined curriculum and a teaching staff that understands their instruction is guided by that curriculum, rather than personal preferences or textbooks.

Level 1: Teaching occurs in isolation. All students are expected to be taught and to learn in the same way. Students with Individualized Education Programs (IEPs) are removed from the general education setting.

Level 2: Students with IEPs are mainstreamed in the general education setting, with accommodations. Some students with IEPs learn in special education classrooms.

Level 3: There is a shared vision with respect to curriculum, instruction, assessment, and a multi-level system of support and prevention. Students with IEPs learn in the general education setting.

Level 4: Regular education and special education staff work seamlessly together to meet the learning needs of all students, through multiple levels of support and prevention.

Level 5: All staff continually monitor every student's achievement and provide relevant instruction so that each student meets or exceeds expected levels of performance.

For instruction, moving across the continuum is contingent on a well-defined curriculum and a teaching staff that understands their instruction is guided by that curriculum, rather than personal preferences or textbooks.

From Assessment of Learning to Assessment for Learning

Assessment is the cornerstone for curriculum and instruction because of the information that can be provided regarding student learning. Many teachers design assessment of learning to answer the question, "what have students learned?" rather than assessment for learning, which should answer the question, "what do students already know and what do they need to learn?"

Level 1: Teachers, individually, give assessments as a result of coming to the end of a unit.

Level 2: Some teachers develop assessments to inform instruction throughout the instructional unit.

Level 3: Together teachers develop or adopt common formative assessments that are aligned to standards, including components of the RtI system with universal screening and progress monitoring, to better inform instruction.

Assessment is the cornerstone for curriculum and instruction because of the information that can be provided regarding student learning.

Level 4: Assessment structures exist for all environments and inform grouping structures for the RtI system.

Level 5: Fully aligned assessments are used by all teachers in all areas of academics and behavior to help student exceed expectations.

From Responding to Behavior to Developing Behavioral Competence

In many schools today, behavioral issues are acknowledged to be directly connected to classroom practices. Developing a system for the explicit instruction of agreed-upon behavioral and social expectations can be one of the more difficult areas to address among staff.

Developing a system for the explicit instruction of agreed-upon behavioral and social expectations can be one of the more difficult areas to address among staff.

Level 1: Behavior is addressed through the principal's office.

Level 2: Some staff understand that the behavior-learning connection is inseparable, and that behavior must be dealt with in the classroom.

Level 3: Staff, together, create a multi-level prevention system of explicit instruction and feedback of behavioral and social expectations.

Level 4: There is a clearly defined prevention system for positive behavioral approaches and the use of evidence-based interventions.

Level 5: Staff recognize that behaviors indicate an instructional need of a student, and address the instructional need as well as assist the student in developing the behavioral competence needed to maintain engagement in learning.

COLLABORATION

The ability of the staff to work together is essential and necessary for systems change to occur; without collaboration there will be neither focused activity, nor comprehensive systemic improvement. The specific skills for collaboration must be developed, and opportunities to collaborate need to be structured, with allocation of time and resources, to achieve desired outcomes.

The ability of the staff to work together is essential and necessary for systems change to occur; without collaboration there will be neither focused activity, nor comprehensive systemic improvement.

From Teaching in Isolation to Learning Communities

We occasionally hear staff refer to "my students," "your students," or "the students" and are thrilled when we hear staff talk about "our students" and speak knowledgeably about the learning characteristics of "our students."

Level 1: General education teachers often send students who are difficult to teach to special education.

Level 2: Teachers independently determine how to differentiate instruction for students who are at risk of failing.

Level 3: Staff collaborate with colleagues to discuss the information gained from curriculum, instruction, assessment, and behavior practices and plan together to address the unique needs of the learners.

Level 4: All teachers collaborate to ensure an RtI system that is implemented with integrity and fidelity.

Level 5: All staff are involved in collaborative structures that inform and help teachers adjust practices and ensure *all* students' growth.

From Separate Practices and Environments to a Collaborative System

As general and special education collaborate in learning communities, they share responsibility for all students. To move from Level 1 requires special and general educators to understand their roles and contributions in developing IEPs, as well as supporting students with IEPs in the regular classroom environment.

As general and special education collaborate in learning communities, they share responsibility for all students.

Level 1: General education and special education teachers are unclear about how to include themselves and/or each other in students' IEPs.

Level 2: Pre-referral strategies and structures are likely to be used; however, they may not be documented until a referral is made.

Level 3: All staff are committed to the implementation of the shared vision. General education teachers are fully involved in the special education process.

Level 4: Staff share information, strategies, and responsibilities for implementing across the lines of special and general education. Peer coaching and feedback are major components of collaborative teaming.

Level 5: The lines between general and special education disappear as practices become blended and staff focus on providing what is needed for continued student learning, engaging in the process of evaluating students for special services when data indicate.

REFERRAL PROCEDURES

Referral procedures may be among the last categories for movement across the continuum because so many pieces, including the process for determining special education eligibility, must be in place in order for the RtI system to be fully utilized.

From Learning Disabilities to learning Differences

Level 1: In a reactive system, students are referred for special education evaluation when learning does not fit the classroom because teaching is not adjusted to the characteristics of students in the school, causing issues of poverty, or language proficiency, or cultural differences to be mistaken for learning disabilities.

Level 2: Some pre-referral strategies and classroom interventions are in place before referral for consideration of special education evaluation.

Level 3: Seeing the success of pre-referral strategies, staff design structures to address student learning needs, and develop a multi-level prevention system for RtI.

Level 4: The system is in place to understand when students are referred for special education.

Level 5: The RtI system becomes *the way we do business* and results in the needs of students with disabilities being met.

From Compliance to Best Practices

With the shift from compliance to best practices, what staff believe about student learning changes, removing the focus on eligibility determinations and disabilities to a focus on providing appropriate instruction to address demonstrated learning characteristics and needs.

Level 1: Staff see those students exhibiting learning difficulties to be in need of special education and become frustrated when students do not qualify.

Level 2: Staff engaged in continuous school improvement planning often have pre-referral teams and strategies in place to monitor and support struggling students. These teams may make a referral for evaluation when needed.

Level 3: Consistent procedures and appropriate documentation of pre-referral strategies are expected prior to special education evaluation.

Level 4: The RtI system is utilized for every referral. Documentation of intervention effectiveness informs the eligibility determination, if evaluation is recommended.

Level 5: Staff recognize that some students continue to struggle even after receiving highly effective instruction on a regular basis and in the prescribed manner, and thus qualify those students for special education services. The necessary documentation and procedures are in place to make this happen.

DATA ANALYSIS AND USE

Data analysis and use are the heart and soul of both the continuous school improvement process and a response to intervention system. If a school is not collecting, analyzing, and utilizing data to inform decisions, it can neither engage in continuous school improvement efforts nor develop a response to intervention system.

From Limited Data Collection to Comprehensive Schoolwide Data Utilization

Proactive schools use multiple measures of data at the school level, classroom level, and at the student level to understand the impact of their processes and strategies on student learning.

Proactive schools use multiple measures of data at the school level, classroom level, and at the student level to understand the impact of their processes and strategies on student learning.

Level 1: In a reactive school, data are not collected in a systematic way, which means informed decisions cannot be made.

Level 2: The value of data analysis and use becomes apparent as some teachers learn to use select data to inform decisions.

Level 3: A system is in place for teachers to use multiple measures of data to inform efforts.

Level 4: Comprehensive data analysis becomes both systematic and systemic, contributing causes for undesirable results are identified and eliminated, and data are used to inform and improve the effectiveness of implementation.

Level 5: Staff realize the power of informed decision making for student learning when data collection, analysis, and use extend beyond the teaching staff to community members and other stakeholders.

From Reactive Problem-Solving to Proactive Decision Making

With quality uses of data, changes in practice move from reacting primarily to gaps in student achievement data, to using multiple measures of data to identify how to meet the learning needs of all students throughout the school.

With quality uses of data, changes in practice move from reacting primarily to gaps in student achievement data, to using multiple measures of data to identify how to meet the learning needs of all students throughout the school.

Level 1: Data are not used to know what needs to change in a school or at the classroom level.

Level 2: Student achievement data are analyzed to determine gaps. Solutions are reactive to the gaps.

Level 3: Teachers know the long-term and short-term impact school has on each student through systematic data analysis and use. Data analysis helps teachers know how to meet the needs of each student.

Level 4: The systematic and systemic use of data defines the multi-level prevention system that provides a continuum of learning that makes sense for students and that helps prevent student failure.

Level 5: The use of data permeates the school system. No student falls through the cracks.

PROFESSIONAL LEARNING

Professional development events are not sufficient for increased staff learning and performance. Schools need to change practices in order to address learning needs of students and staff and to implement a robust RtI system.

Professional development events are not sufficient for increased staff learning and performance. Schools need to change practices in order to address learning needs of students and staff and to implement a robust RtI system.

From Professional Development Events to Professional Learning Experiences

Staff use analysis of student learning, information from the evaluation of school processes, perceptions data, and demographics to plan professional learning directed toward implementing the shared vision and the RtI system.

Level 1: When professional development occurs primarily for compliance reasons, the events planned are often different for groups of teachers, such as special educators and general educators, because the same topics are not seen as relevant to both groups.

Level 2: Teachers seek professional development for personal growth, including book studies that are often applicable to the classroom, but not always aligned with the vision. While professional development may be evaluated at this stage, it is not evaluated in a way that informs the vision.

Level 3: In order to implement the vision and the RtI system, continuously improving schools need to provide the professional learning for staffs that will help them collaborate and implement the vision and the RtI system with integrity and fidelity.

Level 4: Linked to the vision, professional learning is job-embedded, collaborative, and supports staff in implementing the vision and a systemic prevention system.

Level 5: Professional learning becomes deep rather than broad, allowing teachers to plan their learning to increase student achievement.

LEADERSHIP

Successful implementation of CSI and RtI hinges on effective leadership. We see the job of leaders as helping everyone in the organization implement the shared vision. All staff are leaders.

Successful implementation of CSI and RtI hinges on effective leadership. We see the job of leaders as helping everyone in the organization implement the shared vision. All staff are leaders.

From Management to Leadership

Level 1: In reactive schools, leadership structures do not exist. Administrators serve as managers of personnel and resources, evaluating personnel and programs when required, and making necessary decisions with limited input from others.

Level 2: Administrators, supportive of improvement efforts, allow some collaboration and engage in discussions to guide decisions, but bear the primary responsibility for decision making and evaluation of programs.

Level 3: A leadership structure to help all staff implement a shared vision is developed and implemented for shared decision making.

Level 4: As leadership structures embed in daily practices, staff experience a climate conducive to CSI and RtI with data informed decision making for achieving the shared vision.

Level 5: *The way we do business* includes a climate of lifelong learning for staff and students; consistent communication regarding implementation of the vision; and comprehensive data analysis to inform decisions, allowing the accurate prediction of professional needs as well as student learning needs.

BOOK STUDY QUESTIONS

- ◆ What is the purpose of having a school assess itself using the RtI Continuums?

- ◆ How helpful do you believe these Continuums would be for getting a school focused on the same goals for improvement? How difficult would it be for schools to identify next steps for improvement planning when using the Continuums?

TEAM STUDY QUESTIONS

- ◆ Review the RtI Continuums. Where is your school right now with RtI?

- ◆ What are the first steps in helping your school use a tool like this?

- ◆ What are next steps for moving your school forward?

Chapter 5

DESIGNING AND *IMPLEMENTING* RtI WITH CONTINUOUS SCHOOL IMPROVEMENT: *THE CSI PART*

---

*Before we can be successful with RtI, we have to get all staff
on the same page with understanding where we are,
where we are going, how we got to where we are right now,
how we are going to get to where we want to be, and how
we will know if what we are doing is making a difference.*

Marylin Avenue School Leadership Team
Education for the Future Summer Data Institute, July 2007

Before a school staff can dramatically redesign regular and special education to create an RtI system that will make a difference for all their students, they need to begin with continuous school improvement. Schools need to answer the five essential continuous school improvement questions, using the methods shown in Figure 5.1, as completely and honestly as possible.

> *Before a school staff can dramatically redesign regular and special education to create an RtI system that will make a difference for all their students, they need to begin with continuous school improvement.*

♦ *Where are we now?* Comprehensive data analyzed and displayed in a data profile.

♦ *Where do we want to be?* A shared vision.

♦ *How did we get to where we are?* Deeper data analysis, using tools such as the problem-solving cycle, to get to contributing causes of undesirable results.

♦ *How are we going to get to where we want to be?* One comprehensive plan to implement the vision complete with implementation strategies such as professional development, leadership, and partnerships with parents and community.

♦ *Is what we are doing making a difference?* Formative and summative evaluation.

By doing this work, a school would get all staff agreeing to the main structure of what they want to do for all students, which would put them on at least a three level on the RtI Continuums shown in Chapter 4. This chapter, and the Appendices, show an example school's data so you can see what it would look like if your school answered each of these questions, and then guides your school through the components of the CSI framework. The chapter describes tools that appear in the appendices to support your school in doing this work.

Figure 5.1
CONTINUOUS IMPROVEMENT PLANNING

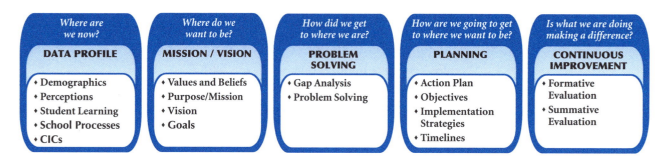

WHERE ARE WE NOW?

The Data Profile

Start with an in-depth appraisal of where your school is right now by creating a comprehensive data profile of the four types of data described in Chapter 3, demographics, perceptions, student learning, and school processes. By laying out these data, over time, your school staff will:

♦ Learn how the student and teaching populations have changed over time.

♦ Gain knowledge of who your students are and what your teachers need to learn about the students to help them learn.

♦ Determine the current health of the organization, and gain ideas to make it healthier.

♦ Understand the impact of philosophies and policies.

♦ Understand how your school is getting the results it is getting now.

♦ Know what staff needs to study, so new approaches to getting better results will be informed by data.

♦ Know if there is instructional coherence.

♦ Understand which programs are working and which programs are not working.

♦ Paint with a broad brush to know how to improve multiple grade levels and subject areas at the same time.

The data profile, first and foremost, tells the story of the school, showing the results the school is getting with the processes that are currently being implemented. The data profile is a needs assessment that assists staffs in knowing what students know and do not know, the health of the organization, and what teachers need to learn to better meet the needs of their students. The data profile is also a beginning of the evaluation of the school and the system.

The data profile is a needs assessment that assists staffs in knowing what students know and do not know, the health of the organization, and what teachers need to learn to better meet the needs of their students.

EXAMPLE: Marylin Avenue Elementary School

Marylin Avenue Elementary School is a typical East San Francisco Bay Area Title 1 school (grades K through 5) that has experienced a rapid increase in the percentage of students coming to school as English Learners and from families living in poverty. Since *No Child Left Behind* was first implemented, California schools have been required to make adequate yearly progress on the *California Standards Tests* (CST) as measured by their *Academic Performance Index* (API)[1]. Unfortunately, between 2001 and 2006, Marylin Avenue's API scores were actually going backward, and not because teachers did not want the scores to improve. Teachers at Marylin Avenue were working very hard, but they could not figure out how to get better results. Considered "under-performing" for four years, Marylin Avenue was placed in Program Improvement in 2006.

API Growth and Targets Met, 2002-03 to 2005-06

Year	Number Tested	Base	Target	Actual	Met Target
2002-03	276	681	6	1	No
2003-04	270	665	6	-17	No
2004-05	313	662	7	-5	No
2005-06	303	651	7	-7	No

In the summer of 2006, seven Marylin Avenue staff members attended a weeklong *Education for the Future Summer Institute* on *Data Analysis and Continuous School Improvement* that assisted them in understanding how to use multiple sources of data to improve student learning. They produced their school data profile, analyzed their data, and created a continuous school improvement plan that they took back and implemented. For the next three years, between two and eleven staff members returned to the Institute to share how they got student achievement increases across the school, what they did to get instructional coherence, and their plans for further improvements. Staff credits the schoolwide gains to the identification of essential standards, comprehensive data analysis, including the creation and/or adoption and implementation of common formative assessments, visioning, structures to implement the vision, and continuous school improvement planning work. The table below shows that, between 2006-07 and 2009-10, Marylin Avenue increased 146 API points (compared to decreasing 28 API points in the previous four years).

API Growth and Targets Met, 2006-07 to 2009-10

Year	Number Tested	Base	Target	Actual	Met Target
2006-07	295	705	6	54	Yes
2007-08	286	745	7	40	Yes
2008-09	280	784	5	40	Yes
2009-10	255	796	5	12	Yes

In beginning its comprehensive data analysis and continuous school improvement journey, Marylin Avenue pulled together its demographic and student learning data, gathered questionnaire data from students, staff, and parents, and began making a list of school processes, to answer the question: *Where are we now?* These data became the foundation for the school's data profile, which they have kept updated over time. The data profile tells the story of the school, helping all staff understand how they are getting the results they are getting.

---

[1]The *Academic Performance Index* (API) measures the academic performance and progress of individual California schools and establishes growth targets for future academic improvement. It is a numeric index (or scale) that ranges from a low of 200 to a high of 1000. A school's score or placement on the API is an indicator of a school's performance level. The interim statewide API performance target for all schools is 800. A school's growth is measured by how well it is moving toward or past that goal.

Create Your Data Profile

Using Appendices B and C as models, and A and D for guidance, create your school's data profile by pulling together your demographic, perceptions, student learning, and school processes data. (If you want a tool to automate the creation of your school's data profile, the *SchoolCity SchoolPortfolio* application uploads your school/district data and creates a data profile, complete with "Look Fors" and "Planning Implications," just like the data profile modeled in Appendix B. The application can also assist you with gathering and graphing questionnaire data, and organizing your school process data.)

SCHOOLPORTFOLIO™

SchoolPortfolio™ is an automated tool that assists with the creation of a school or district portfolio to support the process of systemic continuous improvement in learning organizations.

The SchoolPortfolio is based on the research of *Education for the Future* (Victoria L. Bernhardt, Executive Director) and the elements of a school portfolio.

The SchoolPortfolio automates the data profile (i.e., *demographics, perceptions, student learning,* and *school processes*) and guides the analysis of these data into the creation of a vision, goals, objectives, plan, leadership structure, professional learning plan, partnership plan, and evaluation plan that will improve teaching and learning. Along with automated templates, the SchoolPortfolio provides examples, suggestions, guiding strategies, and activities to complete the entire continuous improvement process.

Source:
http://www.schoolcity.com/html/sp.html

RESOURCES

Appendix B shows our example school's data profile. Appendix C shows what we saw in the data—how each type of data was analyzed for strengths, challenges, and implications for the school improvement plan, and then analyzed and aggregated to inform the vision and continuous school improvement plan. Appendix D provides the process protocol for gathering, analyzing, and aggregating your data for continuous school improvement planning. Appendix A provides the Continuous Improvement Continuums for schoolwide self-assessment.

WHERE DO WE WANT TO BE?

The Vision

A school defines its destination through its mission, vision, goals, and student expectations. The school's vision, goals, and student expectations must also reflect the core values and beliefs of the staff, merged from personal values and beliefs. This level of reflection is paramount. If educators are not cognizant of what they value and believe about being educators, it is impossible to create a shared mission/vision. Creating a vision from core values and beliefs ensures a vision to which all staff members can commit. Without a vision to which all staff members commit, a school's collective efforts have no target.

Staff need to discuss and study the implications of teaching to the current student population, and the changes needed in the school's curriculum, instruction, and assessment approaches to implement best practices before creating a vision.

After analyzing the school data profile, *clarifying where we are right now,* it is important for staff to study different approaches to improving results. Staff need to discuss and study the implications of teaching to the current student population, and the changes needed in the school's curriculum, instruction, and assessment approaches to implement best practices before creating a vision. With new knowledge, a staff can implement new thinking and new strategies—as opposed to signing up for the same thing, or signing up for add-ons.

EXAMPLE: Marylin Avenue Elementary School Vision

Upon reviewing their data, Marylin Avenue staff saw that their staff demographics had stayed essentially the same, even though the student population was changing dramatically. In 2006, staff prepared to create a vision that would be embraced by all staff, and shared with all staff, students, parents, and the community. To learn how to better meet the needs of all of their students, staff read about best practices, reviewed student learning standards/expectations, and created, adopted, and implemented common formative assessments to measure where students were several times throughout the year with respect to the standards.

The analysis of the schoolwide data in 2006 helped all Marylin Avenue staff see that they needed to study how to meet the needs of whom they had as students. They implemented book study groups and read best practices for teaching all subjects. From this groundwork, they knew they needed to revisit their student standards and establish common formative assessments (CFAs). Four questions guided their study: *What do we want our students to learn? How will we know if they have learned it? What will we do if they do not learn it?* and *What will we do if they already know it?* (DuFour, DuFour, Eaker, Many, 2006).

It was also this groundwork that laid the foundation for the first schoolwide vision formed in the fall of 2006. Each year, the vision was reworked. In fall 2009, after implementing their first vision, studying their results, and continuing with their reading of best practices, staff created another vision. This time, the vision was more specific, and based on best practice research and their experiences. The 2009 vision follows. The refinement of the vision to specify an RtI system was done after the analyses of the next three sections were completed, and is shown in Chapter 6. The plan was updated, with additional RtI specifics, for 2010.

EXAMPLE: Marylin Avenue Shared Vision, September 2009

Staff began creating their vision by revisiting their values and beliefs about the *curriculum, instruction, assessment, and environmental* factors that support effective learning for Marylin Avenue students. Core (consensus) values and beliefs follow.

MARYLIN AVENUE CORE VALUES AND BELIEFS

Curriculum	*Instruction*	*Assessment*	*Environment*
• Essential standards unwrapped • Meaningful materials are developmentally appropriate • Modified, as appropriate • Curriculum maps • Tools (Open Court) • Vertical and horizontal alignment • Comprehension, Accuracy, Fluency, and Expand Vocabulary (CAFÉ) • Freedom to use district curriculum as a tool • Research based • Use strategies instead of programs • Include fine arts • Choice and independence (social and emotional)	• RtI system • Spiraling—extra time and support because we believe all kids can learn • Focus on the four questions • Students know what they're learning, their individual goals, and why they are important • Whole group, small group, individual • Checking for understanding throughout the lesson • Background knowledge—build on it or develop it • Writing, writing, writing • Increase nonfiction • Manipulatives to build conceptual knowledge • Students on carpet for mini-lessons and guided practice • Data informed • Flexible, modified • Instructional coherence across all grade levels • All learning modalities used • Student centered • Comprehension, Accuracy, Fluency, and Expand Vocabulary (CAFÉ) • Targeted instruction (Level 1) • Team time (Level 2) • Guided Language Acquisition Design (GLAD) • Lucy Calkins • Academic language • Heads Together • Wait Time • Cooperative learning • Math/Language review • Student/individual goals • Differentiated • Daily 5 • Literacy Studio • Ample time for guided and individual practice towards mastery • Time for students to communicate and cooperate with each other • Foster thinkers	• Common Formative Assessments (CFAs) • Developmental Reading Assessment (DRA) • Checking for understanding (Explicit Direct Instruction [EDI], pre-planned, non volunteer) • Timely and specific feedback. • Data teams at grade levels • Data wall—staff room • Shared protocols for assessments • Benchmarks • Constant monitoring • Administered by trained staff • Pre-assess • Content valid • Engaging multiple measures • Manageable, meaningful, valuable • Balanced with instruction • Easily supported by technology • Discreet balance with application • Students and Parents informed • Targeting instruction • Individual conferencing • Continuum (Reading, Math, Writing) • Criterion-based (skills) • Standards based	• Caring • Structured • Choice • High expectations • Safe • Void of pre-conceived notions • All staff share in responsibility for all students • Student created • FUN! • Common elements in all classrooms • Parent, Teacher, and Community Connections • Everyone is a teacher and learner • Celebrate student success • High expectations that all students can learn • Sense of urgency • Communication across grade level and within each grade level • Collegial • Collaborative • Frequent use of norms • Students feel ownership • Collaboration on curriculum, instruction, and assessment • Calm • Equitable • Goal oriented • Predictable for adults and children • Respectful for all • Everyone can succeed and grow • Love of learning instilled • Encouraging, positive • Clean, orderly, organized • Adult commitment pushes us toward improvement • Professional reading • Highly qualified teachers • Inviting • Large gathering place • Table groups • Shared materials • Class meetings • Purposeful resources, posters on wall • Awareness of student and staff needs • Basic needs met • Time for reflection

EXAMPLE: Marylin Avenue Shared Vision, September 2009

Staff also revisited their mission and came to consensus on this mission statement:

THE MISSION OF MARYLIN AVENUE ELEMENTARY SCHOOL
*is for **all** to develop the confidence to risk, to accept challenges, and to succeed.*
We will learn from our experiences, show compassion for others,
and grow through the joy of discovery. Learning at Marylin Avenue Elementary School
*will enable **all** to achieve their personal best and to be respectful, thoughtful, and independent learners.*

Given what their data told them about their current results, what they learned in their research studies, their core values and beliefs, and mission, Marylin Avenue staff agreed that the following curriculum, instruction, assessment, and environmental strategies would assist them in carrying out their mission.

CURRICULUM: *Marylin Avenue teachers plan instructional content and learning goals based on California State Standards.*

COMPONENTS	WHAT IT WOULD LOOK LIKE
Curriculum is standards based.	• Teachers plan instruction that meets California state standards for literacy, mathematics, social studies, and science.
The collaborative planning of instruction, and the implementation of instruction, for Marylin Avenue students is deep, not just broad.	• All grade-level teams have defined Essential Standards and Super-Power Standards.
The collaborative planning of instruction, and the implementation of instruction, for Marylin Avenue students takes into account the prerequisite skills and concepts required for successful learning (unwrapped standards).	• All grade level teams have unwrapped the Essential and Super-Power Standards to feature the needed prerequisite skills and concepts. • As part of instruction, teachers inform students of the standard being taught, the objective of the lesson that addresses the standard, and the importance of the standard.
Instruction at Marylin Avenue School is horizontally (agreement among grade level team members) and vertically (agreement across the grades) aligned.	• Grade-level teams come to agreement about the meaning and content of standards, Essential Standards, and Super-Power Standards. • Cross-grade-level teams have aligned the Essential Standards. • Literacy Leads act as the cross-grade-level communication structure for agreement in reading and writing standards.
Curriculum is mapped and paced for the school year.	• Grade-level teams draft and agree on year-long curriculum maps to pace instruction.

Curriculum implementation is based on researched-based programs and systems.	Literacy programs and resources include:
	• District-adopted language arts program.
	• District-adopted Step Up to Writing program.
	• Systemic Instruction in Phonics and Phonemic Awareness (SIPPS).
	• Comprehension, Accuracy, Fluency, and Expand Vocabulary (CAFÉ).
	
	Mathematics programs and resources include:
	• District-adopted math program.
	• Math review.
	• Specific and agreed-upon grade-level resources may include such strategies as:
	  * Board language.
	  * Board math.

EXAMPLE: Marylin Avenue Shared Vision, September 2009	
INSTRUCTION: *Students at Marylin Avenue Elementary School are engaged in intellectually demanding tasks that require higher order and critical thinking skills.*	
COMPONENTS	**WHAT IT WOULD LOOK LIKE**
Instruction is based on essential standards.	• Instructional coherence is in place across all grade levels.
Instruction is targeted.	• Learning objectives are based on assessments that assess student standards. • Learning objectives are clearly stated. • Students understand the importance of the learning objective. • Teachers frequently check for understanding and adjust instruction as needed.
Instruction is differentiated to address needs of students.	• Teachers plan for whole group instruction with students on the carpet for mini-lessons and guided practice. • Classroom teachers plan for small group instruction through invitational groups. • Classroom teachers plan for individual instruction through one-on-one conferences. • Students know their individual goals. • All learning styles are addressed. • Multiple exposure through multi-modality instruction. • Teachers provide additional opportunities to learn and practice essential concepts and skills.
A wide variety of instructional strategies are used.	• Effective strategies for English Language Learners include Heads Together, Cooperative Learning, and Wait Time. • Strategies focus on developing schema and building on students' background knowledge. • Tools for developing students' conceptual knowledge include manipulatives, realia, and graphic organizers. • Instruction includes math and language review. • Team time is a structure to provide additional time and support.
Schoolwide instructional practices are research based; grade-level teams agree to the levels of use for instructional practices in their collaborative planning.	Classroom practices for literacy include those supported by: • The district-adopted language arts program. • Literacy Studio management (Daily 5, First 20 Days). • Comprehension, Accuracy, Fluency, and Expand Vocabulary (CAFÉ) Strategies. • Lucy Calkins: Units of Study. • Step Up to Writing. • Developmental Reading Assessment (DRA)-Focus for Instruction. • Guided Language Acquisition Design (GLAD) strategies. Classroom practices for math include those supported by: • The District-adopted math program. • Math review. • Agreed-upon grade-level specific resources.
Instruction is intellectually demanding.	Focus: • Academic language. • Nonfiction reading and writing. • Developing critical-thinking skills.

EXAMPLE: Marylin Avenue Shared Vision, September 2009	
ASSESSMENT: *Marylin Avenue Staff use multiple sources of data from formative and summative assessments to target instruction and measure program effectiveness.*	
COMPONENTS	**WHAT IT WOULD LOOK LIKE**
Our assessments are common, formative, and administered frequently.	• Grade levels agree on which assessments to administer and when. • Grade levels assess each essential standard and conduct data team meetings for most of them. • Teachers use the data from assessments to target instruction for all students. • We look at data from our assessments to determine the effectiveness of instructional strategies and programs. • Our Common Formative Assessments (CFAs) are administered by trained staff every 2 to 3 weeks.
All assessments are based on our unwrapped essential standards, and are content valid.	• Grade levels assess and conduct data team meetings for each essential standard. • All concepts and skills of essential standards are assessed. • Teachers will assess essential concepts and skills.
Assessments will be supported by technology.	• Data Director and the school server will support classroom teachers to collect and analyze data.. • Classroom teachers will receive timely support.
Results from assessments will be shared with students and parents.	• Feedback to students will be timely and specific. • Proficiency and growth will be acknowledged and celebrated on a regular basis. • Student goals will be based on assessments, and will be shared with students and parents at goal setting conferences.
Assessments must be varied.	• Multiple measures (multiple choice, short answer, essay, etc.) need to be used to accurately assess what students know and don't know.

EXAMPLE: Marylin Avenue Shared Vision, September 2009	
ENVIRONMENT: *The learning environment at Marylin Avenue Elementary School is caring, inviting, and safe. It is achieved as staff members model the way for students, for each other, and for the community.*	
COMPONENTS	**WHAT IT WOULD LOOK LIKE**
Learning environment is structured and predictable.	• Routines that are explicitly taught to students are in place for instructional and non-instructional environments. • Common language is used to teach academic, social, and emotional skills. • Processes and procedures are in place so the operation of the school runs smoothly. These are developed as needed. • Traditions are in place, such as the monthly Students Committed to Excellence (SCE) assembly and perfect attendance awards. • All adults implement the behavior plan so that there is consistency for children. • Days are scheduled so that our students' time is structured and predictable.
Interactions are friendly.	• We greet each other. • We greet all students. • We greet parents and members of the community.
Interactions are respectful.	• We use calm voices. • We speak quietly in the hallways and walkways. • We listen and seek to understand. • We encourage each other and cheer for each other. • We focus on the positive.
Campus is clean, orderly, and organized.	• We keep common areas free of clutter, removing obsolete items for which we are responsible. • We leave common areas cleaner than we found them. • We teach students to care for the classroom and for the campus.
Learning is engaging.	• We model the love of learning and the joy of being in school. • A variety of effective instructional strategies are used to address different learning styles. • Students have choices, as guided by teachers.
All staff members are teachers.	• We collaborate with a focus on student achievement. • We conduct ourselves in a professional, collegial manner. • We send minutes of meetings to all staff members. • We keep others informed of pertinent information. • We revise, refer to, and use our norms. • We use the issues bin and the anonymous comments envelope to voice concerns; issues are addressed promptly. • We share leadership. • We assume roles that help share the load of work. • We capitalize on and celebrate the strengths of others. • All adults take responsibility for all children.

EXAMPLE: Marylin Avenue Shared Vision, September 2009

Goals are the outcomes of the vision. Given the staff's core values and beliefs, mission, and vision, the following goals represent what staff believe will result from implementing the vision.

MARYLIN AVENUE SCHOOL GOALS

- All students will exhibit their best effort for themselves, their families, and the community, including a demonstration of respect for their peers and for property.
- We will create an environment where every student, family, staff member, and community member will be excited to be at Marylin Avenue School; and we will be flexible in order to accommodate the educational needs of all.
- All students will be *Proficient* or *Advanced* in Language Arts and Math by the end of fifth grade.

Once the vision was clear and shared, in discussion and on paper, Marylin Avenue staff created a visual of how the parts of the vision work together so all staff can understand it in the same way. The visual of Marylin Avenue's Shared Vision follows.

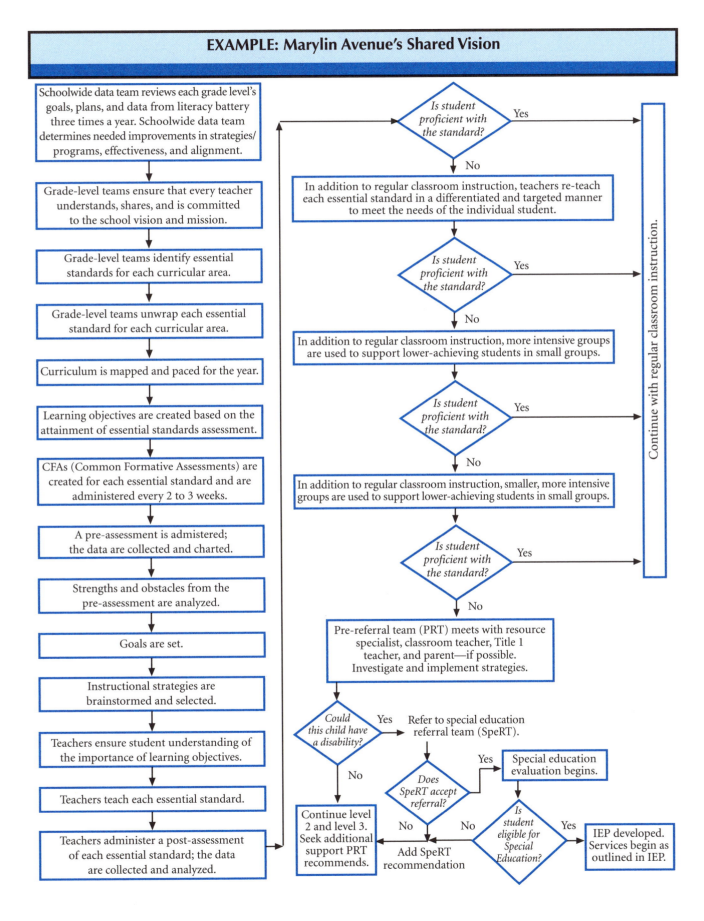

EXAMPLE: Marylin Avenue's Shared Vision

Inspiring a Shared Vision

To create a school vision that is truly shared—committed to unanimously and understood in the same way—we must build on the values and beliefs of the school staff to create core values and beliefs, a core purpose, and a mission for the school. With core values and beliefs, purpose and mission, a vision can be created for the school. We must begin with the personal and move to the collective. Systems thinker Peter Senge (2006) sums up the rationale:

> *Shared visions emerge from personal visions. This is how they derive their energy and how they foster commitment.... If people don't have their own vision, all they can do is "sign up" for someone else's. The result is compliance, never commitment.*

Visions that get implemented are specific and clear so everyone can understand them in the same way.

Visions that get implemented are specific and clear so everyone can understand them in the same way. That is what shared means. We want to see staff members' values and beliefs reflected in the curriculum, instruction, assessment, and environment agreements. If staff members believe certain strategies will impact learning for all students, they will implement them, leading to a truly shared vision that gets implemented. Appendix E contains an activity for creating a shared vision.

RESOURCES

Appendix E houses "Creating a Shared Vision Activity."

HOW DID WE GET TO WHERE WE ARE?

Problem-Solving Cycle

Gaps are the differences between where the school is now (data analysis) and where it wants to be (vision).

After a vision is created, and the data analyzed, staff can determine the gaps in results. Gaps are the differences between where the school is now (data analysis) and where it wants to be (vision). In order to eliminate a gap, staff need to understand the underlying reasons the gap exists; otherwise, they might just be "solving" a symptom.

EXAMPLE: Marylin Avenue Problem-Solving Cycle

As they did every year since the creation of their first vision in 2006, in 2009, staff looked at the difference between where they wanted to be-their vision and goals-and where they are right now, their results. From these analyses, they created their school objectives; they also used the *Education for the Future Problem-Solving Cycle* to study how they got their results, and to think more broadly about issues before they "solved" them. (*The Problem-Solving Cycle Activity* appears as Appendix F.)

In 2006, Marylin Avenue staff defined one of the "problems" they wanted to understand better as "Not enough students are proficient in English Language Arts and Math." Staff brainstormed 20 reasons they thought this problem existed.

Staff's first hunches were external. Eventually, their hunches got more internal. They felt the last four were really close to the contributing causes of their problem.

IDENTIFY THE PROBLEM:
Not enough students are proficient in English Language Arts and Math.

List hunches and hypotheses about why the problem exists.

1. Too many students live in poverty.
2. There is a lack of parent support.
3. There is too much student mobility in our school.
4. The students aren't prepared for school.
5. Many of our students are not fluent in English.
6. Even if the students don't speak English, they have to take the test in English.
7. Students don't do their homework.
8. Students do not like to read.
9. There is no district support.
10. There are budget problems at the school and district levels.
11. We don't know what data are important.
12. We don't know how to use the data.
13. We don't get the data soon enough to make a difference.
14. Not all our curricula are aligned to the standards.
15. Teachers don't know how to set up lessons to teach to the standards.
16. We need to know sooner what students know and don't know.
17. We are not teaching to the standards.
18. Our expectations are too low.
19. We need to collaborate to improve instruction.
20. Teachers need professional learning to work with students with backgrounds different from our own.

EXAMPLE: Marylin Avenue Problem-Solving Cycle

As a third step in the problem-solving cycle, staff reconsidered the problem, "Not enough students are proficient in English Language Arts and Math." Enlightened by their hunches and hypotheses, staff created a list of the questions they would need to answer with data to know more about the problem, before they came up with solutions.

What questions do we need to answer to know more about the problem and what data do we need to gather?

Questions	Data Needed
1. Who are the students who are not performing?	Student achievement results by student groups.
2. What do the students know and what do they not know?	Student achievement results by standards.
3. Are all teachers teaching to the standards?	Standards questionnaire.
4. How are we teaching Mathematics, ELA—actually everything?	Teacher reports about teaching strategies to grade-level teams.
5. What is the impact of our instruction?	We need to follow student achievement by teachers and by course.
6. What do teachers, students, and parents think we need to do to improve?	Teacher, student, and parent questionnaires and follow-up focus groups.
7. What does our data analysis tell us about what we need to do to improve?	Study data analysis results.

It is imperative to follow through with this process by gathering the data and answering the questions. Because staff is a part of learning more about the problem, they will also become a part of the solution. This information is used to refine the vision and the continuous school improvement plan.

Using the Problem-Solving Cycle

The purpose of the problem-solving cycle is to get all staff involved in thinking through a gap and understanding its origins before jumping to solutions. The first three steps in the problem-solving cycle are key and the focus of this activity.

The problem-solving cycle is an outstanding way to get all staff understanding how they are getting the results they are getting now. It is a way to learn what staff are thinking about the problem. The questions and the data required to answer the questions lead to comprehensive data analysis related to the problem, and to new solutions. After completing the problem-solving cycle, you might want to refine your vision to include information gained during this process.

"How can anyone be sure that a particular set of new inputs will produce better outputs if we don't at least study what happens inside?"
(Black & Wiliam, 1998)

RESOURCES

"The Problem-Solving Cycle Activity" appears in Appendix F.

HOW ARE WE GOING TO GET TO WHERE WE WANT TO BE?

The Plan

A school improvement plan lays out how to implement a vision, and includes strategies and activities, person(s) responsible, measurement, expenditures, estimated costs, funding sources, and timelines.

It is not necessary to have every staff member involved in creating a school improvement plan. While it is important that all staff agree with the strategies, it can become cumbersome and inefficient if too many people are working on the plan at the same time. We recommend that the Leadership Team draft the plan, take it to staff for review, improvement, acceptance, and commitment to its implementation. An activity for creating a school improvement plan appears in Appendix G.

EXAMPLE: Marylin Avenue Continuous School Improvement (CSI) Plan

With information from the data profile, the school vision and goals, and knowledge about how they are getting the results they are getting right now, Marylin Avenue staff created a plan to implement their vision. The vision and plan included their leadership structure and professional development as their main supports for implementing the vision and plan. The plan includes strategies and activities, person(s) responsible, measurement, timelines, estimated costs, and funding sources. The Leadership Team drafted the plan, took it to the staff for review, improvement, acceptance, and commitment to its implementation.

(*Note:* This version does not show funding sources or timelines due to space considerations.)

EXAMPLE: Marylin Avenue Continuous School Improvement (CSI) Plan

Goal 1: All students will exhibit their best effort for themselves, their families, and the community, including a demonstration of respect for their peers and for property.

Goal 2: Create an environment where every student, family, staff member, and community member will be excited to be at Marylin Avenue School; and be flexible in order to accommodate the educational needs of all.

Goal 3: All students will be *Proficient* or *Advanced* in Language Arts and Math by the end of fifth grade.

Objective 1: The percentage of students achieving proficiency in ELA, as measured by CSTs, will increase from 51% to 61% by Spring of 2010, measured through student learning results.

Objective 2: The percentage of students achieving proficiency in Math, as measured by CSTs, will increase from 63% to 70% by Spring of 2010, measured through student learning results.

Objective 3: The percentage of English learner students achieving proficiency in ELA, as measured by CSTs, will increase from 36% to 46% by Spring of 2010, measured through student learning results.

Planned Improvements in Student Performance

Strategies and Activities	Person(s) Responsible	Measurement	Expenditures	Estimated Cost
Alignment of instruction with content standards: All grade levels have identified essential standards for all curricular areas. Each essential standard has been unwrapped (in order to feature needed prerequisite skills and concepts), vertically aligned, mapped, and paced for all curricular areas.	Whole Staff / Ongoing	Essential standards are documented for all curricular areas for all grade levels. Grade-level teams agree on the standards. Cross-grade-level teams agree on the standards. Documentation of all essential standards show them to be unwrapped, mapped, vertically aligned, and paced.		
I. Improvement of instructional strategies and materials: A. All teachers will use the unwrapped essential standards to target instruction. 1. Learning objectives will be based on assessment data. 2. Learning objectives will be clearly stated. 3. Students will understand the importance of each learning objective. 4. Teachers will frequently check for understanding and adjust instruction as needed.	Teachers / Ongoing	Classroom observations that describe what instruction and the classroom would look like if RtI implemented will also determine if teachers are: • using the unwrapped essential standards to target instruction • creating clear learning objectives to teach the unwrapped essential standards and to make sure students understand their importance • checking for understanding and adjusting instruction as needed • using grade level assessments of each essential standard • attending data team meetings about the assessment of each essential standard • using CAFÉ/Literacy Studio system with fidelity focusing on nonfiction reading and writing		
B. Each grade level uses balanced assessments that are common, formative, and administered frequently. Assessment will be varied—performance, multi-choice, short answers. 1. Grade levels assess each essential standard and conduct data team meetings for most of them. 2. Grade levels and our schoolwide-data team look at the data from our assessments to determine the effectiveness of instructional strategies and programs. 3. Grade levels administer CFAs every 2-3 weeks.	Grade-Level Teams Ongoing		Grade-Level articulation— two articulation days per grade level Leadership Team Stipends	$7,000 $9,000
C. All teachers K-5 will use CAFÉ/Literacy Studio system with fidelity. D. All grades will focus on nonfiction Reading and Writing and will provide students with more opportunities for authentic writing. E. All grade levels (1-5) will use Board Language in their classrooms.	Teachers / Ongoing	• providing students with more opportunities for authentic writing using Board Language in their classrooms. Documentation exists that grade-level teams and then schoolwide-data-team meetings review the results of the assessments, and check for alignment. Evidence exists that the meeting minutes are shared with all teachers.	Literacy Leads Stipends	$7,000

CAFÉ – *Comprehension, Accuracy, Fluency, and Expand Vocabulary*
CAPE – *Coalition for Affordable Public Education*
CFAs – *Common Formative Assessments*
ELAP – *English Language Acquisition Program*
EIA – *Economic Impact Aid*
QEIA – *Quality Education Investment Act*
SCE – *Students Committed to Excellence*

EXAMPLE: Marylin Avenue Continuous School Improvement (CSI) Plan

Planned Improvements in Student Performance

Strategies and Activities	Person(s) Responsible	Measurement	Expenditures	Estimated Cost
F. Extended learning time: Kindergartners will participate in an extended day program (8:30 am–1:45 pm).		Learning time is extended for Kindergartners.		
II. Increased educational opportunity:				
A. Instruction is differentiated to address students' needs.	Teachers / Ongoing	Classroom observations that describe what instruction and the classroom would look like if RtI implemented will also determine if teachers have a plan for and implement:		
1. Classroom teachers plan for small-group instruction through invitational groups.		◆ small-group instruction through invitational groups		
2. Classroom teachers plan for individual instruction through one-on-one conferences.		◆ individual instruction through one-on-one conferences		
3. Classroom teachers provide additional opportunities to learn and practice essential concepts/skills in the regular classroom (Level 1).		◆ additional opportunities to learn and practice essential concepts and skills in the regular classroom (Level 1)		
B. The school will have policies and procedures in place for addressing school readiness: appropriate placement for entering and at-risk students.	Staff / March 2010	School policies and procedures are in place for enrolling students in Kindergarten.		
1. Develop proactive policies and procedures in place for enrolling students in Kindergarten.		A parent outreach program and Spring intervention program for entering Kindergarten students are created.		
a. Investigate and develop an entrance assessment to be administered at Spring Kindergarten orientation.				
b. Develop a parent outreach program and Spring intervention program for entering Kindergarten students.				
2. Develop common agreements on the skill levels and benchmarks for at-risk students in Math and ELA.	Whole Staff	Agreements are made on the skill levels and benchmarks for at-risk students in Math and ELA for all grades.		
3. Add an after-school program for students who need extra help and a place to be.	After-school program staff	What does the after-school program look like?	After-School Program Staffing and Supplies	$48,965
C. Schoolwide, we will have Levels 2 and 3 of our *Response to Intervention* (RtI) system in place.	Whole Staff	Levels 2 and 3 are in place, and everyone knows what it looks like in her/his classroom.	.4 Science Teacher Instructional Aide Salaries	$84,800
1. Grade-level teams will use data from CFAs to place students in small flexible groups. Instruction will be targeted for a period of 2-3 weeks.	Teachers, Instructional Aides, Science Specialists	Process flowcharts detail how RtI will work for teachers, and how it will work for students.		
2. Classroom teachers, Resource Specialist, Title I Specialist, and classroom assistants will be used to provide small-group targeted instruction (Level 2).				
3. Classroom teachers, Resource Specialist, and Title I Specialist will be used to provide more intensive (smaller group, longer duration) instruction (Level 3).				
4. Universal screening is conducted three times per year to identify students in need of intensive support to meet standards/expectations.				
5. Progress monitoring of student responses to Level 2 or Level 3 instruction will inform instructional decisions for individual students.				

EXAMPLE: Marylin Avenue Continuous School Improvement (CSI) Plan

Planned Improvements in Student Performance

Strategies and Activities	Person(s) Responsible	Measurement	Expenditures	Estimated Cost
III. Staff development and professional collaboration:				
A. Staff development and professional collaboration is frequent and ongoing.	Grade Levels	Are all grade level teams meeting from 1:45 to 3:00?		
1. Grade levels meet every Wednesday from 1:45 to 3:00. Collaboration is focused on results from CFAs and on effective instructional strategies.	Staff / Ongoing	Does the whole staff meet once a month for Professional Development? Is the Professional Development tied to the plan?		
2. Whole staff meet once a month for ongoing professional development tied to our plan.		How often do teachers coach each other? Do they support deep implementation of CAFÉ strategies? What is deep implementation? What does it look like? How would you spot it? How do you coach it? Does every teacher know?		
3. Schoolwide, we will use peer coaching to support deep implementation of CAFÉ strategies.	Whole Staff		Subs for periodic teacher observations	$2,000
4. Develop and implement peer coaching system, including documentation.	Whole Staff	Is a system in place to research and conduct similar school visits with a focus on grades K-2?	Subs and travel expenses for similar school visits	$2,000
5. We will continue to research and conduct similar school visits with a focus on grades K-2.				
IV. Involvement of staff, parents, and community (including interpretation of student assessment results to parents):		What do the assessment reports for students and parents look like? When are the assessments given and when are the results provided for students and parents? How is proficiency and growth acknowledged and celebrated?		
A. Results from assessments will be shared with students and parents.	Teachers / February 2010			
B. Feedback to students will be timely and specific.		Are student goals created on the basis of assessments? Are they shared with students and parents at goal-setting conferences? How often do the goal-setting conferences happen?		
C. Proficiency and growth will be acknowledged and celebrated on a regular basis.				
D. Student goals will be based on assessments, and will be shared with students and parents at goal-setting conferences.				
V. Auxiliary services for students and parents (including transition from preschool to elementary, and elementary to middle school):	Staff / Ongoing	Partnerships among Marylin Avenue, CAPE, and Migrant Preschool are created and carried out.		
A. We will develop a partnership with CAPE and Migrant Preschool as one of our goals for our incoming Kindergarten students.				
VI. Monitor program implementation and results:	Grade Levels	Do the grade levels conduct CFAs every 2-3 weeks to differentiate instruction, and to measure effectiveness of instructional strategies?		
A. Grade levels will conduct CFAs every 2-3 weeks to differentiate and target instruction, and to measure effectiveness of instructional strategies.		Do grade level teams review the CFAs and assist teachers in differentiating instruction and in measuring the effectiveness of instructional strategies?		
B. Conduct universal screening three times per year.				
C. Conduct progress monitoring (Levels 2 and 3).	Whole School	Do schoolwide data teams meet after each literacy battery to measure program effectiveness? Are resources allocated on the basis of these meetings? Are grade-level goals and plans monitored and evaluated during the schoolwide-data-team process?		
D. Schoolwide, we will conduct a data team meeting after each literacy battery (3 times a year) to measure program effectiveness, and to decide on allocation of school resources.				
E. Grade-level goals and plans will be monitored and evaluated during the schoolwide-data-teams process.	Teachers	Is the School Portfolio maintained and used for progress monitoring and continuous improvement?	Updating School Portfolio	$1,400
E. Utilize curriculum associates benchmark assessments 2-3 times a year.	Leadership Team			
F. Continue to use our school portfolio with the various tools we have learned (*Continuous Improvement Continuums, Gallery Walk,* and other data).				
VII. Implement positive behavior system:	Staff / Ongoing	Does everyone know the behavior system and how to record behaviors? Are student behaviors treated consistently?		
A. Agree on behavior approach.				
B. Develop systems for recording.				
C. Teach students the system.				

RESOURCES

"Developing a Continuous School Improvement Plan Activity"
is found in Appendix G.

A Leadership Structure With Clear Roles And Responsibilities For All Staff

We believe the job of leaders is to help everyone in the organization implement the vision. We also believe that each teacher is a leader. Every school should have a structure in place that will help every staff member implement the vision, as well as collaborate with colleagues to help each other implement the vision. These structures are often called "leadership structures" because they also support shared decision making. The important elements of effective leadership structures include:

> ### CREATE A LEADERSHIP STRUCTURE
> ♦ **Partitioning of the school staff in a manner tha makes sense for supporting the implementation of the vision.**
> ♦ **Clarifying purposes and roles and responsibilities of all teacher teams.**
> ♦ **Identifying times to meet and keeping them sacred.**

- *Partitioning of the school staff in a manner that makes sense for supporting the implementation of the vision.* For example, in elementary schools, establishing grade-level teams and cross-grade-level teams to implement the vision makes sense. This is especially effective since the focus is to make sure each teacher is implementing grade level standards, and to ensure that the standards are calibrated across grade levels. Most traditional high schools and middle schools have departments, which could represent an effective leadership structure—if that structure supports the implementation of the vision. However, if the middle school or high school is trying to integrate subjects, individual subject-specific departments might keep the school from implementing its vision. The leadership structure must reflect the vision.

- *Clarifying purposes and roles and responsibilities of all teacher teams.* Getting the teachers to create and agree on the purpose and roles and responsibilities of each team helps them know the intricacies of the team as well as contribute to the successful implementation of each team. A part of identifying roles and responsibilities is to set structures for norms, timed agendas, and rotating roles (facilitator, timekeeper, and recorder) to keep the team focus on student learning.

- *Identifying times to meet and keeping them sacred.* The teams meet no matter what. There can be no cancellations because of other meetings. It is important to not put the principal as lead of any team. We find that the principal is often pulled out at the last minute, and then the team thinks the meeting has to be cancelled. However, the principal should participate in as many meetings as possible. To implement the vision with a strong leadership structure, the team meeting times and agendas must be adhered to. At least one hour a week needs to be dedicated to grade level or subject-area teams to review data and update instruction. Additional time needs to be protected for leadership team meetings and other leadership teams. Time must be created. Many schools bank time by extending the school day four days a week, providing an early dismissal or late start for students so teachers can meet part of one day a week.

EXAMPLE: Marylin Avenue School Leadership Structure

Marylin Avenue Elementary School created a leadership structure in order to clarify how the vision will be implemented. The leadership structure, complete with roles/responsibilities, and meeting times, follows.

EXAMPLE: Marylin Avenue School Leadership Structure

Marylin Avenue Elementary School's (MAS) leadership structure is four-pronged:

- Grade-Level Teams
- Marylin Avenue Leadership Team (MALT)
- Literacy Leads
- Principal

All leadership components are guided by the Mission and Vision statements for the school, and the work of each leadership component is guided by data and the school plan.

All meetings are scheduled on the school calendar. All meetings are open to all staff members; therefore, every attempt will be made to send agendas in advance or with the current meeting minutes. In the event of additions and/or deletions to agendas, staff will be informed by e-mail.

MAS staff are working to strengthen cross-grade-level leadership. Currently, Literacy Leads are the most systematic method of articulating expectations for literacy across grade levels.

Schoolwide focus is student learning and is guided by four important questions:

- *What do we want our students to learn?*
- *How will we know if they have learned it?*
- *What will we do if they don't learn it?*
- *What will we do if they already know it?*
  (DuFour, DuFour, Eaker, and Many, 2006)

Instruction is based on content standards and is delivered through well-designed lessons. Planning for instruction includes goal-setting by teachers and with students, accountability-based assessments, and implementing a response to intervention system for students needing extra time and support to learn.

Meeting Times

Team	Time	Day
Grade-Level Teams	1:45 to 3:00 PM	Wednesdays
Marylin Avenue Leadership	3:15 to 4:30 PM	Wednesdays
Literacy Leads	3:00 to 4:00 PM	Alternate Wednesdays *(calendered by the group)*

Roles and Responsibilities

It is the collective responsibility of all teachers, working in grade-level teams and cross-grade-level teams, to implement instruction that addresses content standards. All classroom teachers participate in grade-level team meetings on a weekly basis.

The Title I Reading Specialist and the Special Education Resource Teacher join grade-level teams weekly to facilitate Pre-Referral Team meetings (PRT), and Special Education Referral Team (SpERT) meetings.

One teacher at each grade level serves as the Grade-Level Lead; this teacher sits on MALT. One teacher at each grade level serves in the role of Literacy Lead for her/his grade level; MAS is attempting to keep this role stable for a number of years in order to build grade-level capacity for leadership in literacy.

EXAMPLE: Marylin Avenue School Leadership Structure

Grade-Level Teams

The purpose of grade-level teams is to maintain the cohesion of curriculum, instruction, and assessment toward the goal of equitable instruction and classroom environment. Grade level teams will:

- create, adopt, review, and revise norms as needed, in support of working effectively together;
- study together, coach each other, and support one another in the implementation of the standards and the school's vision;
- seek support from one another;
- study and support each other's implementation of best practices;
- seek support from specialists on staff, as needed;
- grade-level meetings will be conducted in each other's classrooms on a rotating basis;
- function as Data Teams;
- organize, manage and monitor Levels 2 and 3 intervention groups;
- work with their respective Grade-Level Aide to organize, manage and monitor Levels 2 and 3 intervention groups; and
- plan and conduct Pre-Referral Team (PRT) and Special Education Referral Team (SPERT) meetings.

Marylin Avenue Leadership Team (MALT)

MALT is a decision-making body and, as such, members must practice clear and objective communication to the staff members whom they represent, and to fellow MALT members as representatives for other staff members.

MALT is made up of the Principal, the Principal's Secretary, the Resource Specialist, and a representative from each grade-level team; the Grade-Level Lead. Input from teachers will be communicated to the Grade-Level Lead, input from Science Teachers will be communicated via the Principal, input from Instructional Assistants will be communicated via the Resource Specialist, and input from classified staff will be communicated via the Principal's Secretary. The Issues Bin and the Anonymous Comments envelope are also avenues for all staff to give input to MALT.

The purposes of MALT are to:

- support the implementation of standards within and across grade levels;
- guide, support, and reinforce the school plan using multiple sources of data;
- plan and conduct the schoolwide data teams to monitor the improvement of instruction and student achievement;
- provide ongoing input into budgetary decisions, all of which are based on data and available resources;
- plan "next steps" toward the improvement of school systems and structures on behalf of student achievement;
- oversee and approve the design of agendas for staff development, which may include cross-grade-level meetings;
- disseminate information;
- troubleshoot the concerns of grade levels and individuals;
- improve and support school climate by modeling effective communication skills and leadership skills; and
- calendar schoolwide assessments and events.

EXAMPLE: Marylin Avenue School Leadership Structure

Literacy Leads

The purpose of Literacy Leads is to focus on literacy standards and the effective learning of the content of the standards. This structure is made up of representative grade-level team members and, as such, must practice clear and objective communication to the grade level they represent. This team's work is facilitated by its members. The responsibilities of the Literacy Leads include:

- focusing on instructional coherence for Level 1 instruction;
- reviewing and clarifying the implementation of state standards as they apply to strengthening effective classroom instruction schoolwide;
- working to strengthen the cross-grade-level alignment of literacy planning, implementation, and assessment;
- sharing best practices and effective lessons toward the goal of bringing these to respective grade-level teams;
- making decisions about schoolwide literacy practices;
- planning and implementing staff development in literacy ;
- making budgetary recommendations to MALT in support of schoolwide literacy development and materials; and
- planning and implementing schoolwide literacy projects such as the Read-a-Thon, Turn Off Your TV Week, and augmenting classroom libraries and library habits that support reading engagement.

Principal

The role of the principal is to ensure:

- the implementation of the vision, plan, and leadership structure;
- that staff receive the professional development they need;
- that all staff use data to impact learning for *all* students;
- quality instruction in every classroom; and
- communication is often and of high quality.

Create Your School's Leadership Structure

Follow the information provided in this section and the Marylin Avenue example to create a leadership structure that helps everyone in the organization implement the vision.

Professional Development Calendar Created from the School Improvement Plan and Leadership Structure

Once the plan, based on the data analysis, vision, and leadership structure, is completed, school staffs can benefit from a Professional Development Calendar. A Professional Development Calendar starts with those agreed upon times for the teams to meet, and then pulls from the plan what the teams should be working on at any point in the school year calendar; thereby setting the topic for each meeting. Many principals have found the Professional Development Calendar to be extremely valuable in keeping the whole school on target with implementing the vision, plan, and leadership structure. Some principals say the use of the calendar makes things happen that have never happened before, even though the activities had been "planned." All the purposes or topics in the calendar are derived from the school improvement plan.

Some principals say the use of the calendar makes things happen that have never happened before, even though they had been "planned."

EXAMPLE: Marylin Avenue Professional Development Calendar

The first month of the Marylin Avenue 2009-10 Professional Development Calendar is shown in the example below.

2009-10 CALENDAR

Date	Who Should Attend	Purpose
July 27-31 All day	Leadership Team and Literacy Leads	Attend the *Education for the Future* Summer Data Institute.
August 20-21 8:00 AM to 4:00 PM	Professional development for all staff	Expectations for the year. Select team members and team leaders. Review standards. Model how to unwrap standards to feature needed prerequisite skills and concepts, how to vertically align, map, pace for all curricular areas, and review assessment data. Grade-level teams continue with standards.
August 25 3:05 to 4:15 PM	Cross-Grade-Level Teams	Establish a system to monitor assessment data and ensure the alignment of standards across grade levels.
September 1	All teachers	Conduct literacy assessment.
September 1 3:00 to 4:00 PM	Literacy Leads	Verify Language Arts standards across grade levels.
September 2 1:45 to 3:00 PM	Grade-Level Team	Map Language Arts standards to the curriculum. Review assessment data. Create learning objectives.
September 2 3:15 to 4:30 PM	Leadership Team	Planning for the year.
September 9 1:45 to 3:00 PM	Grade-Level Team	Map Math standards to the curriculum. Review assessment data. Create learning objectives.
September 9 3:15 to 4:30 PM	Leadership Team	Continue planning for the year.
September 14	All teachers	Content standards English Language Arts and Math Practice.
September 15 3:00 to 4:00 PM	Literacy Leads	Verify Language Arts standards across grade levels.
September 16 1:45 to 3:00 PM	Whole staff	Work on Vision with Vickie and Brad from *Education for the Future*.
September 21	All teachers	District writing assessment.
September 22 3:05 to 4:15 PM	Cross-Grade-Level Teams	Monitor assessment data and ensure the alignment of standards across grade levels.
September 23 1:45 to 3:00 PM	Grade-Level Team	Review progress.
September 23 3:15 to 4:30 PM	Leadership Team	Determine assessment reports that will assist staff in implementing and assessing standards.
September 24 3:15 to 4:30 PM	Data Team	Determine how to lead staff in developing common formative assessments.
September 28 3:45 to 4:45 PM	Professional development for all staff	Inservice on ELA/RtI/Assessments.
September 29 3:00 to 4:00 PM	Literacy Leads	Translate inservice idea to all grade levels.
September 30 1:45 to 3:00 PM	Grade-Level Team	Ensure implementation.
September 30 3:15 to 4:30 PM	Leadership Team	Ensure implementation.

Create Your Professional Development Calendar

Create your Professional Development Calendar by laying out the dates of team meetings and professional development and who should attend. From the continuous school improvement plan, determine the purpose of the meetings. If the calendar looks undoable, you will need to revise your school plan.

HOW ARE WE GOING TO GET TO WHERE WE WANT TO BE?

Plan for Parent Involvement

Continuous school improvement calls for real partnerships among the schools and families—partnerships that are consistent, organized, and centered on meaningful communication.

Continuous school improvement calls for real partnerships among the schools and families—partnerships that are consistent, organized, and centered on meaningful communication. This communication allows parents to play important roles in their children's education across academic, behavioral, and social domains, and to inform the evaluation of effectiveness and continuous improvement efforts.

EXAMPLE: Marylin Avenue Elementary School Partnerships

Marylin Avenue staff members are aware that parents have unique insights about their child's strengths and challenges and are eager to help with interventions at home. Involvement at school begins with communication. Marylin Avenue has developed good relationships with frequent communication among classroom teachers, support staff, and parents. Teachers do not hesitate to ask colleagues and support personnel for assistance in communicating with families, or in seeking clarification when miscommunications happen. (Throughout, the use of the term "parent" includes guardians.)

Marylin Avenue has realized this communication is critical for continued implementation of effective RtI processes and even more critical for evaluating the system. With this in mind, teachers are formally communicating with parents the multi-level interventions and the strategies or approaches used to address areas of concern for individual students. During parent-teacher conferences, individual student data are shared in visual form to highlight areas of progress and areas of concern. Teachers can then describe specific locations, frequencies, durations, and focuses of interventions that will be delivered for a student determined in need. Parents can also learn of specific activities for supporting these efforts from home. To learn more about parent perceptions, Marylin Avenue School administers parent questionnaires.

Teachers discuss additional ways to communicate with parents and give them strategies as a part of primary instruction-before students are in need of additional intervention. Ideas involve hosting strategy workshops for parents in the evening or game nights where the focus is for parents and students to learn games and activities that can be done at home to support the learning as it occurs in the classroom.

This could involve making or purchasing some board games, card games, music CDs, and other materials that allow early literacy, comprehension and vocabulary building, writing, and numeracy or math skills to be practiced at home. These materials are available at school for parents or students to check out, or for teachers to send home at strategic times based on individual student needs.

To better accommodate parent involvement, Marylin Avenue is looking to expand opportunities for parents to be at the school. Conferences are held during extended hours for parents who work; school personnel team up and make home visits to ensure parents are included whenever possible; and planning parent contacts and communication with awareness and sensitivity to community or other grade level activities, especially for families with multiple children, are just a few examples. Staff continually explore and discuss ways to enhance this component with each other, with the community, and especially with families.

Create Your School Partnership Plan

Start with your standards. What do you want students to know and be able to do?

With potential partners, brainstorm what each can do to support students in achieving the standards.

IS WHAT WE ARE DOING MAKING A DIFFERENCE?

Continuous Improvement and Evaluation

By making a listing of all the programs and processes used in the school, along with their intents, Marylin Avenue staff members have started the hard work of knowing if what they are doing is making a difference. They are also, in effect, evaluating the implementation of their vision. The Marylin Avenue data profile, vision, problem-solving cycle work, plan, and evaluation data are used to answer the question, *Is What We Are Doing Making A Difference?*, and to create the overall evaluation plan discussed in Chapter 7.

Evaluate Your Continuous School Improvement Efforts

See Chapter 7 for detailed information on evaluation.

BOOK STUDY QUESTIONS

♦ Why is it important to start the creation of an RtI system with comprehensive data analysis?

♦ How will looking across all types of data help a school create an effective vision?

♦ How will looking across all types of data help a school create an effective RtI system?

♦ What is the importance of having a shared vision before specifying RtI details?

TEAM STUDY QUESTIONS

♦ If your school does not have a data profile, pull your data together to answer the question: *Where are we now?* (Use Appendix D for guidance.)

♦ If your school does not have a shared vision in place, set a time to produce one with your staff. (An activity for creating a shared vision is provided in Appendix E.)

♦ After identifying gaps, use the problem-solving cycle to understand more about how your school is getting the results it is getting now. (See Appendix F for the problem-solving cycle activity.)

♦ Create a continuous school improvement plan to implement the vision that is based on your comprehensive data analysis and vision. (See Appendix G for an action plan activity.)

♦ Describe your leadership structure that would ensure the implementation of the vision.

♦ Create a professional development calendar that spells out when the parts of your vision and plan will be implemented.

♦ Create a partnership plan that begins with what you want students to know and be able to do.

Chapter 6

DESIGNING AND IMPLEMENTING RtI WITH CONTINUOUS SCHOOL IMPROVEMENT: THE RtI PART

"We found that if every teacher implements our vision as intended, using identified research-based instruction and assessment strategies, we have an excellent start on implementing the intent of RtI. We did the hardest part already—we got staff agreement and alignment of research-based classroom practices we all need to implement. We agreed on how and when students would be assessed and what we will do instructionally with students on the basis of the assessments. What we have to do now is make clear to everyone what she/he needs to do to ensure implementation fidelity, monitor what everyone is doing so we can support each other, and understand how to be most effective; and then we need to evaluate the impact of our implementation. It will be a lot of work, but well worth the effort."

Marylin Avenue staff as they worked together to design and implement their RtI system.

Designing an RtI system with continuous school improvement calls for a vision that is implemented through the continuous school improvement plan, with the support of data, leadership, professional learning, and parent involvement, as described in Chapter 5. With these structures in place, schools can refine the vision to include the specifics of RtI and ensure the implementation of a responsive prevention system. This chapter describes the specifics of RtI and shows how our example school refined its vision to include these RtI specifics.

RtI COMPONENTS

One of the best reasons for setting up continuous school improvement before identifying and implementing the specifics of RtI is that the structures to implement a schoolwide RtI system are already created, and hopefully in place. The schoolwide plan, leadership structures, professional learning, and partnership development all work together to ensure the implementation of the vision and RtI system. RtI cannot be implemented schoolwide without agreements and implementation of specific elements and the clarification of the roles of staff.

> *RtI cannot be implemented schoolwide without agreements and implementation of specific elements and the clarification of the roles of staff.*

Much of what is needed for a successful RtI system includes:

- clarification of the intent of RtI,
- what RtI would look like when it is implemented,
    - refinement of an assessment system,
    - identification of research-based curriculum and instructional practices that address learning and behavioral needs of students in the school,
    - determination of interventions,
    - student support teams,
- the documentation of the assessments and interventions,
- definition of roles and responsibilities, and
- a plan for parent involvement.

INTENT OF RtI

As schools refine their visions to design RtI systems, it is imperative for them to clarify the intent of RtI with all staff members, which will help define the specifics. While identifying the intent, it is helpful to describe how you will know the intent will be met.

EXAMPLE: Marylin Avenue Elementary School RtI Intent

Marylin Avenue staff agreed that the intent of RtI at Marylin Avenue Elementary School is to:

- Implement, in every classroom, quality, research-based instruction and assessment strategies that address students' needs and differences, and are based on essential learning standards.
- Maximize all students' learning.
- Reduce behavior problems.
- Ensure that all students are primarily educated in the general education environment, with access to the general education content, materials, and expectations.
- Ensure the appropriate identification of students with special needs.

They also determined how they will know the intent is being met:

- When RtI is implemented as intended, instructional coherence and a continuum of learning that makes sense for all students will be evident.
- What students learn in one grade level will build on what they learned in the previous grade level.
- Individual student achievement results will improve each year. All students will be proficient in all areas. No students will need to be retained.
- Progress monitoring and common formative assessments, conducted within the classroom setting, during the school day, will be utilized to identify struggling students and why they are struggling.
- Interventions matched to student needs will result in student learning increases for all students.
- The number of office referrals will be minimal.
- Students will not be placed in special education for the wrong reasons, such as teachers wanting students out of the classroom because of behavior or lack of learning response, poor test-taking skills, English language proficiency levels, or not having received high-quality instruction or adequate interventions.
- Attendance will improve.

WHAT RtI WOULD LOOK LIKE IF IT IS IMPLEMENTED

Figure 6.1 outlines the essential components, their definitions, and considerations for designing an RtI system, which include:

- refinement of an aligned, comprehensive assessment system to continually inform practice;
- identification of research-based curriculum and instructional practices that address learning and behavioral needs of students in the school;
- determination of prevention levels and evidenced-based interventions;
- and student support teams and referral procedures.

Figure 6.1
ESSENTIAL COMPONENTS FOR DESIGNING AN RtI SYSTEM

RtI Components		Definitions	Consideration
ASSESSMENT SYSTEM	**Universal screening**	Universal screenings are assessments used to identify students who may be at risk for poor learning outcomes. Universal screening tests are brief; conducted with all students at a grade level; and followed by additional testing or short-term progress monitoring to corroborate students' risk status. (National Center on RtI, April 2009.)	What assessment tools will be used to screen students in designated areas of performance (i.e., Literacy, Writing, Math, Behavior)?
	Progress monitoring assessment	Progress monitoring is used to assess students' academic performance, to quantify a student's rate of improvement or responsiveness to instruction, and to evaluate the effectiveness of instruction. Progress monitoring can be implemented with individual students or an entire class. (National Center on RtI, April 2009.)	What assessment tools will be used to monitor student performance and progress in designated areas of performance (i.e., Literacy, Writing, Math, Behavior)?
	Cut point	A cut point is a score on the scale of a screening tool or a progress monitoring tool. For universal screeners, educators use the cut point to determine whether to provide additional intervention. For progress monitoring tools, educators use the cut point to determine whether the student has demonstrated adequate response, whether to make an instructional change, and whether to move the student to more or less intensive services. (National Center on RtI, April 2010.)	At what performance level will students receive secondary level interventions? At what performance level will students receive tertiary level interventions?
	Benchmarks or formative assessments	Formative assessment is a form of evaluation used to plan instruction in a recursive way. With formative assessment, student progress is systematically assessed to provide continuous feedback to both the student and the teacher concerning learning successes and failures. With formative assessment, teachers diagnose skill, ability, and knowledge gaps, measure progress, and evaluate instruction. Formative assessments are not necessarily used for grading purposes. Examples include (but are not limited to): Curriculum Based Measurements (CBM), Classroom Based Assessments (CBA), pre/post tests, portfolios, benchmark assessments, quizzes, teacher observations, and teacher/student conferencing. (National Center on RtI, April 2010.)	What benchmarks or formative assessments will be developed and used by the teachers? When will assessments be administered? Will teachers have help in scoring assessments? When and how will scores be shared with students, parents, etc.?

Figure 6.1 *(Continued)*
ESSENTIAL COMPONENTS FOR DESIGNING AN RtI SYSTEM

RtI Components		Definitions	Consideration
INSTRUCTION AND INTERVENTIONS	**Multi-level prevention system (primary, secondary, tertiary) with evidence-based instruction and interventions in academics and behavior for each level.**	*Primary prevention,* the least intensive level of the RtI prevention framework, typically includes the research-based core curriculum and the instructional practices used for all students. Students who require interventions due to learning difficulties continue to receive instruction in the core curriculum. *Secondary prevention* typically involves small-group instruction that relies on evidence-based interventions that specify the instructional procedures, duration (typically 10 to 15 weeks of 20 to 40-minute sessions), and frequency (3 or 4 times per week) of instruction. Secondary prevention has at least three distinguishing characteristics: it is evidence-based (rather than research-based); it relies entirely on adult-led small-group instruction rather than whole-class instruction; and it involves a clearly articulated, validated intervention, which should be adhered to with fidelity. *Tertiary prevention* is the most intensive of the three levels and is individualized to target each student's area(s) of need. At the tertiary level, the teacher begins with a more intensive version of the intervention program used in secondary prevention (e.g., longer sessions, smaller group size, more frequent sessions). The teacher conducts frequent progress monitoring (i.e., at least weekly) with each student. When the progress monitoring data indicate the student's rate of progress is unlikely to achieve the established learning goal, the teacher engages in a problem-solving process. By continually monitoring and modifying (as needed) each student's program, the teacher is able to design effective, individualized instruction.) (National Center on RtI, April 2010.)	How will instruction be delivered at each level? Whole group, individual, specified numbers in each group, etc.? Who will provide and/or assist with the delivery of instruction?
	Evidence-based instruction and interventions. (Includes procedures, duration, frequency, and length of sessions.)	Evidence-based practices are educational practices and instructional strategies that are supported by scientific research studies. Intensive academic and/or behavioral interventions are characterized by their increased focus for students who fail to respond to less intensive forms of instruction. Intensity can be increased through many dimensions including length, frequency, and duration of implementation. Within RtI, intensive is sometimes referred to as tertiary intervention. (National Center on RtI, April 2010.)	Who will provide the intervention sessions? Where will the sessions take place? How frequent will the sessions occur? How long will each session be? How many sessions will occur before evaluating effectiveness? How often will progress be monitored? How and when will decisions to change intervention intensity occur; or to remove students from intervention? How will implementation fidelity and integrity be monitored/ instructional coherence be maintained? What are the instructional materials and resources to be used at each level of prevention/intervention? What are the specific strategies and approaches to be used?
	Standard Protocol Intervention	Standard protocol intervention relies on the same, empirically validated intervention for all students with similar academic or behavioral needs. Standard protocol interventions facilitate quality control. (National Center on RtI.)	Will we use a standard protocol intervention? What similar academic and/or behavioral needs do our students demonstrate? How will implementation fidelity and integrity be monitored?

Figure 6.1 *(Continued)*
ESSENTIAL COMPONENTS FOR DESIGNING AN RtI SYSTEM

RtI Components		Definitions	Consideration
SUPPORT TEAMS	**Support team membership and procedures.**	Support teams are a designated group of teachers who review student performance data to monitor students assigned to intervention groups and assist with decisions to change intervention intensity. Support teams also engage in problem solving to determine additional interventions prior to referral, making the decision to refer only when a lack of acceptable progress, after multiple evidence-based intervention, is demonstrated. (National Center on RtI, April 2010.)	Whom should our Support Team include? How often, when, and where will they meet? How will the team document level, frequency, duration and effectiveness of interventions?
	Referral criteria for consideration of special services.	If a student fails to respond to intervention, the student may have a learning disability or other disability that requires further evaluation. Progress monitoring and other data collected over the course of the provided intervention should be examined during the evaluation process, along with data from appropriately selected measures (e.g., tests of cognition, language, perception, and social skills). (National Center on RtI, April 2010.)	What is the process for determining if students should be considered for special services? How many different interventions? How many sessions? What demonstrates a lack of acceptable progress or failure to respond?

Assessment System

An effective RtI system requires designing a multi-level prevention system of evidence-based interventions to address the needs of students who are at risk for poor learning outcomes.

An effective RtI system requires designing a multi-level prevention system of evidence-based interventions to address the needs of students who are at risk for poor learning outcomes. This requires the identification of universal screening and progress monitoring instruments, benchmark or formative assessments, some of which are administered to every student every two to three weeks. Assessments should be evaluated to determine if they are reliable and valid; and to determine if they are aligned with curriculum and standards outcomes. Assessments that are reliable, valid, and aligned will assist with predicting how students will perform on annual assessments and, therefore, assist in preparing students for these assessments. Additionally, students need to be assigned to intervention groups and progress needs to be monitored with an assessment instrument that is reliable, valid, brief, sensitive to small amounts of growth, and easily administered in the classroom.

EXAMPLE: Marylin Avenue Elementary School RtI Assessment

To help them with the RtI considerations and to ensure common understandings of the implementation and use of assessment data, Marylin Avenue staff implemented their shared vision for assessment (outlined in Chapter 5). Staff utilize multiple assessments across academic and behavioral areas to continually inform instruction and flexible grouping, and to assist with decisions regarding referral.

ASSESSMENT SYSTEM AT MARYLIN AVENUE ELEMENTARY SCHOOL

Type of Assessment	Instrument(s)/Tool(s) or Definition	Administration

Universal screening.	• California State Test scores (Annual Performance Test)
	 • Literacy Battery
	   * Developmental Reading Assessment (DRA)
	   * Basic Phonic Skills Test (BPST)
	   * Spelling Inventory
	   * Common Formative Assessments
		Literacy Battery is administered 3 times per year (fall, winter, and spring) to all students.

Progress monitoring assessment.	• Common Formative Assessments • Systematic Instruction in Phoneme Awareness, Phonics, and Sight Words (SIPPS) Mastery Assessments • Read Naturally Assessments	Common Formative Assessments are administered every 2 weeks for all students and inform progress; SIPPS and Read Naturally assessments are used with students in those programs.
Cut point.	Cut points from the published assessments are used for each grade level in DRA, BPST, SIPPS and Read Naturally to determine placement in secondary or tertiary levels, and to assist in determining adequate progress.	
Benchmarks or formative assessments.	Vertically and horizontally aligned standards have informed the development of common formative and/or benchmark assessments that are also accumulative of skills across time.	Administered every 2 weeks to all students.

Determination of Interventions

Staffs must agree upon and establish procedures and evidence-based practices for each prevention level as well as determine the location, frequency, length, and number of intervention sessions for each level. Additionally, student support team members need to be identified to meet regularly to review assessment data, assign students to intervention levels or adjust those assignments, and eventually make decisions regarding referral for consideration of special services.

EXAMPLE: Marylin Avenue Elementary School RtI Assessment

During the initial year of implementation, Marylin Avenue staff completed a grid defining the components of the RtI system for the school and for each grade level in order to assist the Leadership Team with planning.

	Secondary Prevention Defined	Tertiary Prevention Defined
Entry criteria (cut point on universal screening).	DRA and BPST established criteria per grade level.	DRA and BPST established criteria per grade level.
Progress-monitoring tools.	Common formative assessments (every 2 weeks); SIPPS Master Assessments.	Common formative assessments; Program-specific assessments.
Number and length of interventions (range or description).	Thirty minutes per day; 10 to 12 days (review progress).	Thirty minutes per day; 10 to 12 days (review progress).
Intervention procedures.	Small-group instruction: not more than 6 students.	Small-group instruction: not more than 3 students.
Materials/instructional resources.	Systematic Instruction in Phonemic Awareness, Phonics, Sight Words. (SIPPS).	SIPPS.
Exit criteria (cut point).	Grade-level performance.	Grade-level performance.
Criteria for consideration of referral for special education evaluation.	Tertiary level required before consideration for referral.	At least two interventions (one change in intervention) and limited or no progress.

GRADE 3 EXAMPLE	Secondary Prevention Defined	Tertiary Prevention Defined
Entry criteria (cut point on universal screening). Teacher requests also considered when classroom performance indicates a need.	DRA / BPST — Fall Below 28 / Below 70; Winter Below 34 / Below 75; Spring Below 38 / Below 85	DRA / BPST — Fall Below 20 / Below 65; Winter Below 24 / Below 70; Spring Below 30 / Below 75
Progress-monitoring tools.	SIPPS mastery assessment; Common Formative Assessments.	Read Naturally Assessments; Common Formative Assessments.
Number and length of interventions (range or description).	Thirty minutes, 4 times per week, 10 to 12 days/sessions (complete 2 cycles with limited progress before moving to Tertiary Level).	Thirty minutes, 4 times per week, 10 to 12 days.
Intervention procedures.	Small-group instruction (3 to 6 students); Direct instruction with SIPPS and specific reading goals on leveled books.	Smaller group instruction (3 or fewer students); Direct instruction with Read Naturally or other materials that target deficit area.
Intervention materials/instructional resources.	Grade-level performance on CBM.	Grade-level performance on CBM.
Exit criteria (cut point).	Tertiary level required before consideration for referral.	Limited or no progress after at least 3 sets/cycles of intervention sessions and 2 or more differing intervention approaches.
Criteria for consideration of referral for special education evaluation.		

Staff must also identify research-based curriculum, instructional practices, and evidence-based interventions for students at risk of poor learning outcome.. While many schools have engaged in practices associated with aligning curriculum to standards and implementing assessments to inform instruction, the work of designing a multi-level prevention system for all areas of academic and behavioral performance involves greater specificity and investigation of evidence-based interventions across all areas. Many schools create their RtI system by focusing on one area at a time. Marylin Avenue has been working primarily in English Language Arts, but is ever mindful of the needs of students in the performance areas of behavior, math, and science. They are defining the multi-level prevention system for each of these performance areas as they acquire resources and expand staff expertise.

EXAMPLE: Marylin Avenue Elementary School RtI Implementation

Marylin Avenue staff created a flowchart of their RtI system that builds from their school vision flowchart (shown in the Vision Example in Chapter 5), to ensure that all staff members understand what it would look like when each staff member is implementing the intent of RtI. As staff become more proficient with their early tries at RtI, they discover that they need to create specific flowcharts for each subject area and sometimes grade levels, because the assessments and instruction may vary and because they want to spell out the details. The grade three reading flowchart follows.

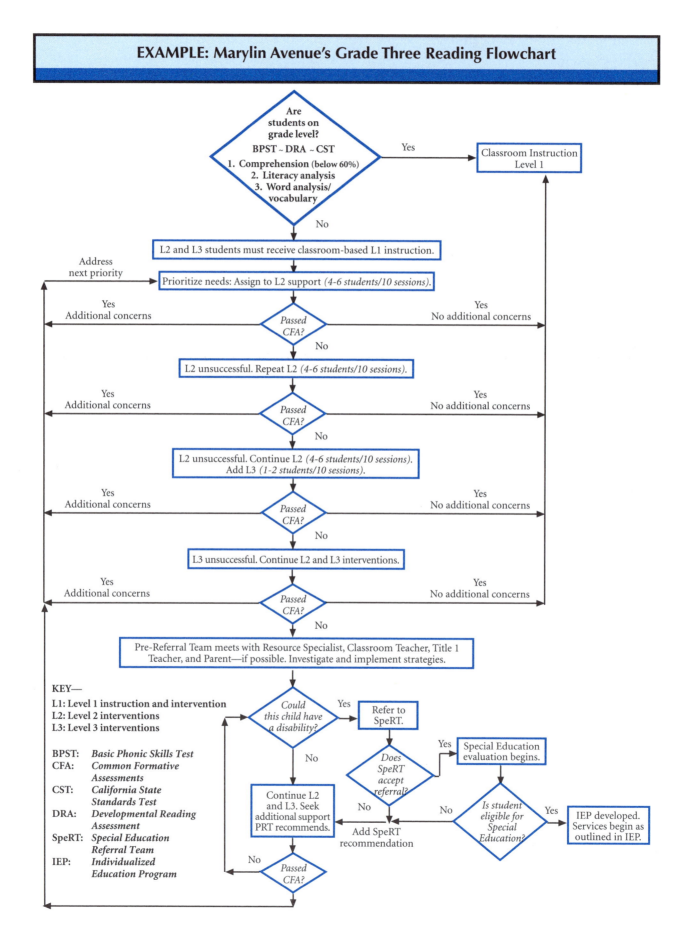

EXAMPLE: Marylin Avenue's Grade Three Reading Flowchart

Are students on grade level?
BPST ~ DRA ~ CST
1. **Comprehension** (below 60%)
2. **Literacy analysis**
3. **Word analysis/ vocabulary**

Yes → Classroom Instruction Level 1

No

L2 and L3 students must receive classroom-based L1 instruction.

Address next priority

Prioritize needs: Assign to L2 support *(4-6 students/10 sessions)*.

Passed CFA?
Yes — Additional concerns
Yes — No additional concerns
No

L2 unsuccessful. Repeat L2 *(4-6 students/10 sessions)*.

Passed CFA?
Yes — Additional concerns
Yes — No additional concerns
No

L2 unsuccessful. Continue L2 *(4-6 students/10 sessions)*. Add L3 *(1-2 students/10 sessions)*.

Passed CFA?
Yes — Additional concerns
Yes — No additional concerns
No

L3 unsuccessful. Continue L2 and L3 interventions.

Passed CFA?
Yes — Additional concerns
Yes — No additional concerns
No

Pre-Referral Team meets with Resource Specialist, Classroom Teacher, Title 1 Teacher, and Parent—if possible. Investigate and implement strategies.

Could this child have a disability?
Yes → Refer to SpeRT.
No

Does SpeRT accept referral?
Yes → Special Education evaluation begins.
No → Add SpeRT recommendation

Continue L2 and L3. Seek additional support PRT recommends.

Is student eligible for Special Education?
No
Yes → IEP developed. Services begin as outlined in IEP.

Passed CFA?
No

KEY—
L1: Level 1 instruction and intervention
L2: Level 2 interventions
L3: Level 3 interventions

BPST:	*Basic Phonic Skills Test*
CFA:	*Common Formative Assessments*
CST:	*California State Standards Test*
DRA:	*Developmental Reading Assessment*
SpeRT:	*Special Education Referral Team*
IEP:	*Individualized Education Program*

RESOURCES

Flowcharting is a valuable way to display the elements and flow of programs, processes, and vision. Use the flowcharting activity in Appendix I to help staff understand how your school is getting the results it is getting now, and to get agreement on the major steps in a process.

DOCUMENTATION

In designing RtI systems, schools need to document interventions and responsiveness to interventions to inform decision making. This documentation will assist with the evaluation of the RtI system by identifying how well the assessments inform instruction and intervention practices. Additionally, individual student documentation is used to meet the requirements to assist in the identification of a student with a disability. Figure 6.2 describes the different levels for data source documentation considerations, what to look for in the data sources, and what the data analysis for those data sources might look like, using our example school's data. Figure 6.3 shows an example *Documentation of Pre-Referral Interventions and Strategies* form. This type of documentation is vital when the team begins to review existing data to determine the need for special education evaluation.

In designing RtI systems, schools need to document interventions and responsiveness to interventions to inform decision making.

Figure 6.2
DATA DOCUMENTATION CONSIDERATIONS FOR DESIGNING AND IMPLEMENTING AN RtI SYSTEM

Data Documentation	Look For...	Looks Like...
1. How many students do we have performing at or above grade level/expected levels of performance?	1. Review to assist with grouping for instruction. Review to inform curriculum and instruction issues through item analysis and sub-group performance. Monitor over time to note change in numbers at each performance level.	1. Bar graph of performance over time.
2. How well do our current practices in curriculum and instruction help students reach expected levels of performance? (primary level)	2. Review numbers of students served at secondary and tertiary levels; length of time or number of sessions before intervention is no longer needed; review to inform intervention match and effectiveness with student needs.	2. Triangle graph for annual data and for each benchmark period.
3. How well do the secondary and tertiary curriculum, materials, instruction, and interventions help students reach expected levels?	3. Number of referrals for consideration of special education; number of students evaluated; number and percentage of students evaluated that are eligible for special education services.	3. Table.

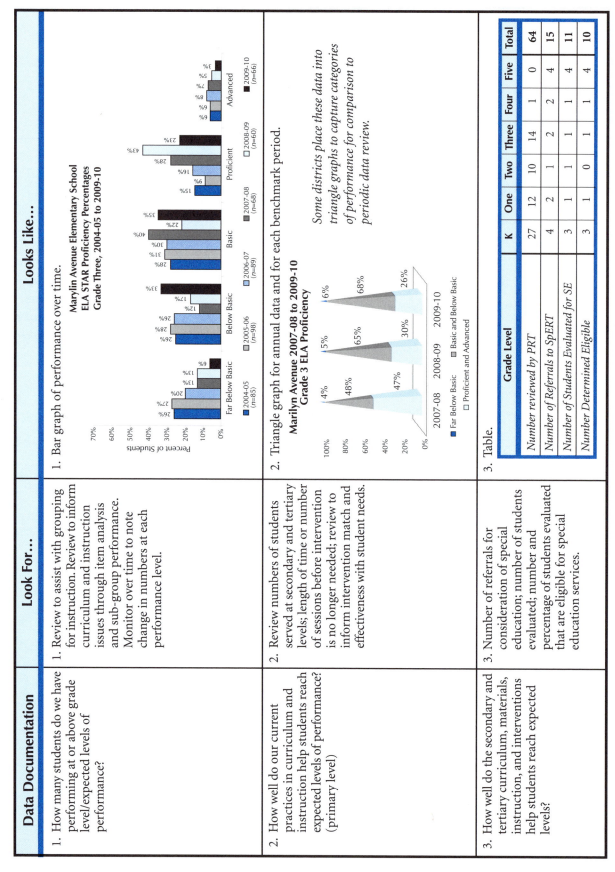

**Marilyn Avenue Elementary School
ELA STAR Proficiency Percentages
Grade Three, 2004-05 to 2009-10**

**Marilyn Avenue 2007-08 to 2009-10
Grade 3 ELA Proficiency**

Some districts place these data into triangle graphs to capture categories of performance for comparison to periodic data review.

Grade Level	K	One	Two	Three	Four	Five	Total
Number reviewed by PRT	27	12	10	14	1	0	**64**
Number of Referrals to SpERT	4	2	1	2	2	4	**15**
Number of Students Evaluated for SE	3	1	1	1	1	4	**11**
Number Determined Eligible	3	1	0	1	1	4	**10**

Figure 6.2 (Continued)
DATA DOCUMENTATION CONSIDERATIONS FOR DESIGNING AND IMPLEMENTING AN RtI SYSTEM

Data Documentation	Look For...	Looks Like...
4. How well do the primary, secondary, and tertiary curriculum/materials, instruction, and interventions help students reach expected levels? (Include number of students in each level and movement among levels from benchmark to benchmark.)	4. Number of students at primary, secondary, and tertiary levels; number of students at or above expected performance on other formative assessments; number below expected level of performance; number far below expected level of performance.	4. Monitor number of students at each level of intervention/ instruction; using the same type of graph as used in annual performance data review is helpful for comparison.
5. How well does our RtI system support the accurate and timely identification of students with disabilities?	5. Number of students at each level of instruction/ intervention in one classroom for individual teachers to monitor class performance/ progress; evaluate instructional match to student needs; and establish instructional groups and assign students to levels of intervention.	5. Classroom-level data (some electronic monitoring systems will provide this type or similar chart for this purpose).

Marilyn Avenue Grade 3 ELA Proficiency

	2008-09	2009-10
Far Below Basic	5%	6%
Basic + Below Basic	65%	68%
Proficient + Advanced	30%	26%

Marilyn Avenue 2009-10 Grade 3 Literacy Battery (DRA, BPST)

	Fall	Winter	Spring
Far Below Target	39%	14%	14%
Below Target	28%	42%	20%
At or Above Target	33%	45%	66%

Grade Level	DRA Level 2009-10 Fall (20/28)	DRA Level 2009-10 Winter (24/34)	DRA Level 2009-10 Spring (30/38)	BPST 2009-10 Fall (70/85)	BPST 2009-10 Winter (70/85)	BPST 2009-10 Spring (80/85)
3	28	40	40	81	85	85
3	28	34	38	79	85	85
3	34	38	38	78	85	85
3	28	34	38	70	85	85
3	34	38	38	82	84	85
3	16	30	38	82	84	85
3	28	34	40	79	84	85
3	20	24	28	76	84	85
3	14	24	34	81	83	85
3	14	24	38	59	83	85
3	24	30	34	72	82	85
3	14	30	34	70	79	80
3	8	24	34	69	77	80
3	14	30	38	65	75	77
3	8	24	28	47	75	77
3	3	12	16	33	73	77
3	3	12	18		68	70

Legend: Far Below Target ■ Below Target ■ At or Above Target □

Figure 6.2 (Continued)
DATA DOCUMENTATION CONSIDERATIONS FOR DESIGNING AND IMPLEMENTING AN RtI SYSTEM

Data Documentation	Look For...	Looks Like...
6. How well do the interventions at the secondary and tertiary levels meet the needs of individual students?	6. Progress monitoring of performance with a measure that informs instruction for the targeted area (reading fluency; phonemic awareness; numeracy skills; etc.). Decision points need to be established, such as frequency of progress monitoring, number of data points above aim line before decreasing intervention, number of data points below aim line before changing interventions for better results (there are specific recommendations in the literature for these decisions if using CBM).	6. Individual student graphing (electronic data monitoring systems may also produce this type or similar graph for same purpose). **Reading Fluency – Words Correct** **Sample Student**
7. How do we know when to refer for consideration of special education?	7. Documentation of individual number and length of interventions, as well as response to interventions used for referral for consideration of special education after continued intervention, or after repeat years of intervention use, to maintain performance.	7. Documentation of pre-referral interventions and strategies (See Figure 6.3).

	PROBLEM IDENTIFICATION		INTERVENTIONS				EVALUATION	
	Specific Performance Concern	Baseline Performance Information	Intervention/ Strategy	Performance Goal (Measurable)	Intervention Frequency and Length (1x/week; 20 minutes)	Time Period for Use (Begin Date / End Date)	Summary of Performance	Intervention Results
INTERVENTION 1								Total # of Sessions: ____ Did student reach goal? Yes☐ No☐ Is student making progress? Yes☐ No☐
INTERVENTION 2								Total # of Sessions: ____ Did student reach goal? Yes☐ No☐ Is student making progress? Yes☐ No☐
INTERVENTION 3								Total # of Sessions: ____ Did student reach goal? Yes☐ No☐ Is student making progress? Yes☐ No☐

Comments/Team Notes/Decisions:

Figure 6.3
DOCUMENTATION OF PRE-REFERRAL INTERVENTIONS AND STRATEGIES

PROBLEM IDENTIFICATION		INTERVENTIONS					EVALUATION	
Specific Performance Concern	Baseline Performance Information	Intervention/ Strategy	Performance Goal (Measurable)	Intervention Frequency and Length (1x/week; 20 minutes)	Time Period for Use		Summary of Performance	Intervention Results
					Begin Date	End Date		
INTERVENTION 1								Total # of Sessions: _____ Did student reach goal? Yes☐ No☐ Is student making progress? Yes☐ No☐
INTERVENTION 2								Total # of Sessions: _____ Did student reach goal? Yes☐ No☐ Is student making progress? Yes☐ No☐
INTERVENTION 3								Total # of Sessions: _____ Did student reach goal? Yes☐ No☐ Is student making progress? Yes☐ No☐

Comments/Team Notes/Decisions:

Student Support Teams

A fully integrated RtI system features partnerships among classroom teachers, administrators, other staff, parents, and students.

A fully integrated RtI system features partnerships among classroom teachers, administrators, other staff, parents, and students. These partnerships—focused on implementing a multi-level prevention system to ensure success for all students—lead to the formation of "teams" who provide ongoing support and professional learning experiences for all of those involved. While these teams may have different names in the school setting, their basic function is to monitor student performance, evaluate, and document interventions.

Student support teams, also known as Student Assistance Teams, Teacher Assistance Teams, Problem-Solving Teams, Learning Needs Teams, or RtI Teams, design specific interventions targeted to a student's deficit, usually based on classroom performance and assessment data. This places the team in an excellent position to document and monitor the interventions, and to identify students who need referral for consideration of special education evaluation.

The two common approaches to implementation of RtI are the *standard treatment protocol* and the *problem-solving* approach. Both approaches require universal screenings (benchmark assessments) for all students to alert teachers to students at risk of academic or behavioral failure. Both approaches include secondary and tertiary instructional and behavioral interventions.

The standard treatment protocol approach utilizes preset interventions for common academic or behavioral difficulties and is applied in secondary or tertiary level interventions.

The standard treatment protocol approach utilizes preset interventions for common academic or behavioral difficulties and is applied in secondary or tertiary level interventions. Predetermined performance levels, or cut points from universal screening assessments, place a student in a designated intervention strategy or program designed to address the most common reasons for poor performance. These programs often have a recommended intervention schedule for number and length of sessions as well as instructional group size. They may also have accompanying progress monitoring assessments to guide instruction as well as monitor student performance for movement between levels.

In contrast, the problem-solving approach requires the team to review each individual student who qualifies for secondary and tertiary interventions and develop an individualized plan based on that student's profile. The plan includes interventions and progress monitoring procedures. Teachers find they often use similar or even the same interventions with students as there are similar reasons for poor performance.

A combined approach usually involves identifying students who reflect a specific performance deficit or learning profile to access specific interventions with designated progress monitoring methods, using the standard treatment protocol. Only students who demonstrate unique performance deficits receive a plan developed with the problem-solving method for individualized programming. This greatly expedites the intervention process and honors the reality that many students have common deficits and benefit from similar intervention programming.

Many existing pre-referral teams have the structures in place that can easily be modified or adjusted to accommodate an RtI model with either the standard treatment protocol approach or the problem-solving approach, or a combination. One major adjustment these teams often have to make is identifying students for intervention based on performance on the universal screening assessment instead of waiting for teacher referral, which requires the Student Support Team to analyze screening data to identify these students.

These teams also serve as the "gate-keepers" to special education for students suspected of having a learning disability. As RtI systems become fluid and effective, all requests for consideration of evaluation for learning disabilities and other high incidence areas are directed to the RtI procedures for proper documentation of student responsiveness to instruction and intervention.

The problem-solving approach requires the team to review each individual student who qualifies for secondary and tertiary interventions and develop an individualized plan based on that student's profile.

A combined approach usually involves identifying students who reflect a specific performance deficit or learning profile to access designated interventions with designated progress monitoring methods.

EXAMPLE: Marylin Avenue Elementary School PRT and SpERT

Marylin Avenue uses Pre-Referral Teams (PRT) and Special Education Referral Teams (SpERT).

PRT: Pre-Referral Team

At Marylin Avenue, the Pre-Referral Teams are grade-level teams that meet to discuss students who continue to struggle after intervention is provided through the multi-level system under supervision of the classroom teacher. The problem-solving model is used to identify additional interventions. Selected interventions are implemented with progress monitoring data collected and reviewed by the team following implementation. The PRT may include classroom teachers, resource specialist, title teachers or other specialists as well as parents when possible. When these interventions are unsuccessful and the student does not make acceptable or adequate progress, the team considers referral for special education evaluation. If this team suspects the student could have a disability, they pass the information acquired from interventions implemented and other relevant information to the Special Education Evaluation Team (SpeRT).

SpERT: Special Education Referral Team

The Special Education Referral Team is the team of professionals that reviews the interventions used and progress made with an individual student to see if there is support to suspect that this could be a student with a disability, therefore requiring a complete evaluation. If this is the case, permission to evaluate is sought from the parents and a Multi-Disciplinary Team (MDT) conducts the evaluation to determine if a disability exists. If the SpeRT determines there is not sufficient information to suspect a disability and, therefore, will not seek permission to conduct the evaluation, or if permission for an evaluation is denied, then the SpeRT generates additional recommendations for the classroom teacher, grade level team, and multi-level intervention providers to use with the student. Likewise, if the student is not found to have a disability and be eligible for special education services, the MDT generates additional recommendations for the classroom teacher, grade level team, and multi-level intervention providers to use with the student.

ROLES OF STAFF IN THE IMPLEMENTATION OF RtI

RtI, implemented with integrity and fidelity, calls for new and/or expanded roles for every staff member in the school and those from the district who work closely with schools.

Successful RtI systems rely on the leadership of a strong principal to bring general educators, special educators, speech and language therapists, school psychologists, school counselors, Title I specialists, and instructional specialists together to learn and share information on how students learn, how to assess what students know, and how to avail themselves of curriculum resources.

Figure 6.4 provides a summary of staff members' roles and responsibilities within an effective RtI system.

Figure 6.4
PRIMARY ROLES AND RESPONSIBILITIES IN AN EFFECTIVE RtI SYSTEM

What is the role of...	in... Assessment (benchmark and progress monitoring)	Instruction	Intervention	Data Analysis	Collaboration	Evaluation of Program/ Services	Evaluation of Student Performances (Secondary or Tertiary Supports)	Evaluation for Special Education Eligibility— Severe Learning Disability (SLD)
District Administrator(s) and School Board	Allocation of resources: funds, staff, materials, calendar.	Allocation of resources: funds, staff, materials, and tools, calendar.	Allocation of resources: funds, staff, materials, and tools.	Allocation of resources: funds, staff, and tools.	Allocation of resources: staff development, calendar (time).	Evaluate building administrators, evaluate program and process data.	Allocation of resources, professional development.	Allocation of resources, professional development.
Building Administrator(s)	Allocation of resources: funds, staff, professional development, schedule, materials, fidelity checks, evaluation, and feedback.	Allocation of resources: funds, staff, professional development, schedule, materials, coherence, evaluation, and feedback/ supervision.	Allocation of resources: funds, staff, materials, tools, scheduling, professional development, evaluation, and feedback.	Allocation of resources: funds, staff, training, tools-knowledgeable of analysis procedures and use of tools; participates in analysis with staff.	Allocation of resources: staff development, schedule, contribute as collaborator in planning, intervention, and teaching assignments; supervision.	Evaluate staff; evaluate program and process data. Utilize these data in analysis for improvement	Allocation of resources; professional development; supervision or oversight.	Allocation of resources; professional development; supervision or oversight.
Special Education Administrator(s)	Allocation of resources: funds, staff, professional development, materials.	Allocation of resources: funds, staff, professional development, materials, evaluation, and feedback/ supervision.	Allocation of resources: funds, staff, professional development, materials, evaluation.	Allocation of resources: funds, staff, training, tools; knowledgeable of analysis procedures and use of tools; participates in analysis with staff.	Allocation of resources for staff development; time and commitment of staff for collaboration; supervision.	Evaluate staff; evaluate program and process data; utilize these data in analysis for improvement.	Allocation of resources; professional development; supervision.	Allocation of resources; professional development; supervision of eligibility determination.
General Education Teacher(s)	Conducting/ interpreting results.	Delivery of core curriculum; differentiating; coherence; providing accommodations.	Delivery of secondary sessions and possibly tertiary sessions for select students or based on expertise.	Collection of data; use of data tools; participate in analysis with staff; translate results for students into interventions.	Participate and contribute to plan for instruction and intervention, using data; seek assistance when needed; provide support in area(s) of expertise.	Assist in process and program effectiveness data and analysis for improvement; contribute additional intervention ideas.	Collect data on students when delivering secondary or tertiary interventions; team member for determining satisfactory progress and next steps.	Representative on collaborative team for determination of eligibility.

Figure 6.4 *(Continued)*
PRIMARY ROLES AND RESPONSIBILITIES IN AN EFFECTIVE RtI SYSTEM

What is the role of...	in... Assessment (benchmark and progress monitoring)	Instruction	Intervention	Data Analysis	Collaboration	Evaluation of Program/Services	Evaluation of Student Performances (Secondary or Tertiary Supports)	Evaluation for Special Education Eligibility—Severe Learning Disability (SLD)
Special Education Teacher(s)	Conducting/interpreting results.	Support to general educators via consultation, push in, direct instruction, provide specially designed instruction. Collaborate with general education teachers to deliver core curriculum to select students.	Delivery of secondary and/or tertiary sessions.	Collection of data; use of data tools; participate in analysis with staff; translate results for students into interventions.	Participate and contribute to plan for instruction and intervention, using data; provide consultation for accommodation; seek assistance when needed; provide support in area(s) of expertise.	Assist in process and program effectiveness data and analysis for improvement; contribute additional intervention ideas.	Collect data on students when delivering secondary or tertiary interventions; team member for determining satisfactory progress and next steps.	Representative on collaborative team for determination of eligibility. May provide additional support during evaluation.
Remedial Teacher(s) (Title, etc.)	Conducting; interpreting results.	Remediation (see intervention).	Delivery of secondary and tertiary sessions.	Collection of data; use of data tools; participate in analysis with staff; translate results for students into interventions.	Participate and contribute to plan for instruction and intervention, using data; provide consultation for accommodation.	Assist in process and program effectiveness data and analysis for improvement; contribute additional intervention ideas.	Collect data on students when delivering secondary or tertiary interventions; team member for determining satisfactory progress and next steps.	Representative on collaborative team for determination of eligibility
Psychologist(s)/ Psychological Examiner/ Diagnosticians	Conducting/interpreting results; training; fidelity checks.	Assist with designing of accommodation; consultation.	Assist with designing, progress monitoring, fidelity checks.	Collection of data; assist with/participate in analysis; translate results for students into interventions.	Consult and provide assistance in collaborative structures.	Assist in collection of process and program effectiveness data and analysis for improvement; contribute additional strategies and intervention ideas.	One team member contributing to determination of satisfactory or lack of progress and next steps, including referral for evaluation.	Administer standard assessments only if necessary; interpret and share results; contribute to collaborative decision for determination of eligibility as one member of team.

Figure 6.4 (Continued)
PRIMARY ROLES AND RESPONSIBILITIES IN AN EFFECTIVE RtI SYSTEM

What is the role of...	in... Assessment (benchmark and progress monitoring)	Instruction	Intervention	Data Analysis	Collaboration	Evaluation of Program/Services	Evaluation of Student Performances (Secondary or Tertiary Supports)	Evaluation for Special Education Eligibility—Severe Learning Disability (SLD)
*Counselor(s)	*Dependent on job description.	Delivery of counseling curriculum.	Possible secondary or tertiary sessions.	Participate in analysis with staff; assist in translating results into instruction.	Participate in and contribute to planning instruction and interventions, using data.	Assist in collection of process and program effectiveness data and analysis for improvement.	*Dependent on job description.	Part of collaborative team for determination of eligibility; or providing additional data depending on additional areas of concern.
Speech/Language Therapist(s)	Conducting (especially early literacy for student with speech issues); interpreting results.	Support general education teachers via consultations; push-in services. Collaborate in area(s) of expertise.	Possible secondary or tertiary sessions, especially for students with speech or language issues.	Participate in analysis with staff; translate results for students into intervention; use data tools.	Participate and contribute to plan for instruction and intervention, using data.	Assist in collection of process and program effectiveness data and analysis for improvement.	Collect data on students when delivering secondary or tertiary interventions; team member for determining satisfactory progress and next steps.	Part of collaborative team for determination of eligibility; provide additional assessment if needed, depending on primary areas of concern.
Paraprofessional/ Classroom Assistant(s)	Conducting assessments (optional).	Supportive role— as directed by supervising teacher (usually small group management/ supervision).	Possible delivery of secondary or tertiary interventions with supervision— especially with "scripted" programs.	Possibly collection of data; participate in analysis with staff.	Participate and contribute to plan for instruction.	Optional— minimally provide feedback or observations on implementation.	Optional team member.	Optional team member.
Music, Art, Library, P.E. (Encore; Auxiliary; etc.)	Optional.	Delivery of general curriculum/ standards; integrating content.	Possible delivery of secondary or tertiary interventions; or enrichment during designated/ scheduled intervention times.	Collection of data; use of data tools; participate in analysis with staff; translate results for students into interventions.	Participate and contribute to plan for instruction using data; provide consultation in areas of expertise.	Assist in process and program effectiveness data and analysis for improvement.	Optional team member.	Optional team member.

*Positions differ from state-to-state in scope and expectation with roles and responsibilities shifting accordingly.

A Plan For Parent Involvement

The focus on preventive, early intervention with frequent data collection to ensure student success requires strong communication and positive relationships among school staffs and families. Continuous school improvement and RtI systems require partnerships among the schools and families that are consistent, organized, and centered on meaningful communication. This communication allows parents to play important roles in their childrens' education across academic, behavioral, and social domains.

Continuous school improvement and RtI systems require partnerships among the schools and families that are consistent, organized, and centered on meaningful communication.

Schools must plan carefully how to initiate and maintain the information flow about RtI systems, and the monitoring and reporting of student progress. Since each level of support calls for more intensive interventions and more frequent data collection, each level should involve more frequent and explicit school-parent communications. These communications need to inform parents about their child's needs, the interventions being delivered, and the progress monitoring results. Providing early, consistent, ongoing communication with parents regarding interventions becomes critical and extremely beneficial if a decision is needed regarding referral for consideration to evaluate for special education.

Schools must consider the characteristics of their communities and parents in order to communicate effectively (e.g., non-English speaking families, diverse). This will require sensitivity in communications, from the earliest stages that describe generally the processes that are being created and implemented for RtI, to the advanced stages of communications about evaluation of the processes, as well as information regarding individual students' needs and progress.

Staff need to be consistent yet flexible when it comes to parent/family involvement. Not all parent involvement will necessitate physically coming to the school, and not all parent involvement will happen during the traditional school day/hours. Schools already design and adjust parent teacher conferences and communications about grades and traditional measures of student performance to accommodate increased involvement; but this creativity and adjustment may need to expand to involve parents in learning strategies and activities to be used at home to support primary, secondary, and tertiary prevention levels. Electronic communications can be powerful approaches to reaching parents.

BOOK STUDY QUESTIONS

♦ What are the components that support a quality RtI system?

♦ What implementation structures would help every teacher implement the school vision and RtI system?

TEAM STUDY QUESTIONS

♦ Complete a program planning worksheet to spell out the intentions and expectations of your RtI process. (The activity for doing this appears in Appendix H.)

♦ List and describe the components that need to be in place to support the implementation of your RtI system by completing the planning chart provided (Figure 6.3). What components are present or missing in your school?

♦ Create a flowchart of an RtI structure for your school. (Use Appendix I for guidance.)

♦ For your RtI implementation, state the roles and responsibilities for—

   * Principals

   * Regular Education Teachers

   * Special Education Teachers

   * School Psychologists

   * Counselors

   * District Administrators

   * Instructional Specialists

   * Paraprofessionals

   * Speech and Language Specialists

   * Title 1 Specialists (e.g., reading)

   * Reading Specialists

   * Resource Specialists

♦ How will these various roles relate to one another differently than before?

♦ How are these roles related to student success with RtI ?

Chapter 7

EVALUATING CSI AND RtI

Having a structure for implementing our schoolwide vision, plan, and RtI system is wonderful. That has helped get all teachers doing the same thing. The work is hard and time slips by. Without an evaluation process in place, the whole year could be gone before we know if there was something we could have done different or better. Luckily we have the metrics identified and planned, and we know that what we are doing is making a difference. We are getting the results! It is very exciting!

A Marylin Avenue teacher

To conduct a comprehensive evaluation of CSI and RtI, schools need to understand the impact of the parts and how the parts align to create the whole. When schools create a data profile such as the one shown in Appendix B, they make a great start with their comprehensive evaluation. They simply need to use the analyses in the data profile to go deeper into the data and to answer the specific questions.

This chapter explores thinking through the evaluation of continuous school improvement and RtI systems, using the Marylin Avenue Elementary School's systems as examples. The evaluation report of Marylin Avenue's first year of implementing RtI in English Language Arts (ELA) is shown at the end of the chapter.

To conduct a comprehensive evaluation of CSI and RtI, schools need to understand the impact of the parts and how the parts align to create the whole.

EVALUATION AND CONTINUOUS SCHOOL IMPROVEMENT

Continuous improvement is the constant adapting of programs and processes by getting and using evaluative information. Through continuous improvement processes, we seek to understand how we are getting our current results and then how to improve our processes and operations to better implement the vision and goals. Evaluation is . . . *the systematic inquiry to judge the merit, worth, and/or significance of a program, policy, innovation, and/or organization, and to support decision-making.* (American Evaluation Association, *www.eval.org*)

Continuous improvement is the constant adapting of programs and processes by getting and using evaluative information.

To continuously improve a school, we need to evaluate the parts and the whole; make sure the parts equal what we are trying to do overall; and ensure that what we are doing overall is what we intend to be doing. In this chapter, we start this process by thinking about how we would evaluate the following:

♦ school improvement plan;

♦ school goals; and

♦ programs and processes.

Evaluating the School Improvement Plan

High quality school improvement plans tell staffs how to implement the school vision. Most school improvement plans have a measurement column that indicates whether or not an activity has been completed. Many staffs think the measurement column also represents an evaluation of the plan. It does not. The measurement column is very important for determining if the parts of the plan are being implemented and are on schedule. It does not, however, tell staff if what they are planning or doing is effective.

To evaluate the implementation of the plan, one needs to think about how staff will know that the planned strategies were implemented. To evaluate the effectiveness of the plan, one needs to consider how staff will know if the plan was effective and if the goals were achieved.

To evaluate their school improvement plan, Marylin Avenue staff placed the first column of activities and strategies from the school improvement plan next to the measurement column, which answers the question *How will we know if this got done?* Staff then created a third column that asks a deeper question than the measurement column addresses: *How will we know if what we are doing is effective?* Figure 7.1 shows the first iteration of the evaluation design of the Marylin Avenue school plan. To complete the effectiveness evaluation, staff will need to analyze the data spelled out in the effectiveness column.

Figure 7.1
EVALUATION OF THE MARYLIN AVENUE SCHOOL IMPROVEMENT PLAN, GOAL 3, JANUARY 2010

Goal 1: All students will exhibit their best effort for themselves, their families, and the community, including a demonstration of respect for their peers and for property.

Goal 2: Create an environment where every student, family, staff member, and community member will be excited to be at Marylin Avenue School; and be flexible in order to accommodate the educational needs of all.

Goal 3: All students will be *Proficient* or *Advanced* in Language Arts and Math by the end of fifth grade.

Objective 1: The percentage of students achieving proficiency in ELA, as measured by CSTs, will increase from 51% to 61% by Spring of 2010, measured through student learning results.

Objective 2: The percentage of students achieving proficiency in Math, as measured by CSTs, will increase from 63% to 70% by Spring of 2010, measured through student learning results.

Objective 3: The percentage of English learner students achieving proficiency in ELA, as measured by CSTs, will increase from 36% to 46% by Spring of 2010, measured through student learning results.

Goal 3—All students will be Proficient or Advanced in Language Arts and Math: Planned improvements in student performance

Description of Specific Actions to Improve Educational Practice	Measurement of Strategies Is It Done?	Evaluation How Effective?
Alignment of instruction with content standards: All grade levels have identified essential standards for all curricular areas. Each essential standard has been unwrapped (in order to feature needed prerequisite skills and concepts), vertically aligned, mapped, and paced for all curricular areas.	Essential standards are documented for all curricular areas for all grade levels. Grade-level teams agree on the standards. Cross-grade-level teams agree on the standards. Documentation of all essential standards show them to be unwrapped, mapped, vertically aligned, and paced.	Have the *most essential* standards been identified? Is there horizontal as well as vertical alignment? Is there vertical and horizontal alignment with the implementation of the standards? Are students proficient? Do student scores continue to increase over time?
I. Improvement of instructional strategies and materials: A. All teachers will use the unwrapped essential standards to target instruction. 1. Learning objectives will be based on assessment data. 2. Learning objectives will be clearly stated. 3. Students will understand the importance of each learning objective. 4. Teachers will frequently check for understanding and adjust instruction as needed. B. Each grade level uses balanced assessments that are common, formative, and administered frequently. Assessment will be varied—performance, multi-choice, short answers. 1. Grade levels assess each essential standard and conduct data team meetings for most of them. 2. Grade levels and our schoolwide-data team look at the data from our assessments to determine the effectiveness of instructional strategies and programs. 3. Grade levels administer CFAs every 2-3 weeks. C. All teachers K-5 will use CAFE/Literacy Studio system with fidelity. E. All grades will focus on nonfiction Reading and Writing and will provide students with more opportunities for authentic writing. F. All grade levels (1-5) will use Board Language in their classrooms.	Classroom observations that describe what instruction and the classroom would look like if RtI implemented will also determine if teachers are: ◆ using the unwrapped essential standards to target instruction ◆ creating clear learning objectives to teach the unwrapped essential standards and to make sure students understand their importance ◆ checking for understanding and adjusting instruction as needed ◆ using grade level assessments of each essential standard ◆ administering CFAs every 2-3 weeks ◆ attending data team meetings about the assessment of each essential standard ◆ using CAFE/Literacy Studio system with fidelity ◆ focusing on nonfiction reading and writing ◆ providing students with more opportunities for authentic writing ◆ using board language in their classrooms Documentation exists that grade-level teams and then schoolwide, data-team meetings review the results of the assessments, and check for alignment. Evidence exists that the meeting minutes are shared with all teachers.	Classroom observations will ensure standards work and the degree of implementation. Alignment can be determined through classroom observations and assessment results. How do students feel about the learning? Do they understand the learning objectives? Do Common Formative Assessments parallel the curriculum and state assessments to predict student performance and inform instruction? What do grade-level teams do when they meet? How effective are the grade level teams? What makes grade level teams most effective?

CAFÉ – Comprehension, Accuracy, Fluency, and Expand Vocabulary; CFAs – Common Formative Assessments; ELA – English Language Arts.

Figure 7.1 *(Continued)*

EVALUATION OF THE MARYLIN AVENUE SCHOOL IMPROVEMENT PLAN, GOAL 3, JANUARY 2010

Goal 3—All students will be Proficient or Advanced in Language Arts and Math: Planned improvements in student performance

Description of Specific Actions to Improve Educational Practice	Measurement of Strategies Is It Done?	Evaluation How Effective?
F. *Extended learning time:* Kindergartners will participate in an extended day program (8:30 am–1:45 pm).	Learning time is extended for Kindergarteners.	What is the effectiveness and impact of increasing the school day for Kindergartners? What is being implemented? What is the attendance?
II. *Increased educational opportunity:* A. Instruction is differentiated to address students' needs. 1. Classroom teachers plan for small-group instruction through invitational groups. 2. Classroom teachers plan for individual instruction through one-on-one conferences. 3. Classroom teachers provide additional opportunities to learn and practice essential concepts / skills in the regular classroom (Level 1).	Classroom observations that describe what instruction and the classroom would look like when RtI is implemented will also determine if teachers have a plan for and implement: ◆ Small-group instruction through invitational groups. ◆ Individual instruction through one-on-one conferences. ◆ Additional opportunities to learn and practice essential concepts and skills in the regular classroom (Level 1).	Does a plan for RtI exist? Is it effective? What is being implemented? Are all students being served? Are the number of students identified for Special Education services decreasing? Are interventions meeting the needs of students?
B. The school will have policies and procedures in place for addressing school readiness: appropriate placement for entering and at-risk students. 1. Develop proactive policies and procedures in place for enrolling students in Kindergarten. a. Investigate and develop an entrance assessment to be administered at Spring Kindergarten orientation. b. Develop a parent outreach program and Spring intervention program for entering Kindergarten students. 2. Develop common agreements on the skill levels and benchmarks for at-risk students in Math and ELA. 3. Add an after-school program for students who need extra help and a place to be.	School policies and procedures are in place for enrolling students in Kindergarten. A parent outreach program and Spring intervention program for entering Kindergarten students are created. Agreements are made on the skill levels and benchmarks for at-risk students in Math and ELA. What does the after-school program look like?	To what degree are effective strategies being implemented? How effective are the implemented strategies? How effective are the policies and procedures for enrolling students in Kindergarten? How effective is the parent outreach program and Spring intervention program for entering Kindergarten students? Are the set skill levels and benchmarks for at-risk students in Math and ELA appropriate? How effective is the after-school program? Who are the students who are attending?
C. Schoolwide, we will have Levels 2 and 3 of our *Response to Intervention* (RtI) system in place. 1. Grade-level teams will use data from CFAs to place students in small flexible groups. Instruction will be targeted for a period of 2–3 weeks. 2. Classroom teachers, Resource teacher, Title I specialist, and classroom assistants will be used to provide small group targeted instruction (Level 2). 3. Classroom teachers, Resource specialist, and Title I Specialist will be used to provide more intensive (smaller group, longer duration) instruction (Level 3). 4. Universal screening is conducted three times per year to identify students in need of intensive support to meet standards/expectations. 5. Progress monitoring of student responses to Level 2 or Level 3 instruction will inform instructional decisions for individual students.	Levels 2 and 3 are in place, and everyone knows what it looks like in her/his classroom. Process flowcharts detail how RtI will work for teachers, other staff, and students. Record of instructional (student) assignments to Level 2, Level 3, and movement to/from each level. Record of time, location, frequency of Level 2 and Level 3.	What is being implemented? Are the concepts being implemented consistently? Do they make a difference? Does every staff member understand the expectations and procedures in the same way? Does the model lead to all students learning? How effective are the three levels? How many students in need of Level 2? How many students are in need of Level 2, after screenings? How many students are in each level? What is the length of time students stay at Level 2 and/or Level 3.

Figure 7.1 (Continued)

EVALUATION OF THE MARYLIN AVENUE SCHOOL IMPROVEMENT PLAN, GOAL 3, JANUARY 2010

Goal 3—All students will be Proficient or Advanced in Language Arts and Math: Planned improvements in student performance

Description of Specific Actions to Improve Educational Practice	Measurement of Strategies Is It Done?	Evaluation How Effective?
III. *Staff development and professional collaboration:* A. Staff development and professional collaboration is frequent and ongoing. 1. Grade levels meet every Wednesday from 1:45 to 3:00. Collaboration is focused on results from CFAs and on effective instructional strategies. 2. Whole staff meet once a month for ongoing professional development tied to our plan. 3. Schoolwide, we will use peer coaching to support deep implementation of CAFE strategies. 4. Develop and implement peer coaching system, including documentation. 5. We will continue to research and conduct similar school visits with a focus on grades K-2.	Are all grade level teams meeting from 1:45 to 3:00 on Wednesdays? Does the whole staff meet once a month for Professional Development? Is the Professional Development tied to the plan? How often do teachers coach each other? Do they support deep implementation of CAFE strategies? What is deep implementation? What does it look like? How would you spot it? How do you coach it? Does every teacher know? Is a system in place to research and conduct similar school visits with a focus on grades K-2?	What do the grade level teams do during their times together? Is it effective? What do they need to make their times more effective? How do staff members feel about these meetings? Is the whole-staff Professional Development effective? Is it tied to the vision and plan? Does the information get implemented? How effective is peer coaching? Are CAFE strategies included in the peer coaching? To what degree are teachers implementing CAFE deeply? How effective is the deep implementation? Is CAFE leading to student achievement increases? Have the research and site visits been effective and helpful?
IV. *Involvement of staff, parents, and community (including interpretation of student assessment results to parents):* A. Results from assessments will be shared with students and parents. B. Feedback to students will be timely and specific. C. Proficiency and growth will be acknowledged and celebrated on a regular basis. D. Student goals will be based on assessments, and will be shared with students and parents at goal-setting conferences.	What do the assessment reports for students and parents look like? When are the assessments given and when are the results provided for students and parents? How is proficiency and growth acknowledged and celebrated? Are student goals created on the basis of assessments? Are they shared with students and parents at goal-setting conferences? How often do the goal-setting conferences happen.	Are the assessment reports for students and parents understandable, timely, and helpful? How effective are the goal-setting conferences? What would make them more effective? How many parents come to the conferences? How effective do the students think the conferences are? How effective do the teachers think the conferences are? How do the conferences impact student achievement?
V. *Auxiliary services for students and parents (including transition from preschool, elementary, and to middle school):* A. We will develop a partnership with CAPE and Migrant Preschool as one of our goals for our incoming Kindergarten students.	Partnerships among Marylin Avenue, CAPE, and Migrant Preschool are created and carried out.	In what ways do the partnerships among Marylin Avenue, CAPE, and Migrant Preschool support incoming Kindergarten students? How effective are the partnerships? How can they be more effective?

Figure 7.1 (Continued)

EVALUATION OF THE MARYLIN AVENUE SCHOOL IMPROVEMENT PLAN, GOAL 3, JANUARY 2010

Goal 3—All students will be Proficient or Advanced in Language Arts and Math: Planned improvements in student performance

Description of Specific Actions to Improve Educational Practice	Measurement of Strategies Is It Done?	Evaluation How Effective?
VI. Monitor program implementation and results: A. Grade levels will conduct CFAs every 2-3 weeks to differentiate and target instruction, and to measure effectiveness of instructional strategies. B. Conduct universal screening three times per year. C. Conduct progress monitoring (Levels 2 and 3). D. Schoolwide, we will conduct a data team meeting after each literacy battery (3 times a year) to measure program effectiveness, and to decide on allocation of school resources. E. Grade-level goals and plans will be monitored and evaluated during the schoolwide–data-teams process. F. Utilize curriculum associates benchmark assessments 2-3 times a year. G. Continue to use our school portfolio with the various tools we have learned (*Continuous Improvement Continuums, Gallery Walk*, and other data).	Do the grade levels conduct CFAs every 2-3 weeks to differentiate instruction, and to measure effectiveness of instructional strategies? Do grade level teams review the CFAs and assist teachers in differentiating and targeting instruction and in measuring the effectiveness of instructional strategies? Do schoolwide data teams meet after each literacy battery to measure program effectiveness? Are resources allocated on the basis of these meetings? Are grade-level goals and plans monitored and evaluated during the schoolwide–data-teams process? Is the *School Portfolio* maintained and used for progress monitoring and continuous improvement?	How effective are the assessments? Do they include multiple ways to assess the students? Do teachers use the data to target instruction for all students? How effective are teachers in using the assessments to differentiate instruction and measure effectiveness of instructional strategies? How is effectiveness measured? What can be done to ensure that the process becomes even more effective? How effective is Data Director in providing appropriate and helpful results to teachers? How effective are the data teams in allocating resources and monitoring grade-level goals and plans? Are the goals and plans consistent across the school? How effective are the parts of the school? Do the parts create the "whole" that the school wants? How effective is the vision of the school?
VII. Implement positive behavior system: A. Agree on behavior approach. B. Develop systems for recording. C. Teach students the system.	Do staff know the behavior system and how to record behaviors? Are student behaviors treated consistently? Do students know the behavior system?	How effective is the positive behavior system? Are all staff members recording behaviors consistently?

Evaluating Achievement of School Goals

While the question, *How will we know if what we are doing is effective?*, helped Marylin Avenue staff get a little closer to a comprehensive evaluation, they felt it was not quite enough. For their comprehensive evaluation, staff laid out the school goals and objectives to answer the question, *How will we know if the goals and objectives are making a difference for our students?* The evaluation plan for goals and objectives follows.

EXAMPLE: Marylin Avenue 2009-10 Evaluation Plan for School Goals

THE MISSION OF MARYLIN AVENUE ELEMENTARY SCHOOL
*is for **all** to develop the confidence to risk, to accept challenges, and to succeed.
We will learn from our experiences, show compassion for others,
and grow through the joy of discovery. Learning at Marylin Avenue Elementary School
will enable **all** to achieve their personal best and to be respectful, thoughtful, and independent learners.*

SCHOOL GOALS

- Students will exhibit their best efforts for themselves, their families, and the community, including a demonstration of respect for their peers and for property.
- We will create an environment where every student, family, staff member, and community member will be excited to be at Marylin Avenue School; and we will be flexible in order to accommodate the educational needs of all.
- All students will be *Proficient* or *Advanced* in Language Arts and Math by the end of fifth grade.

Marylin Avenue Staff believe that the three school goals are very closely related, and that the achievement of the first two goals is critical for the staff and students to be successful with the third goal.

SCHOOL GOAL	WHEN THIS GOAL IS IMPLEMENTED—
Students will exhibit their best efforts for themselves, their families, and the community, including a demonstration of respect for their peers and for property.	• Behavior routines that are taught to the students will be in place in every classroom, and observable with the classroom observation tool. • Discipline incidents will decrease (be minimal), as measured by the number of office referrals. • Students, at all grade levels, will strongly agree with the questions on the student questionnaire that relate to exhibiting their best efforts and respect for peers, teachers, and for property, feelings of belonging to the school, and being cared for by staff. Students will also feel treated fairly by all people associated with the school. • Adults will implement the behavior plan with consistency, as measured through self-reflection, classroom observations, and student behavior incidences. • Students in hallways and walkways will show respectful behavior and volume, as measured through staff and student report. • All interactions will be friendly and respectful, as measured through staff and student report, and student questionnaire results. • Our campus will look clean, orderly, and organized, as measured through observation.

We will create an environment where every student, family, staff member, and community member will be excited to be at Marylin Avenue School; and we will be flexible in order to accommodate the educational needs of all.	• There will be high student attendance.
	• There will be high staff attendance.
	• There will be a decrease in mobility because students will want to stay at Marylin Avenue.
	• Student questionnaire results will show that students feel that:
	  ∗ they belong to the school,
	  ∗ they are challenged,
	  ∗ their teachers believe they can learn,
	  ∗ their teachers and principal care about them,
	  ∗ they are doing the best they can,
	  ∗ they know what they are supposed to be learning in their classes,
	  ∗ they have choice in what and how they learn, and
	  ∗ their family believes they can do well in school.

EXAMPLE: Marylin Avenue 2009-10 Evaluation Plan for School Goals	
SCHOOL GOAL	**WHEN THIS GOAL IS IMPLEMENTED—**

We will create an environment where every student, family, staff member, and community member will be excited to be at Marylin Avenue School; and we will be flexible in order to accommodate the educational needs of all.	• Staff questionnaire results will show that staff feel that:
	  ⋆ they belong at the school,
	  ⋆ staff care about them,
	  ⋆ they are clear about what their job is at the school,
	  ⋆ people they work with treat them, and each other, with respect,
	  ⋆ they collaborate to create a continuum of learning across grade levels,
	  ⋆ there is shared decision-making in the school,
	  ⋆ communication is good throughout the school,
	  ⋆ they love working at this school,
	  ⋆ they love seeing the results of their work with students,
	  ⋆ they believe the instructional program at this school is challenging, and provides an atmosphere where every student can succeed,
	  ⋆ quality work is expected of everyone at the school,
	  ⋆ the school has a good public image, and
	  ⋆ all staff morale is high.
	• Parent questionnaire results will show that parents feel that:
	  ⋆ they are welcome at the school,
	  ⋆ they are informed about their child's progress,
	  ⋆ their child is safe at school,
	  ⋆ the school meets the social and academic needs of its students,
	  ⋆ the teachers help them know how to help their child learn at home, and
	  ⋆ the school has a good public image.

All students will be "Proficient" or "Advanced" in Language Arts and Math by the end of fifth grade.	• All students will be proficient by the end of fifth grade, as measured by the California Standards Test (CST). • The percentage of students proficient in ELA and Math will increase, by Spring 2010, as indicated in the content area objectives, as measured by the CST. • English learner achievement will increase, from 36% to 46%, as measured by the CST, by Spring 2010. • There will be evidence that each teacher is implementing all aspects of the school vision and plan, as measured by the *Marylin Avenue Teacher Observation Tool.* • All questions in the "how effective" part of the evaluation of the school plan will be answered positively.

EVALUATING THE RTI SYSTEM

Evaluation of RtI involves regularly analyzing the data generated by benchmark assessments, universal screening instruments, and ongoing progress monitoring of student performance. These analyses assist in determining if acceptable student progress is occurring and if appropriate instruction is being provided at each level of instruction. Additionally, to ensure desired results, schools have to ensure integrity and fidelity of implementation for each level of instruction and intervention. Consideration for changes in instructional practices, cut points for assignment of students to instructional groups, or even changes in assessments used to inform the processes need to be considered as a part of the analysis and data-informed decisions.

To design the evaluation, we must consider what we want to know about RtI. At minimum, we want to understand if, within the structure of RtI, there is—

♦ integrity and fidelity of implementation;

♦ acceptable progress being made; and

♦ the impact of RtI implementation.

Is the RtI Process Being Implemented With Integrity and Fidelity?

To know if RtI interventions are effective, we must know what was implemented; specifically, were the strategies implemented as they were intended—with integrity and fidelity. Integrity of RtI implementation is the adherence to the intent and purpose. Fidelity of implementation is the delivery of content and instructional strategies in the way in which they were designed and intended to be delivered—accurately and consistently.

One way to evaluate implementation with integrity and fidelity is to design and compile a classroom assessment/observation tool that lists what one would expect to see when the program is implemented. In addition, schools may find integrity checklists provided with intervention materials or as part of professional development for specific strategies. These checklists can help inform and ensure accurate, consistent implementation of materials and strategies. Figure 7.2 shows an implementation instrument drafted to reflect what the vision and RtI should look like in Marylin Avenue classrooms.

The tool in Figure 7.2 reminds teachers of what to implement in their classrooms, and can be used for teacher self-assessment, peer coaching dialogues, and principal-teacher feedback.

Figure 7.2

MARYLIN AVENUE ELEMENTARY SCHOOL
CLASSROOM OBSERVATION AND IMPLEMENTATION TOOL

In order to implement the Marylin Avenue vision, classroom teachers are using the unwrapped essential standards to target instruction as demonstrated by—

	Needs Improvement	Present	About Half the Time	Most of the Time	Exemplary
1. Creating and communicating clear learning objectives to teach the unwrapped essential standards and to make sure students understand their importance. Comments:	①	②	③	④	⑤
2. Checking for understanding, providing feedback, and adjusting instruction. Comments:	①	②	③	④	⑤
3. Focusing on non-fiction reading and writing. Comments:	①	②	③	④	⑤
4. Providing students with more opportunities for authentic writing. Comments:	①	②	③	④	⑤
5. Using Board Language in their classrooms. Comments:	①	②	③	④	⑤
6. Small-group instruction through invitational groups. Comments:	①	②	③	④	⑤
7. Individual instruction through one-on-one conferences. Comments:	①	②	③	④	⑤
8. Additional opportunities to learn and practice essential concepts and skills in the regular classroom. Comments:	①	②	③	④	⑤
9. Multiple exposure through multi-modality instruction. Comments:	①	②	③	④	⑤
10. Use of tools for developing conceptual knowledge such as manipulatives, realia, and graphic organizers. Comments:	①	②	③	④	⑤

Figure 7.2 *(Continued)*

MARYLIN AVENUE ELEMENTARY SCHOOL
CLASSROOM OBSERVATION AND IMPLEMENTATION TOOL

In order to implement the Marylin Avenue vision, classroom teachers are planning, implementing, and using information that includes—

Please check all that apply; note source(s) of evidence.

	Teacher Report	Student or Classroom Product	Data or Scores	Other
1. Grade-level assessments of each essential standard. *Comments:* _____	❏	❏	❏	❏
2. Administering *Common Formative Assessments* (CFAs) every 2 to 3 weeks. *Comments:* _____	❏	❏	❏	❏
3. Attending grade-level meetings about the assessment of each essential standard. *Comments:* _____	❏	❏	❏	❏
4. Following curriculum map and pacing for school year. *Comments:* _____	❏	❏	❏	❏
5. Providing a classroom schedule that is structured and predictable. *Comments:* _____	❏	❏	❏	❏
6. Student achievement celebrated on the walls in classrooms and throughout the school. *Comments:* _____	❏	❏	❏	❏
7. Class meetings held regularly in order to build community and to provide a voice for students. *Comments:* _____	❏	❏	❏	❏

Additional observation notes and comments: _____

_____

_____

Observer Name: _____   **Title:** _____

Observer Location: _____   **Date:** _____

Is Acceptable Progress Being Made?

How will you know if acceptable progress is being made by students? No matter the local specifics or content area, each RtI system has a similar purpose and structure, such as an initial or universal screening of students' skills and knowledge and a multi-level prevention system. It is from the screening, with its cut scores, that students move into different levels of intervention or intensive instruction. How well students do in these levels is dependent upon the *quality and appropriateness* of the instruction being provided.

To know if students are making adequate progress, school staffs need to consider both overall progress as well as individual progress. At the individual level, this requires staff to ask if they have moved the appropriate students to the correct levels for their student learning concerns, and whether they have provided them with the proper instruction and intervention. This is first informed by ongoing progress monitoring of each student while secondary and tertiary interventions are provided. Knowing if there is adequate progress overall requires comprehensive study of student performance on universal screening and performance assessments administered throughout the year to understand what students know and do not know.

Figure 2 in the Marylin Avenue RtI Evaluation Summary Example shows the major components of RtI implementation, the evaluation questions that need to be asked to know if adequate progress is being made, and the data required to answer the questions, and a summary of results.

What is the Impact of RtI Implementation?

To determine the impact of RtI implementation, one must consider the expected/intended outcomes of RtI, preferably as the system is designed. The Marylin Avenue RtI Evaluation Summary Example shows intended impact, how impact was measured, and a summary of results.

EXAMPLE: Marylin Avenue RtI Evaluation Summary Report

Marylin Avenue's comprehensive evaluation report has three parts:

+ Goals
+ Plan/vision
+ RtI in English Language Arts (ELA)

What follows is a summary evaluation report for Marylin Avenue's evaluation of RtI in ELA.

MARYLIN AVENUE FIRST YEAR OF RTI IMPLEMENTATION IN ELA

Introduction and Purpose

During the 2009-10 school year, Marylin Avenue staff refined their shared vision, based on comprehensive data analysis and professional learning, to include the design of a Response to Intervention (RtI) system for English Language Arts (ELA). The purpose of this report is to provide a summary of the evaluation of this first year of RtI implementation, and to understand how to make its implementation more effective in 2010-11.

RtI at Marylin Avenue

The intent of RtI at Marylin Avenue Elementary School is to:

+ Implement, in every classroom, quality, research-based instruction and assessment strategies that are based on essential learning standards, and address students' needs and differences.
+ Maximize all students' learning.
+ Reduce behavior problems.
+ Ensure that all students are primarily educated in the general education environment, with access to the general education content, materials, and expectations.
+ Ensure the appropriate identification of students with special needs.

Evaluation of RtI Implementation at Marylin Avenue Elementary School

A comprehensive evaluation of the implementation of RtI in ELA was conducted at Marylin Avenue Elementary School. The following data sources were used to study the results:

+ RtI Implementation Questionnaire.
+ Summary of interviews with individual staff members, the Leadership Team, and grade level teams.
+ Summary of classroom observations.
+ Demographic data.
+ California Standards Test (CST) and formative assessment results.
+ Longitudinal individual student learning results, by teacher.
+ Student achievement results, by teacher, over time.
+ Staff, student, and parent school improvement questionnaire results.
+ Process data.

The results of this study were shared in meetings with staff to discuss next steps in improving the implementation and impact of RtI in ELA at Marylin Avenue, which appear after the summary of results.

This report summarizes the results for the first year of RtI implementation in ELA, in terms of—

+ fidelity of implementation;
+ acceptable progress; and
+ impact.

EXAMPLE: Marylin Avenue RtI Evaluation Summary Report

MARYLIN AVENUE FIRST YEAR OF RTI IMPLEMENTATION IN ELA

Is the RtI System for English Language Arts (ELA) at Marylin Avenue Elementary School Being Implemented with Fidelity?

Fidelity of implementation means that the RtI system is being implemented as it is intended. When the RtI system is implemented with fidelity, we can understand the impact of the system on student achievement. We then know what staff need to adjust, and what they need to keep doing.

To determine implementation fidelity, half of the Marylin Avenue teachers (all grade levels represented) piloted a questionnaire designed to determine where they were with RtI implementation. The questionnaire was followed-up with interviews and classroom observations about how RtI was implemented in 2009-10. Highlights of the questionnaire follow, as Figure 1.

FIGURE 1

Implementation of RtI Questionnaire Results

In September 2010, 14 Marylin Avenue Elementary School Staff were asked to respond to an anonymous, online questionnaire, containing 11 questions (6 multiple choice and 5 open-ended) designed to elicit their attitudes about implementation of RtI. The highlights of the results follow.

A. *How well do you know the components of RtI?*

The majority of the 13 staff responding to this question, about 54% (*n=7*), said they knew the components *About Halfway.* No staff responded to *Very Well* or *Not At All,* 31% (*n=4*) said they knew the components *Well,* and 15% (*n=2*) said *Little Bit.* Write-in comments included:

a. I've done a lot of reading and have taken classes, but there is still so much to learn.

b. I know what I think I know, but I don't know what I don't know, so how do I know how much I know?

B. *What do you need to help you better know the components of RtI?* (Select all that apply.)

The majority of the 14 respondents, about 71%, said they needed clarification of what RtI should look like in their classrooms.

Answer Options	Response Percent	Response Count
Workshop on the components.	14.3%	2
Staff meeting about the components.	28.6%	4
Book study.	24.4%	3
A flowchart of how the components work together.	50.0%	7
Clarification of what RtI should look like in my classroom.	**71.4%**	**10**
Peer coaching.	50.0%	7
Visiting another classroom.	42.9%	6
Visiting another school.	21.4%	3
Demonstration lessons.	28.6%	4
I know the components: it is just making them work together that is difficult.	57.1%	8

EXAMPLE: Marylin Avenue RtI Evaluation Summary Report

MARYLIN AVENUE FIRST YEAR OF RTI IMPLEMENTATION IN ELA

FIGURE 1 *(Continued)*
Implementation of RtI Questionnaire Results

C. *What "one thing" would help the most?*

The majority of the 13 staff responding to this question, about 31%, again said they needed clarification of what RtI should look like in their classrooms.

Answer Options	Response Percent	Response Count
Workshop on the components.	7.7%	1
Staff meeting about the components.		0
Book study.	7.7%	1
A flowchart of how the components work together.	7.7%	1
Clarification of what RtI should look like in my classroom.	**30.8%**	**4**
Peer coaching.		0
Visiting another classroom.	15.4%	2
Visiting another school.	7.7%	1
Demonstration lessons.		0
Someone to talk with to understand how to make the components work together.	23.1%	3

D. *What percentage of the time do you feel you implemented the components of RtI in English Language Arts (ELA), the way they were intended to be implemented, in your classroom during the 2009-10 school year?* (Overall, indicate 0% to 100% on the scale.)

The graphs that follow show staff responses for Levels 1, 2, and 3.

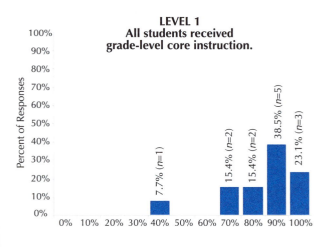

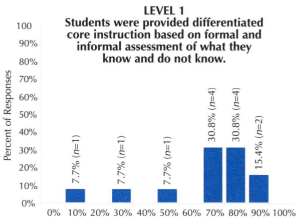

EXAMPLE: Marylin Avenue RtI Evaluation Summary Report

MARYLIN AVENUE FIRST YEAR OF RTI IMPLEMENTATION IN ELA

FIGURE 1 *(Continued)*

Implementation of RtI Questionnaire Results

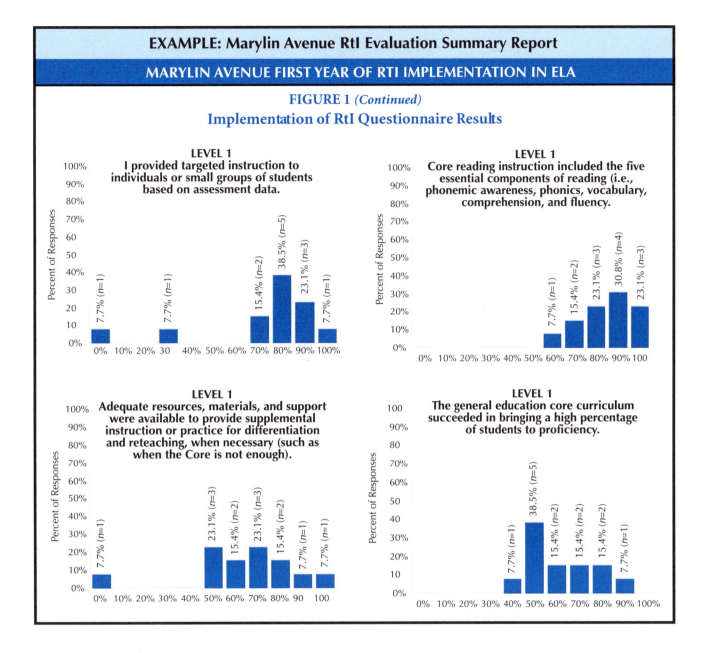

EXAMPLE: Marylin Avenue RtI Evaluation Summary Report

MARYLIN AVENUE FIRST YEAR OF RTI IMPLEMENTATION IN ELA

FIGURE 1 *(Continued)*
Implementation of RtI Questionnaire Results

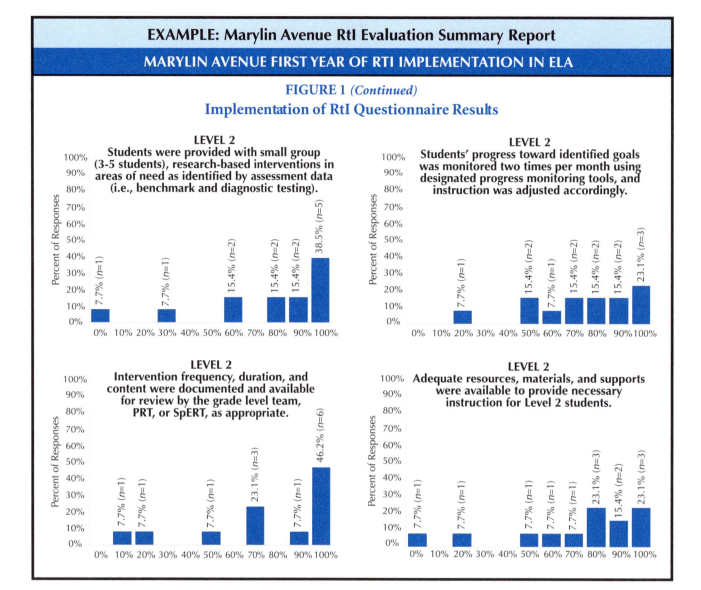

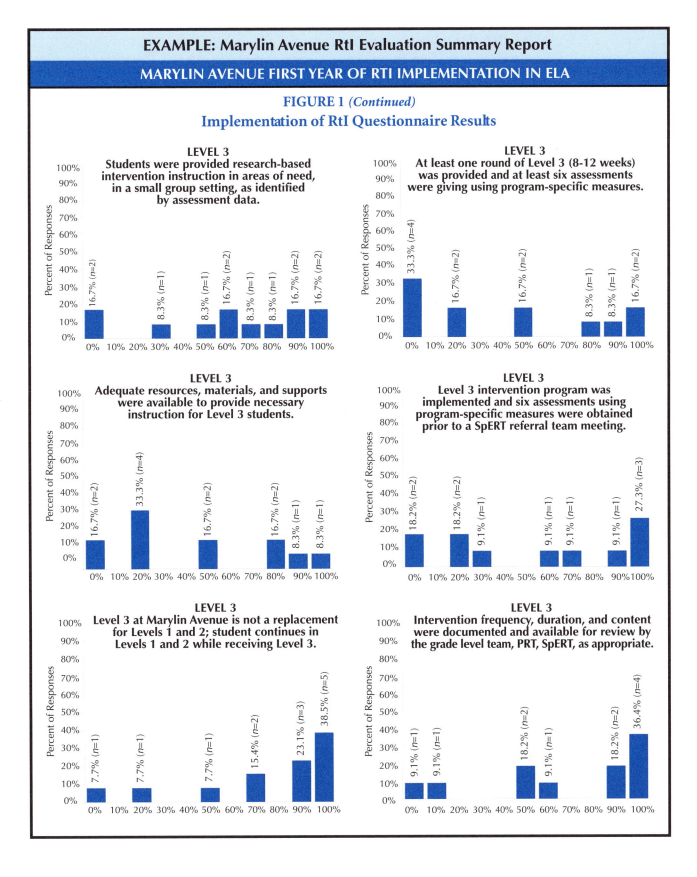

EXAMPLE: Marylin Avenue RtI Evaluation Summary Report

MARYLIN AVENUE FIRST YEAR OF RTI IMPLEMENTATION IN ELA

FIGURE 1 (Continued)
Implementation of RtI Questionnaire Results

EXAMPLE: Marylin Avenue RtI Evaluation Summary Report

MARYLIN AVENUE FIRST YEAR OF RTI IMPLEMENTATION IN ELA

FIGURE 1 *(Continued)*
Implementation of RtI Questionnaire Results

E. *How effective do you feel you were with the following statements?*

The graph that follows shows staff average responses on a five-point scale: 1=extremely ineffective; 2=ineffective; 3=neither effective nor ineffective; 4=effective; and 5=extremely effective.

Marylin Avenue Elementary School Staff Responses
RtI Implementation Questionnaire, September 2010

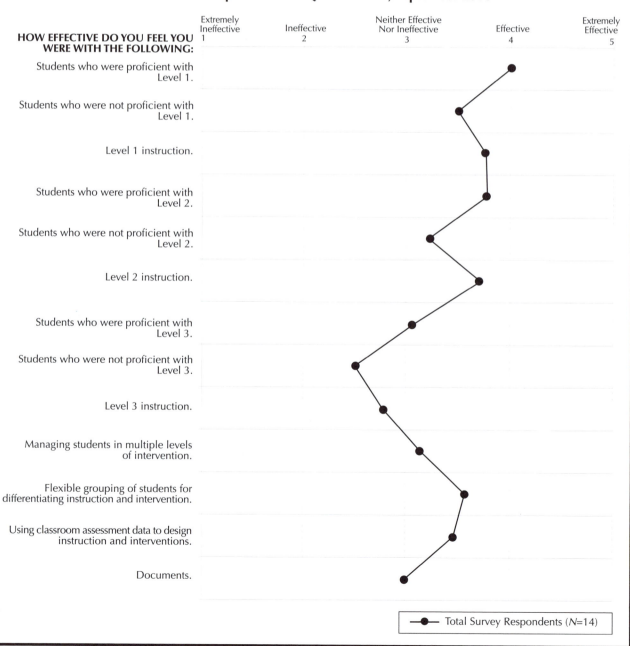

HOW EFFECTIVE DO YOU FEEL YOU WERE WITH THE FOLLOWING:	Extremely Ineffective 1	Ineffective 2	Neither Effective Nor Ineffective 3	Effective 4	Extremely Effective 5
Students who were proficient with Level 1.					
Students who were not proficient with Level 1.					
Level 1 instruction.					
Students who were proficient with Level 2.					
Students who were not proficient with Level 2.					
Level 2 instruction.					
Students who were proficient with Level 3.					
Students who were not proficient with Level 3.					
Level 3 instruction.					
Managing students in multiple levels of intervention.					
Flexible grouping of students for differentiating instruction and intervention.					
Using classroom assessment data to design instruction and interventions.					
Documents.					

Total Survey Respondents (*N*=14)

EXAMPLE: Marylin Avenue RtI Evaluation Summary Report

MARYLIN AVENUE FIRST YEAR OF RTI IMPLEMENTATION IN ELA

FIGURE 1 *(Continued)*
Implementation of RtI Questionnaire Results

F. *How helpful would the following be for implementing RtI in 2010-11?*

The graph that follows shows staff average responses on a five-point scale: 1=definitely would not be helpful; 2=not so helpful; 3=neither helpful nor unhelpful; 4=helpful; and 5=extremely helpful.

Marylin Avenue Elementary School Staff Responses
RtI Implementation Questionnaire, September 2010

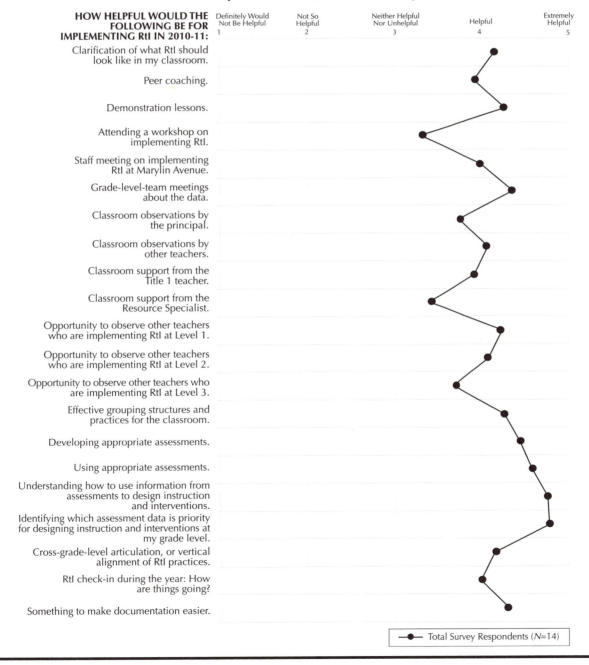

EXAMPLE: Marylin Avenue RtI Evaluation Summary Report

MARYLIN AVENUE FIRST YEAR OF RTI IMPLEMENTATION IN ELA

FIGURE 1 *(Continued)*
Implementation of RtI Questionnaire Results

Open-Ended Responses

Aggregated responses to the five open-ended questions follow:

G. *What are the celebrations or victories at Marylin Avenue as a result of RtI implementation?*
- Big movement.
- Students are learning!!
- Students are in more flexible groups that have a targeted goal for instruction. The groups are fluid.
- We have been able to raise the benchmarks, students achieving higher scores.
- Help a broader scope of students.
- Students have made academic progress.
- That we actually jumped in and started RTI, it is a process! Some students needs are being met, but we have too many Level 3 students and not enough teachers for them.
- ELA CST scores keep improving, not great yet.
- The aide attached to our grade level is excellent.
- More focused intervention for students not at grade level. PRTs are helpful for strategies for helping kids with Level 1 and Level 2 interventions.
- Increased literacy as measured by DRA and CSTs.
- Not as many kids at the very low levels.

H. *What are the benefits of RtI implementation?*
- More students are getting the help they need. More students are getting help. It is seen as the norm to go to small group instruction.
- Having a system in place for students who are not moving in the classroom.
- Students do not have to wait until they are in second grade to get help. More involvement from the classroom teacher in goals.
- Much more efficient team-time groupings.
- Being able to help students without the limitations of special education.
- Help with differentiation in the classroom-it being one component.
- Some students' needs are being met. We're using assessments to guide instruction. We really know what our students know and don't know.
- The benefits of RtI are that we are trying to understand the causes of low student achievement, implement multiple remedies, and monitor each student's progress toward increased student achievement post intervention.
- Students receive multiple levels of instruction in a variety of formats.
- Helps teachers to develop an intervention plan based on assessments, more effective for students than data team meetings. Collaboration around intervention strategies helpful for many students, not just targeted students.
- Targeting instruction.
- Meeting kids' specific needs, improvement in Level 1.
- Targeted level instruction for all students.

EXAMPLE: Marylin Avenue RtI Evaluation Summary Report

MARYLIN AVENUE FIRST YEAR OF RTI IMPLEMENTATION IN ELA

FIGURE 1 *(Continued)*
Implementation of RtI Questionnaire Results

Open-Ended Responses *(Continued)*

I. *What are the challenges of RtI Implementation?*
- Documentation and continuity of instruction. (4)
- Managing all the small groups, keeping track of the interventions, resources for Level 2 and Level 3. Knowing what to do next. (4)
- Assessments taking over Level 1 instruction. (2)
- Human resources for Level 3. (2)
- Knowing what to do when Levels 2 and 3 don't work. (2)
- Too much data entry. Too much assessment.
- Using and understanding all the components effectively and the learning curve.
- The challenges of RtI are creating the best assessment and then using the data to differentiate instruction.
- Juggling so many components.
- Time, money, time, time, time.

J. *What are the roadblocks to full RtI implementation?*
- Time. (6)
- Understanding. (2)
- Level 2 and 3 assessing, analyzing, regrouping, and planning are getting in the way of a strong Level 1.
- Systematic communication cross-grade level.
- Students who need services have to wait much longer to get help.
- Schoolwide and community-wide understanding and trust in the RTI system.
- Not sure-questions arise as the process unfolds.
- Lack of assessments that match instruction. A management system for assessments.
- Qualified staff for Level 3 support.
- Number of students who need intervention.
- Money.

K. *What next steps are most important for Marylin Avenue Elementary School?*
- Strengthening teaching practices in Level 1. (2)
- Streamlining our assessments and data entry.
- To create a program that is systematic and successful.
- Better understanding of how the program works and what it looks like.
- More shared knowledge regarding procedures that bridge special and general education in regards to RtI.
- Making sure everyone understands what to do and are on the same page.
- How to differentiate in our own classroom (Level 1).
- Ways to manage all the information, grade-level and cross-grade-level collaboration about how to meet the needs of more students in Levels 1 and 2 interventions in the classroom.
- Ways to evaluate Level 1 instruction.
- Time to observe RtI in practice in other classrooms.

EXAMPLE: Marylin Avenue RtI Evaluation Summary Report

MARYLIN AVENUE FIRST YEAR OF RTI IMPLEMENTATION IN ELA

Questions, Data Required, and Results Related to Acceptable Progress

FIGURE 2

The major components of RtI implemented at Marylin Avenue in 2009-10, the questions that need to be answered to know if there has been acceptable progress, the data required, and the results are shown in Figure 2 below.

Components of RtI	Questions	Data Required	Results
Universal Screening (3 or 4 times per year) *Curriculum-Based Assessment Common Formative Assessment*	• How many students do we have performing above, at, or below expected levels of performance? • What do the students know and what do they not know? • How many students need extra help in small groups? • How many students need more than small group instruction/assistance?	• Universal screening and formative assessment results, by standard, or learning criteria. • Cut points that will help staff know which intervention is most appropriate for each level of student performance.	• Teachers like the universal screening tools they are currently using. They can identify what students know and what they do not know, which students need more assistance, and what type of assistance they need.
Cut Points	• Based on the cut scores that determine which level of intervention each student receives, are students successful? • Have all students who need more intensive instruction been identified with the universal screening and cut scores? Should the cut scores be altered? Should a different screening instrument be considered?	• Student achievement results for all students from ongoing assessments, including frequent progress monitoring. • Number of students at each proficiency level, over time.	• Staff feel the current cut scores on their progress monitoring assessments are appropriate.

Periodic Review of Performance Data
• Beginning, middle, and end-of-year (or to coincide with benchmark/formative assessment schedule).
• Performance on benchmark and formative assessments by building, grade level, and/or classroom.
  • Classroom level—each student's performance on all formative/benchmark assessments.
  • Progress monitoring of individual student performance in secondary and tertiary interventions.
	• How well do our current practices in curriculum and instruction help students reach expected levels of performance? (Primary level)
	• Are all students responding to the level of instruction that the universal screening, formative assessments, and corresponding cut scores suggest? Should the cut scores be altered? Should a different screening instrument be considered?
	• How well do the secondary and tertiary interventions help students reach expected levels?
	• How do we know when to refer students for consideration of special education sources?
	• Are we able to provide support to all students who meet criteria for services at secondary and tertiary levels— enough slots or groups?
	• Are students exiting secondary and/or tertiary levels efficiently?
	• Are students moved among levels efficiently for highest benefit in accelerating learning?
	• How well aligned/correlated are assessments with annual assessments?
		• Student achievement results for all students on ongoing assessments.
		• Prediction of where students are expected to be compared to where they perform.
		• Number of students at secondary and tertiary levels is decreasing over time.
		• Number of students meeting criteria for secondary or tertiary interventions compared to number receiving services.
		• Length of time students remain in secondary and tertiary levels is reasonable and changes are made as soon as data indicate the need.
		• Review of individual student progress monitoring data to ensure interventions are having desired impact or changes are made to achieve desired outcome.
			• Students made tremendous progress at every grade level with the Developmental Reading Assessment (DRA), which led teachers to believe the students would do well on the California Standards Test (CST).
			• The number of students at secondary and tertiary levels decreased over time.
			• Student achievement, as measured by the summative, CST, by grade level, showed students in grades 2 and 5 made great progress. Students in grades 3 and 4 did not make good progress, overall.
			• The length of time students remained in secondary and tertiary levels was reasonable. Changes were made as soon as data indicated the need.
			• At grades 3 and 4, the master teachers worked hard to bring up the lowest performing students. Many of the students on the higher end of proficiency showed decreases in their scores. Results indicate that Level 1 needs to be strengthened for all students.

Multi-Level Prevention System *Primary, Secondary, and Tertiary instruction and intervention*	• Are the preventions effective for students?	• Student achievement results on annual assessment compared to benchmark and universal assessments. • Percentages of students receiving each level of instruction are at, or near, expected levels (80% at primary; 15% at secondary; 5% at tertiary).	• CST results showed that Level 1 instruction at most grade levels needs to become more effective. Teachers want to know how to be effective with students who are already proficient, while working intensively with students who are not proficient.

EXAMPLE: Marylin Avenue RtI Evaluation Summary Report

MARYLIN AVENUE FIRST YEAR OF RTI IMPLEMENTATION IN ELA

FIGURE 3

Impact of the First Year of Implementation of RtI in English Language Arts (ELA)

The intended impact of the first year of RtI implementation in ELA, how impact is measured, and the results are summarized in Figure 3.

Intended Impact	How Impact Will Be Measured	Results
◆ When RtI is implemented, as intended, there will be instructional coherence and a continuum of learning that makes sense for all students. What students learn in one grade level will build on what they learned in the previous grade level(s), and will set them up for learning in the following grade levels. Individual student achievement results will improve each year. All students will be proficient in all areas. No students will need to be retained.	◆ Individual and schoolwide student achievement results will show student growth over time, and a larger percentage of students proficient each year. There will be no "dips" in achievement. ◆ Number of students retained, by grade level, will be low or zero. ◆ Data brought to bear in the RtI flowcharts show that RtI processes are working as intended.	◆ There were schoolwide decreases overall and for all significant subgroups (numbers greater than 40) in 2009-10. ◆ There were larger percentages of students proficient in ELA in grades 2 and 5; however, there were fewer students proficient in grades 3 and 4. ◆ In grades 3 and 4, even though the overall percentage of students proficient did not show it, many students starting at Far Below Basic and Below Basic moved up one or more proficiency levels, albeit not all the way to proficiency. ◆ There were only 2 students retained in Kindergarten in 2009-10, down from higher numbers in the previous four years. ◆ Formative assessments show increases in student learning throughout the year. The referral data show there were fewer students referred to special education during the year, and that the evaluations for eligibility were accurate.
◆ Students will not be placed in special education for the wrong reasons, such as teachers wanting students out of the classroom because of behavior or lack of learning response, poor test-taking skills, not having received high-quality instruction or adequate interventions. ◆ Students will want to come to school to learn.	◆ Which students are identified for special education services, and why, will be analyzed. ◆ Accurate identification of need for special education will be demonstrated by number of students evaluated being similar to or the same as the number determined eligible for special education. ◆ Attendance rates will improve for the school and every classroom. ◆ Student perceptions will show that students love to learn at this school, that they are challenged by the work they are expected to perform, that they belong, and that they feel teachers care about them.	◆ Special education referral data show the Pre-Referral and Special Education Referral Team processes accurately screened appropriate students for special education services. ◆ The number of students determined eligible for special education was one less than the number evaluated. ◆ Attendance rates continue to be high schoolwide. ◆ Student perception results continue to show that students mostly strongly agree with all statements on the questionnaire about learning at Marylin Avenue. The lowest items, although in high agreement, relate to students being friendly and respecting each other.
◆ Teachers will understand how to make schoolwide improvements.	◆ Teacher perceptions will show that teachers feel that they belong at the school, that colleagues work well together, that there is a shared vision at the school, and that they can make a difference in all students' learning because all staff are working together.	◆ 2009-10 teacher perceptions show the majority of responses to items in the questionnaire to be in strong agreement. Teachers share the school vision, collaborate and know how to improve results, overall. The lowest items, although in agreement, relate to students communication and morale.
◆ Parents will be knowledgeable of, and effectively support, the school's RtI process.	◆ Parent perceptions will show that they feel involved with their child's learning at home and at school. Parents will feel that communication with the school is highly effective.	◆ Parent perception results continue to show that parents responding strongly agree with all statements on the questionnaire about learning at Marylin Avenue. Parents express that the strengths of the school are the caring staff and environment, and the communication between teachers and parents. The lowest item, although in high agreement, relates to students showing respect for each other.

EXAMPLE: Marylin Avenue RtI Evaluation Summary Report

MARYLIN AVENUE FIRST YEAR OF RTI IMPLEMENTATION IN ELA

FIGURE 3 *(Continued)*

Impact of the First Year of Implementation of RtI in English Language Arts (ELA)

Intended Impact	How Impact Will Be Measured	Results
◆ The number of students referred to the office for behavior will be minimal.	◆ The number of office referrals by school, by classroom, by number and type of offenses will be minimal.	◆ The number of students referred to the office has decreased over time. However, there is evidence that a behavior plan needs to be created, implemented, and documented with consistency.
◆ Progress monitoring and common formative assessments, conducted within the classroom setting and the school day, will be utilized to identify struggling students and to focus on why they are struggling. ◆ Interventions matched to student needs will result in student learning increases for all students.	◆ Review of assessment results will show that those students struggling to learn are properly placed in corresponding intensity levels of instruction/intervention. ◆ Review of the assessment results will show student learning increases for all students.	◆ Grade level process measurement and documentation show that those students struggling to learn were properly placed in corresponding intensity levels of instruction. Many students who scored Far Below Basic on the CST in previous years moved up. ◆ In some grade levels, the focus on the struggling students took the quality teaching away from the non-struggling students, and their proficiency levels dropped
◆ High-quality instruction and appropriate interventions will be provided for all students. ◆ Interventions occur for all students, no matter what teacher the student has. RtI is a schoolwide system and not a teacher-specific process.	◆ The student achievement results all show there is instructional coherence throughout the school, and that every student is achieving in every subject area. ◆ Classroom observations show that teachers are effectively implementing the components of RtI. ◆ All students demonstrate a minimum of one year's growth each year	◆ Throughout the school there is high-quality instruction and appropriate interventions are taking place. After reviewing the 2009-10 data, teachers know they must strengthen core instruction for every student while improving the interventions for struggling students.

EXAMPLE: Marylin Avenue RtI Evaluation Summary Report

OVERALL FINDINGS AND RECOMMENDATIONS FOR IMPROVEMENT

Overall Findings

In 2009-10, Marylin Avenue Elementary School staff worked hard to understand, design, and implement RtI in ELA. Teachers, in grade level teams, reviewed their periodic assessments and identified which students needed extra support in specific concepts. These teachers placed students in small learning groups. When the small group approach was not enough for some students, they received one-on-one intensive assistance, in most cases by the most qualified professional - the classroom teacher.

The results were mixed: The progress monitoring showed student learning in all classrooms with most students. The CST showed proficiency increases in two of the four grade levels assessed. In these cases, the classroom teacher made sure she/he was teaching all Level 1 students in the spring before CST testing. The other two grade levels focused more on moving the Far Below Basic and Below Basic students to proficiency. Most of these students did not make it all the way to proficiency, while many of the advanced and proficient students from the year before fell to proficient or basic.

The 2009-10 results helped teachers see how to implement RtI to get the results they want for all students.

Recommendations for Improvement

Staff agreed to the following recommendations as ways to improve the implementation for RtI throughout the school, which include—

- *Professional Learning.* Marylin Avenue teachers need to continue to learn about RtI, and specifically clarification of what RtI should look like in their classrooms. The following would be most helpful:
  * The refinement and use of the classroom self-assessment and observation tool that reinforces what RtI implementation looks like in the classroom.
  * A flowchart of how the components work together, for each grade level.
  * Peer coaching to support the implementation.
  * Ongoing professional learning on RtI in grade level team meetings and with the entire staff.
  * Visiting other classrooms.
  * Time to talk with each other about implementing RtI.
  * Time to talk and prepare with the other teachers and specialists who help with interventions.
  * Improving core instruction in Level 1, through peer coaching, classroom visits, and demonstration lessons.
  * Expanding strategies for differentiating and targeting Level 1 instruction to address learning needs of students at or above grade level.
  * Improving Level 3 interventions, through peer coaching, classroom visits, and instructional support.
- *Assessments.* Marylin Avenue staff need to take a serious look at the assessments they are using to predict the CST, standards attainment, and to help them understand how students are doing during instruction. Their current Common Formative Assessments and universal screeners in ELA are not good predictors of the CST and of standards attainment.
- *Instruction.* Marylin Avenue teachers need to strengthen their Level 1 instruction to ensure that all students receive the highest quality core instruction, including those already proficient.
- *Interventions.* Marylin Avenue staff need to strengthen their most intensive intervention level, Level 3. Equity in Level 3 assistance needs to be addressed. Currently, in some grades, students receive Level 3, based on available personnel, rather than need for instruction.
- *Data Tool.* A quality data analysis tool will help teachers analyze their formative and summative student achievement data easier and quicker; and, at the same time, help with the documentation will free teachers to concentrate on their instruction.

Evaluation starts with the clarification of intent, brainstorming how you know it is implemented and making a difference, and then following through to understand the results.

Designing the Evaluation of Your Systems

While evaluating the implementation of the school improvement plan, vision, goals, and RtI might seem so overwhelming that your school just does not do it, reconsider. As you can see in this chapter, evaluation starts with the clarification of intent, brainstorming how you know it is implemented and making a difference, and then following through to understand the results. If you have created a data profile, much of the data have already been gathered. You merely need to make meaning of the data with respect to the evaluation questions. To get the evaluation work started with the design, use the "program/process evaluation form" in Appendix H.

RESOURCES

How to evaluate a program or process is described in Appendix H.

BOOK STUDY QUESTIONS

♦ What components of CSI and RtI need to be evaluated?

♦ How can you know if there is integrity and fidelity of RtI implementation?

♦ How can you know if acceptable progress is being made with an RtI system?

♦ How can you know the impact of RtI implementation?

TEAM STUDY QUESTIONS

♦ Develop an evaluation plan for your programs and processes, including RtI.

♦ Determine how you will know if acceptable progress is being made in your school's RtI system.

♦ Determine how you will know if there is integrity and fidelity of RtI implementation in your school's RtI system.

♦ Determine how you will know the impact of your school's RtI implementation.

Chapter 8

SUMMARY AND CONCLUSIONS

RtI is a dramatic redesign of general and special education; both need to change and the entire system needs reform.... Tweaking will not be sufficient.

The National Association of State Directors of Special Education (NASDSE)

Response to Intervention (RtI) represents one of the first times in many of our educational careers that a nationally supported process has led staffs in schools and in districts—large and small—to proactive measures, as opposed to reactive solutions. RtI is about school staffs providing many structured options to students to ensure their success and to prevent them from failing so much that they are required to obtain special services.

Starting with continuous school improvement—reviewing the school's data, getting all staff believing the same instructional and assessment strategies will make a difference for their collective students, creating a shared vision, getting communication and collaboration structures in place to implement the vision—is the best way to rethink regular and special education, and to get accelerated change. Incremental change is simply not enough to meet the needs of *all* students.

This book supports the philosophy that all students can be successful; and it shows what an actual school has done, and is continuing to do, to engage in continuous school improvement with a Response to Intervention focus.

RtI is about school staffs providing many structured options to students to ensure their success and to prevent them from failing so much that they are required to obtain special services.

TRANSFORMING GENERAL AND SPECIAL EDUCATION WITH RtI AND CSI

To implement the concept and intent of RtI as described and exemplified in this book, staffs will need to shift their thinking and behavior. To truly transform general and special education, staff members need to embrace the following:

- ♦ Truly believe that all students can learn.

- ♦ Take a comprehensive and honest look at all data to understand where the school is as an organization, and how the organization is doing with respect to ensuring that all students learn.

- ♦ Understand how the school is getting its current results to know which processes need to improve, and which processes need to be kept or eliminated to get different results.

- ♦ Read best practices and engage in professional learning when the data show that they need to learn more about meeting the needs of their students.

- ♦ Believe in and understand the mission of the school. A shared vision, based on the core values and beliefs of the staff, describes what it will look like when the mission of the school is being carried out by all staff—because they believe in the vision.

- ♦ Complete a school improvement plan to implement the vision and put the RtI specifics into motion.

- ♦ Once a vision is created, or as a part of creating the vision, specific details of RtI need to be clarified and agreed to, such as, which students will receive which interventions, when, where, and provided by whom.

- ♦ Rethink roles and responsibilities so the entire system can undergo dramatic change. Roles and responsibilities must be spelled out so everyone understands them in the same way.

- ♦ Leaders must become more knowledgeable of RtI and able to translate the intent into action. They must become master collaborators, observers, and interveners, when necessary.

- ♦ Teachers must become knowledgeable of RtI and able to translate the intent into action. They must also become leaders, collaborators, data analysts, assessors, and multi-taskers.

- ♦ Create flowcharts of the vision and the RtI system to help lay out the parts and show how the parts work together to create the whole. This is important so every teacher can see what is expected of her/him.

- ♦ Realign existing resources such as personnel, time, and budgets.

♦ Be sure that structures are in place to support the system and to assist teachers with the implementation of strategies to help struggling learners.

♦ Establish collaborative teams that come together through a leadership team to assist staffs in implementing the vision and carrying out the intent and components of RtI.

♦ Participate in professional learning for collaborative teaching techniques and instructional strategies that meet different student learning styles and needs.

♦ Embed schoolwide professional learning, book studies, shared readings, peer coaching, demonstration lessons, and shared experiences within the school day to help all teachers learn how to meet the needs of students, and to assist with the implementation of the vision, including RtI.

♦ Create and follow a professional development calendar with collaborative and leadership team meeting dates, and what the teams should be discussing at that time, to help implement the vision, and to keep the flow of the work continuing as planned.

♦ Create classroom observation tools that include elements of the vision and the RtI system to assist teachers in implementing the vision, and in knowing what the vision and RtI look like in their classrooms.

♦ Having classroom data accessible and easy to understand are a must for helping teachers know which students are not proficient on a standard, what they know and do not know, and what instructional strategies would help them become proficient on the standard. Standard data reports give teachers the time to review the reports and do something about the results, as opposed to teachers using their time creating the reports. Data tools are necessary for doing this work.

♦ Parents have unique insights about their child's strengths and challenges and are frequently eager to help with interventions at home. Parents need continuous updates on their child's progress, and about how they can support their child's learning so they can be true partners in the teaching/learning process.

♦ Evaluate the parts and assess the alignment of the parts that create the whole. This work helps staffs know they are on the right track, what needs to change to improve results, and adds accountability to the entire process of redesign.

♦ Assess the integrity and fidelity of implementation, determine if acceptable progress is being made, and verify the impact of RtI implementation.

What RtI Is Not

While we have written in terms of what to do with RtI, we want to make clear that some of the ways we are seeing RtI implemented is *not* the way RtI is intended to be implemented. Response to Intervention (RtI) is a comprehensive delivery system in which teachers use researched-based instructional strategies and assessments to meet the needs of *every* student. RtI is *not:*

Response to Intervention (RtI) is a comprehensive delivery system in which teachers use researched-based instructional strategies and assessments to meet the needs of "every" student.

- A pre-referral system for special education, alone.

- A system that prevents the timely identification of special education.

- Whole group instruction 80% of the time; 15% of the time small group instruction, by ability groupings, or one-on-one instruction; and 5% of the time referring the lowest performing students to special education.

- Adding after-school programs to do interventions.

- Hiring an RtI teacher.

- Buying an intervention program.

- Securing an intervention room.

- Starting or ending the day with a 45-minute intervention class, with students grouped by abilities.

Many teachers, schools, and entire districts struggle with the creation, implementation, and evaluation of their multi-level prevention systems. We are often surprised at how quickly faculty or team meetings turn to the identification of students with learning disabilities as part of designing their RtI systems. While RtI must be sensitive to this need in order to best serve all students, it is not the true purpose and intent of RtI. It is merely one outcome for a small percentage of students when the RtI system is implemented correctly.

Perhaps the word "intervention" is getting in the way. Or perhaps it is that some staffs do not have a vision (no big picture) that clarifies how they can measure and meet the needs of all students.

Too often, school staffs study the gaps that appear in the high stakes test scores of students and attempt too quickly and superficially to determine solutions for their undesirable results. Consequently, the "solutions" most often involve "fixing" the students and do not include process improvement or targeted professional learning for staff related to the consistent implementation of a vision and RtI.

WARNING!

RtI and CSI can be upsetting to your organization.

As schools redesign regular and special education together to implement robust RtI systems, some unforeseen changes may occur. One of the best-anticipated changes is that there should be fewer students identified for special services, and those who are identified will be students who will benefit most from special services. Following are some of the unexpected changes that could happen as your school reinvents itself. These may be unpleasant, but they do not mean stop.

♦ Some teachers will not like the idea that someone is forcing them to work differently. This could lead to teachers becoming uncooperative, or even leaving the job. Keep going—RtI will provide better learning for students, and what teacher does not want that?

♦ Other teachers may not like the idea that someone is *forcing them to work differently.* Listen carefully and ask questions. Often it is veteran teachers who say "been there, done that." They may be loud, but they also may not be saying they will not do it. They need to know that the new way of doing business is going to last, and that it will benefit students.

♦ Some specialists, like School Psychologists, Counselors, and Special Educators, will not like the idea that someone is *forcing them to work differently.* Because they are often employees of the school district, and not the school, it becomes difficult to implement a schoolwide RtI system with integrity and fidelity when the district might not be "there" yet. Sometimes schools have to work around these individuals if the district level supervisors are not willing to understand and support the true implementation of RtI.

♦ Some teachers may try to pressure school staff to stop the RtI system because they *do not want to work so hard.* Hopefully, the other teachers who believe the intent and result of RtI is to reach *all* students will get the others back on track. If the teachers do not speak up, the principal must.

♦ Even though staff might be working extremely hard to implement the elements of RtI as agreed upon, student achievement scores could go down at first. That is when a strong evaluation that helps staff understand the impact of their actions needs to take place. It could be the assessment system was not comprehensive enough and/or the interventions were not implemented with fidelity. It could also be an indicator that teachers need to learn more about the students they have in their classrooms and look closely at the processes they are using to implement the strategies they are delivering.

♦ Even though the whole RtI system is spelled out, some staff may focus most of their efforts on the lowest achieving students to the detriment of the higher achieving students. Every school implementing a multi-level prevention system needs to make sure the primary level of instruction is robust and provides quality instruction for the students who are already proficient, as well as the ones they want to get to proficiency.

♦ As new concepts are identified, clarified, and implemented, *we need better communication from the Principal* may be heard throughout the school— often to the dismay of the school leader. Take that as a call for help and feedback—that teachers want to get the system right in the classrooms, that they want help in knowing what it would look like in their classrooms, and/or that they want to know if they really have to do this.

General and special education teachers/specialists need to be patient and flexible as they include each other as collaborators and partners in learning new strategies. A strong RtI system requires that roles will need to change. Everyone needs to remember that RtI will improve teaching and learning for everyone. When the school staff does the right things for students, they will see differences in student and teacher attitudes, expectations, and results.

> *When the school staff does the right thing for students, they will see differences in student and teacher attitudes, expectations, and results.*

RECOMMENDATIONS

Start with the mission and vision, and keep them at the center of everything that you do. Do the right thing for the benefit of every child—in every classroom, in every building, in every school in the district.

Be clear so every staff member understands all the components of RtI, and what the components will look like when fully implemented. Put multiple structures in place to help every teacher implement RtI with integrity and fidelity.

Leaders: Only let go long enough to get a better grip. What others have described as an implementation dip is sometimes leadership backing off because the going gets tough with the implementation of continuous school improvement. When the going gets tough, model the way with intensity, and encourage the hearts of those who are involved in implementing new processes to ensure student success.

Sometimes the *implementation dip* during the implementation of RtI is related to teachers' need for more knowledge of RtI—specifically, what it should look like in "my" classroom. Flowcharts, clarified intentions, peer coaching, demonstration lessons, and classroom visits are sometimes all necessary to help teachers implement RtI with integrity and fidelity.

Recovering from a "dip," or decrease in performance, requires vigilant efforts. Teachers and administrators must recognize the hard work that produces desired results and inspire each other to continue to engage in honest reflection and evaluation that will allow the school to continuously improve.

In this book, we have described and shown an example of one school implementing RtI by starting with continuous school improvement. We have also described how schools can get started with the same or similar processes.

While RtI involves hard work and may be difficult to implement, teachers will find renewed confidence in their abilities to make a difference in students' learning when they are working in a school in which RtI is the way we do business.

We wish you much success in your journey. Feel free to contact us with your questions and comments.

While RtI involves hard work and may be difficult to implement, teachers will find renewed confidence in their abilities to make a difference in students' learning when they are working in a school in which RtI is the way we do business.

BOOK STUDY QUESTIONS

- If you are doing CSI right, how does it lead you to the development of an RtI system?

- If you are doing RtI right, how does it move you to CSI?

TEAM STUDY QUESTIONS

- What are the anticipated and unanticipated changes you are seeing because of RtI implementation?

- What are your next steps?

Appendix A

EDUCATION FOR THE FUTURE CONTINUOUS IMPROVEMENT CONTINUUMS ACTIVITY

OVERVIEW OF THE CONTINUUMS

Measuring the school's progress against identified criteria—such as the *Education for the Future Continuous Improvement Continuums*—provides a benchmark that schools can use to see if their actions have created the results they intended. These measures are supported by analyzing data gathered through questionnaires, performance measures, and observations of the learning environment. When these measures are used on a regular basis, the data clearly document trends and provide information that assist schools in deciding next steps for improvement. Again, the school's guiding principles must be kept in mind to understand the true impact of the data.

There are seven *Education for the Future Initiative Continuous Improvement Continuums* that represent the theoretical flow of systemic school improvement. The Continuous Improvement Continuums take the theory and spirit of continuous school improvement, interweave educational research, and offer practical meaning to the components that must change simultaneously and systematically.

These *Education for the Future Continuous Improvement Continuums,* adapted from the *Malcolm Baldrige Award Program for Quality Business Management,* provide an authentic means for measuring schoolwide improvement and growth. Schools use these Continuums as a vehicle for ongoing self-assessment. They use the results of the assessment to acknowledge their accomplishments, to set goals for improvement, and to keep school districts and partners apprised of the progress they have made in their school improvement efforts.

Understanding the Continuums

These Continuums, extending from one to five horizontally, represent a continuum of expectations related to school improvement with respect to an *Approach* to the Continuum, *Implementation* of the approach, and the *Outcome* that results from the implementation. A one rating, located at the left of each Continuum, represents a school that has not yet begun to improve. Five, located at the right of each Continuum, represents a school that is one step removed from "world class quality." The elements between one and five describe how that Continuum is hypothesized to evolve in a continuously improving school. Each Continuum moves from a reactive mode to a proactive mode— from fire fighting to prevention. The five in outcome in each Continuum is the target.

Vertically, the *Approach, Implementation,* and *Outcome* statements, for any number one through five, are hypotheses. In other words, the implementation statement describes how the approach might look when implemented, and the outcome is the "pay-off" for implementing the approach. If the hypotheses are accurate, the outcome will not be realized until the approach is actually implemented.

Using the Continuums

Use the *Continuous Improvement Continuums* (CICs) to understand where your school is with respect to continuous improvement, and to determine next steps. The results will hopefully provide that sense of urgency needed to spark enthusiasm for your school improvement efforts.

Remember that where your school is at any time is just where it is. Do not worry about being lower than you thought. The important thing is what you do with this information. Continuous improvement is a never-ending process which, when used effectively, will ultimately lead your school, or district, toward providing a quality program for all children.

Purpose

Assessing on the *Continuous Improvement Continuums* will help staffs see where their systems are right now with respect to continuous improvement, and ultimately show that they are making progress over time. The discussion that leads to consensus is the most valuable piece of this activity. In addition to helping the entire staff see where the *school or district* is, the discussion begins to write the sections of the *Continuous Improvement Portfolio* for them.

Target Audience

School or district staff

Time

Three hours for the first assessment; 90 minutes for subsequent assessments.

Materials

One set of the school or district *Continuous Improvement Continuums* (CICs), enlarged to poster size, a copy of the CICs for staff members, chart pad paper, markers, masking tape or tacks to hang the large *Continuums*, colored dots, 3x5 post-its, and computer for notetaking—or use the *SchoolCity Portfolio* Continuum Section to record your results as you go.

Process Protocol

Hang the enlarged posters of the *Continuous Improvement Continuums* around the room. Read about where the *Continuous Improvement Continuums* came from, that they represent the theoretical flow of continuous improvement, going from reactive (1) to proactive (5). Have a person available to record the highlights of the conversation in the comment section of the *SchoolCity SchoolPortfolio*.

1. Establish ground rules for the assessment. We want to make sure everyone understands that the conversation is safe and confidential. Also clarify why it is important to do this activity.

2. Introduce the first section of the *Continuums—Information and Analysis*. Ask staff members to independently read the *Information and Analysis Continuous Improvement Continuum* and see if they can recognize where the *school or district* is right now, with respect to *Approach, Implementation,* and *Outcome*. Ask them to start with a one and move to a five. Keep the group moving and try to avoid rewording the descriptions of the continuums. Also ask them to select a whole number (2), as opposed to a "between" number like 2.5.

Process Protocol

3. Direct staff to walk over to the *Information and Analysis Continuum* on the wall and place a colorful dot or flag where they believe the school/district is with respect to *Approach, Implementation,* and *Outcome*. We call this "dot mocracy."

4. After everyone has placed her or his dot, review what you see. Focusing on *Approach*, ask for discussion of why staff thought the school/district was a 1, 2, 3, 4, or 5. Record the highlights of the discussion.

5. After the discussion, if one number is becoming clearly favored, ask if there is anyone who could not live with this number as a baseline assessment of this school's or district's *Approach* to *Information and Analysis*. If no one opposes, write that number on a post-it and place it on the large continuum to represent the consensus decision of the group. If there is not a number that is clearly favored after the first discussion, continue the discussion. You can assist if there is a stalemate by systematically asking what the organization has for *Information and Analysis*, and walking through each number in *Approach*, clarifying what the organization would have to have to be a specific number. Ask again for a show of hands.

6. Continue with *Implementation* and *Outcome*.

7. When consensus on the three sections is complete, ask for the "Next Steps." *What do we need to do to move up? Or to become the next solid number?*

8. Continue with the next six *Continuums*. After *Information and Analysis*, you can usually introduce two *Continuums* at a time. (If you are familiar with the *Continuums*, you could read and dot two or three at the same time. You will need to discuss each one separately to list "Next Steps.") It is effective to have one-half of the room read one *Continuum*, place their dots, and then come back and read the next *Continuum*, while the other half of the room is reading the second *Continuum* first, putting up their dots, and then reading the first *Continuum*.

Process Protocol

9. As staff is reading the next *Continuum,* use the time to type highlights of the discussion on the just completed *Continuum.* You will be able to leave with a complete report that summarizes the assessment results that day.

10. Add digital pictures of the assessment charts to the report to watch the staff thinking come together over time.

Comments to the Facilitator

We want the *Continuous Improvement Continuums* to add a sense of urgency for improvement. To that end, do not let staff members average their scores or rate themselves too high. Make sure they think about, and write, next steps.

Averaging the scores does not inspire change—especially on the first assessment. If the discussion hangs between two numbers, go to the lower number, and write solid *Next Steps* to become the next number.

Make sure everyone knows the emphasis is on *consensus* and not just a vote. We want everyone to win!

Periodic (regular) assessment sessions will help staffs see that they are making progress. We recommend at least once a year.

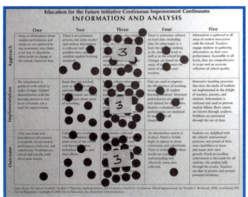

Fall Assessment

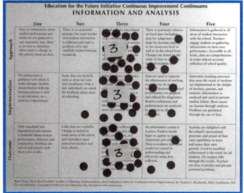

Spring Assessment

The *Education for the Future Continuous Improvement Continuums* for schools and districts are shown on the pages that follow.

School Continuous Improvement Continuums
INFORMATION AND ANALYSIS

	One	Two	Three	Four	Five
Approach	Data or information about student performance and needs are not gathered in any systematic way; there is no way to determine what needs to change at the school, based on data.	There is no systematic process, but some teacher and student information is collected and used to problem solve and establish student learning standards.	School collects data related to student performance (e.g., attendance, achievement) and conducts surveys on student, teacher, and parent needs. The information is used to drive the strategic quality plan for school change.	There is systematic reliance on hard data (including data for subgroups) as a basis for decision making at the classroom level as well as at the school level. Changes are based on the study of data to meet the needs of students and teachers.	Information is gathered in all areas of student interaction with the school. Teachers engage students in gathering information on their own performance. Accessible to all levels, data are comprehensive in scope and an accurate reflection of school quality.
Implementation	No information is gathered with which to make changes. Student dissatisfaction with the learning process is seen as an irritation, not a need for improvement.	Some data are tracked, such as drop-out rates and enrollment. Only a few individuals are asked for feedback about areas of schooling.	School collects information on current and former students (e.g., student achievement and perceptions), analyzes and uses it in conjunction with future trends for planning. Identified areas for improvement are tracked over time.	Data are used to improve the effectiveness of teaching strategies on all student learning. Students' historical performances are graphed and utilized for diagnostics. Student evaluations and performances are analyzed by teachers in all classrooms.	Innovative teaching processes that meet the needs of students are implemented to the delight of teachers, parents, and students. Information is analyzed and used to prevent student failure. Root causes are known through analyses. Problems are prevented through the use of data.
Outcome	Only anecdotal and hypothetical information is available about student performance, behavior, and satisfaction. Problems are solved individually with short-term results.	Little data are available. Change is limited to some areas of the school and dependent upon individual teachers and their efforts.	Information collected about student and parent needs, assessment, and instructional practices is shared with the school staff and used to plan for change. Information helps staff understand pressing issues, analyze information for "root causes," and track results for improvement.	An information system is in place. Positive trends begin to appear in many classrooms and schoolwide. There is evidence that these results are caused by understanding and effectively using data collected.	Students are delighted with the school's instructional processes and proud of their own capabilities to learn and assess their own growth. Good to excellent achievement is the result for all students. No student falls through the cracks. Teachers use data to predict and prevent potential problems.

© Education for the Future Initiative, Chico, CA (http://eff.csuchico.edu)

School Continuous Improvement Continuums
STUDENT ACHIEVEMENT

	One	Two	Three	Four	Five
Approach	Instructional and organizational processes critical to student success are not identified. Little distinction of student learning differences is made. Some teachers believe that not all students can achieve.	Some data are collected on student background and performance trends. Learning gaps are noted to direct improvement of instruction. It is known that student learning standards must be identified.	Student learning standards are identified, and a continuum of learning is created throughout the school. Student performance data are collected and compared to the standards in order to analyze how to improve learning for all students.	Data on student achievement are used throughout the school to pursue the improvement of student learning. Teachers collaborate to implement appropriate instruction and assessment strategies for meeting student learning standards articulated across grade levels. All teachers believe that all students can learn.	School makes an effort to exceed student achievement expectations. Innovative instructional changes are made to anticipate learning needs and improve student achievement. Teachers are able to predict characteristics impacting student achievement and to know how to perform from a small set of internal quality measures.
Implementation	All students are taught the same way. There is no communication with students about their academic needs or learning styles. There are no analyses of how to improve instruction.	Some effort is made to track and analyze student achievement trends on a school-wide basis. Teachers begin to understand the needs and learning gaps of students.	Teachers study effective instruction and assessment strategies to implement standards and to increase their students' learning. Student feedback and analysis of achievement data are used in conjunction with implementation support strategies.	There is a systematic focus on implementing student learning standards and on the improvement of student learning schoolwide. Effective instruction and assessment strategies are implemented in each classroom. Teachers support one another with peer coaching and/or action research focused on implementing strategies that lead to increased achievement and the attainment of the shared vision.	All teachers correlate critical instructional and assessment strategies with objective indicators of quality student achievement. A comparative analysis of actual individual student performance to student learning standards is utilized to adjust teaching strategies to ensure a progression of learning for all students.
Outcome	There is wide variation in student attitudes and achievement with undesirable results. There is high dissatisfaction among students with learning. Student background is used as an excuse for low student achievement.	There is some evidence that student achievement trends are available to teachers and are being used. There is much effort, but minimal observable results in improving student achievement.	There is an increase in communication between students and teachers regarding student learning. Teachers learn about effective instructional strategies that will implement the shared vision, including student learning standards, and meet the needs of their students. They make some gains.	Increased student achievement is evident schoolwide. Student morale, attendance, and behavior are good. Teachers converse often with each other about preventing student failure. Areas for further attention are clear.	Students and teachers conduct self-assessments to continuously improve performance. Improvements in student achievement are evident and clearly caused by teachers' and students' understandings of individual student learning standards, linked to appropriate and effective instructional and assessment strategies. A continuum of learning results. No students fall through the cracks.

School Continuous Improvement Continuums
QUALITY PLANNING

	One	Two	Three	Four	Five
Approach	No quality plan or process exists. Data are neither used nor considered important in planning.	The staff realize the importance of a mission, vision, and one comprehensive action plan. Teams develop goals and timelines, and dollars are allocated to begin the process.	A comprehensive school plan to achieve the vision is developed. Plan includes evaluation and continuous improvement.	One focused and integrated schoolwide plan for implementing a continuous improvement process is put into action. All school efforts are focused on the implementation of this plan that represents the achievement of the vision.	A plan for the continuous improvement of the school, with a focus on students, is put into place. There is excellent articulation and integration of all elements in the school due to quality planning. Leadership team ensures all elements are implemented by all appropriate parties.
Implementation	There is no knowledge of or direction for quality planning. Budget is allocated on an as-needed basis. Many plans exist.	School community begins continuous improvement planning efforts by laying out major steps to a shared vision, by identifying values and beliefs, the purpose of the school, a mission, vision, and student learning standards.	Implementation goals, responsibilities, due dates, and timelines are spelled out. Support structures for implementing the plan are set in place.	The quality management plan is implemented through effective procedures in all areas of the school. Everyone commits to implementing the plan aligned to the vision, mission, and values and beliefs. All share responsibility for accomplishing school goals.	Schoolwide goals, mission, vision, and student learning standards are shared and articulated throughout the school and with feeder schools. The attainment of identified student learning standards is linked to planning and implementation of effective instruction that meets students' needs. Leaders at all levels are developing expertise because planning is the norm.
Outcome	There is no evidence of comprehensive planning. Staff work is carried out in isolation. A continuum of learning for students is absent.	The school community understands the benefits of working together to implement a comprehensive continuous improvement plan.	There is evidence that the school plan is being implemented in some areas of the school. Improvements are neither systematic nor integrated schoolwide.	A schoolwide plan is known to all. Results from working toward the quality improvement goals are evident throughout the school. Planning is ongoing and inclusive of all stakeholders.	Evidence of effective teaching and learning results in significant improvement of student achievement attributed to quality planning at all levels of the school organization. Teachers and administrators understand and share the school mission and vision. Quality planning is seamless and all demonstrate evidence of accountability.

School Continuous Improvement Continuums
LEADERSHIP

	One	Two	Three	Four	Five
Approach	Principal as decision maker. Decisions are reactive to state, district, and federal mandates. There is no knowledge of continuous improvement.	A shared decision-making structure is put into place and discussions begin on how to achieve a school vision. Most decisions are focused on solving problems and are reactive.	Leadership team is committed to continuous improvement. Leadership seeks inclusion of all school sectors and supports study teams by making time provisions for their work.	Leadership team represents a true shared decision-making structure. Study teams are reconstructed for the implementation of a comprehensive continuous improvement plan.	A strong continuous improvement structure is set into place that allows for input from all sectors of the school, district, and community, ensuring strong communication, flexibility, and refinement of approach and beliefs. The school vision is student focused, based on data, and appropriate for school/community values, and meeting student needs.
Implementation	Principal makes all decisions, with little or no input from teachers, the community, or students. Leadership inspects for mistakes.	School values and beliefs are identified; the purpose of school is defined; a school mission and student learning standards are developed with representative input. A structure for studying approaches to achieving student learning standards is established.	Leadership team is active on study teams and integrates recommendations from the teams' research and analyses to form a comprehensive plan for continuous improvement within the context of the school mission. Everyone is kept informed.	Decisions about budget and implementation of the vision are made within teams, by the principal, by the leadership team, and by the full staff as appropriate. All decisions are communicated to the leadership team and to the full staff.	The vision is implemented and articulated across all grade levels and into feeder schools. Quality standards are reinforced throughout the school. All members of the school community understand and apply the quality standards. Leadership team has systematic interactions and involvement with district administrators, teachers, parents, community, and students about the school's direction. Necessary resources are available to implement and measure staff learning related to student learning standards.
Outcome	Decisions lack focus and consistency. There is no evidence of staff commitment to a shared vision. Students and parents do not feel they are being heard. Decision-making process is clear and known.	The mission provides a focus for all school improvement and guides the action to the vision. The school community is committed to continuous improvement. Quality leadership techniques are used sporadically.	Leadership team is seen as committed to planning and quality improvement. Critical areas for improvement are identified. Faculty feel included in shared decision making.	There is evidence that the leadership team listens to all levels of the organization. Implementation of the continuous improvement plan is linked to student learning standards and the guiding principles of the school. Leadership capacities for implementing the vision among teachers are evident.	Site-based management and shared decision making truly exists. Teachers understand and display an intimate knowledge of how the school operates. Teachers support and communicate with each other in the implementation of quality strategies. Teachers implement the vision in their classrooms and can determine how their new approach meets student needs and leads to the attainment of student learning standards. Leaders are standards-driven at all levels.

School Continuous Improvement Continuums
PROFESSIONAL LEARNING

	One	Two	Three	Four	Five
Approach	There is no professional development. Teachers, principals, and staff are seen as interchangeable parts that can be replaced. Professional development is external and usually equated to attending a conference alone. Hierarchy determines "haves" and "have-nots."	The "cafeteria" approach to professional development is used, whereby individual teachers choose what they want to take, without regard to an overall school plan.	The shared vision, school plan, and student needs are used to target focused professional development for all employees. Staff is inserviced on relevant instructional and leadership strategies.	Professional development and data-gathering methods are used by all teachers and are directed toward the goals of the shared vision and the continuous improvement of the school. Teachers have ongoing conversations about student achievement data. Other staff members receive training in their content areas. Systems thinking is considered in all decisions.	Leadership and staff continuously improve all aspects of the learning organization through an innovative, data-driven, and comprehensive continuous improvement process that prevents student failures. Effective job-embedded professional development is ongoing for implementing the vision for student success. Traditional teacher evaluations are replaced by collegial coaching and action research focused on student learning standards. Policies set professional development as a priority budget line-item. Professional development is planned, aligned, and lead to the achievement of student learning standards.
Implementation	Teacher, principal, and staff performance is controlled and inspected. Performance evaluations are used to detect mistakes.	Teacher professional development is sporadic and unfocused, lacking an approach for implementing new procedures and processes. Some leadership training begins to take place.	Teachers are involved in year-round quality professional development. The school community is trained in shared decision making, team building concepts, effective communication strategies, and data analysis at the classroom level.	Teachers, in teams, continuously set and implement student achievement goals. Leadership considers these goals and provides necessary support structures for collaboration. Teachers utilize effective support approaches as they implement new instruction and assessment strategies. Coaching and feedback structures are in place. Use of new knowledge and skills is evident.	Teams passionately support each other in the pursuit of quality improvement at all levels. Teachers make bold changes in instruction and assessment strategies focused on student learning standards and student learning styles. A teacher as action researcher model is implemented. Staffwide conversations focus on systemic reflection and improvement. Teachers are strong leaders.
Outcome	No professional growth and no staff or student performance improvement. There exists a high turnover rate of employees, especially administrators. Attitudes and approaches filter down to students.	The effectiveness of professional development is not known or analyzed. Teachers feel helpless about making schoolwide changes.	Teachers, working in teams, feel supported and begin to feel they can make changes. Evidence shows that shared decision making works.	A collegial school is evident. Effective classroom strategies are practiced, articulated schoolwide, are reflective of professional development aimed at ensuring student achievement, and the implementation of the shared vision, that includes student learning standards.	True systemic change and improved student achievement result because teachers are knowledgeable of and implement effective, differentiated teaching strategies for individual student learning gains. Teachers' repertoire of skills are enhanced, and students are achieving. Professional development is driving learning at all levels.

© Education for the Future Initiative, Chico, CA (*http://eff.csuchico.edu*)

School Continuous Improvement Continuums
PARTNERSHIP DEVELOPMENT

	One	Two	Three	Four	Five
Approach	There is no system for input from parents, business, or community. Status quo is desired for managing the school.	Partnerships are sought, but mostly for money and things.	School has knowledge of why partnerships are important and seeks to include businesses and parents in a strategic fashion related to student learning standards for increased student achievement.	School seeks effective win-win business and community partnerships and parent involvement to implement the vision. Desired outcomes are clearly identified. A solid plan for partnership development exists.	Community, parent, and business partnerships become integrated across all student groupings. The benefits of outside involvement are known by all. Parent and business involvement in student learning is refined. Student learning *regularly* takes place beyond the school walls.
Implementation	Barriers are erected to close out involvement of outsiders. Outsiders are managed for least impact on status quo.	A team is assigned to get partners and to receive input from parents, the community, and business in the school.	Involvement of business, community, and parents begins to take place in some classrooms and after school hours related to the vision. Partners begin to realize how they can support each other in achieving school goals. School staff understand what partners need from the partnership.	There is a systematic utilization of parents, community, and businesses schoolwide. Areas in which the active use of these partnerships benefit student learning are clear.	Partnership development is articulated across all student groupings. Parents, community, business, and educators work together in an innovative fashion to increase student learning and to prepare students for the 21st Century. Partnerships are evaluated for continuous improvement.
Outcome	There is little or no involvement of parents, business, or community at-large. School is a closed, isolated system.	Much effort is given to establishing partnerships. Some spotty trends emerge, such as receiving donated equipment.	Some substantial gains are achieved in implementing partnerships. Some student achievement increases can be attributed to this involvement.	Gains in student satisfaction with learning and school are clearly related to partnerships. All partners benefit.	Previously non-achieving students enjoy learning with excellent achievement. Community, business, and home become common places for student learning, while school becomes a place where parents come for further education. Partnerships enhance what the school does for students.

© Education for the Future Initiative, Chico, CA (*http://eff.csuchico.edu*)

School Continuous Improvement Continuums
CONTINUOUS IMPROVEMENT AND EVALUATION

	One	Two	Three	Four	Five
Approach	Neither goals nor strategies exist for the evaluation and continuous improvement of the school organization or for elements of the school organization.	The approach to continuous improvement and evaluation is problem solving. If there are no problems, or if solutions can be made quickly, there is no need for improvement or analyses. Changes in parts of the system are not coordinated with all other parts.	Some elements of the school organization are evaluated for effectiveness. Some elements are improved on the basis of the evaluation findings.	All elements of the school's operations are evaluated for improvement and to ensure congruence of the elements with respect to the continuum of learning students experience.	All aspects of the school organization are rigorously evaluated and improved on a continuous basis. Students, and the maintenance of a comprehensive learning continuum for students, become the focus of all aspects of the school improvement process.
Implementation	With no overall plan for evaluation and continuous improvement, strategies are changed by individual teachers and administrators only when something sparks the need to improve. Reactive decisions and activities are a daily mode of operation.	Isolated changes are made in some areas of the school organization in response to problem incidents. Changes are not preceded by comprehensive analyses, such as an understanding of the root causes of problems. The effectiveness of the elements of the school organization, or changes made to the elements, is not known.	Elements of the school organization are improved on the basis of comprehensive analyses of root causes of problems, client perceptions, and operational effectiveness of processes.	Continuous improvement analyses of student achievement and instructional strategies are rigorously reinforced within each classroom and across learning levels to develop a comprehensive learning continuum for students and to prevent student failure.	Comprehensive continuous improvement becomes the way of doing business at the school. Teachers continuously improve the appropriateness and effectiveness of instructional strategies based on student feedback and performance. All aspects of the school organization are improved to support teachers' efforts.
Outcome	Individuals struggle with system failure. Finger pointing and blaming others for failure occurs. The effectiveness of strategies is not known. Mistakes are repeated.	Problems are solved only temporarily and few positive changes result. Additionally, unintended and undesirable consequences often appear in other parts of the system. Many aspects of the school are incongruent, keeping the school from reaching its vision.	Evidence of effective improvement strategies is observable. Positive changes are made and maintained due to comprehensive analyses and evaluation.	Teachers become astute at assessing and in predicting the impact of their instructional strategies on individual student achievement. Sustainable improvements in student achievement are evident at all grade levels, due to continuous improvement.	The school becomes a congruent and effective learning organization. Only instruction and assessment strategies that produce quality student achievement are used. A true continuum of learning results for all students and staff. The impact of improvements is increasingly measurable.

© Education for the Future Initiative, Chico, CA (http://eff.csuchico.edu)

District Continuous Improvement Continuums
INFORMATION AND ANALYSIS

	One	Two	Three	Four	Five
Approach	Data or information about school student performance and needs are not gathered in any systematic way. The district does not provide assistance in helping schools understand what needs to change at the school and classroom levels, based on data.	There is no systematic process for data analysis across the district. Some school, teacher, and student information are collected and used to problem solve and establish student-learning standards across the district.	School district collects data related to school and student performance (e.g., attendance, enrollment, achievement), and surveys students, staff, and parents. The information is used to drive the strategic quality plan for district and school improvement.	There is systematic reliance on hard data (including data for subgroups) as a basis for decision making at the district, school, and classroom levels. Changes are based on the study of data to meet the educational needs of students and teachers.	Information is gathered in all areas of student interaction with the school. The district engages administrators and teachers in gathering information on their own performance. Accessible to all schools, data are comprehensive in scope and an accurate reflection of school and district quality.
Implementation	No information is gathered with which to make district or school changes. Student dissatisfaction with the learning process is seen as an irritation, not a need for improvement.	Some data are tracked, such as attendance, enrollment, and drop-out rates. Only a few individuals are asked for feedback about areas of schooling and district operations.	The district collects information on current and former students (e.g., student achievement and perceptions), analyzes and uses it in conjunction with future trends for planning. Identified areas for improvement are tracked over time.	Data are used to provide feedback to improve the effectiveness of teaching strategies on all student learning. Schools' historical performances are graphed and utilized for diagnosis by the district.	Innovative teaching processes that meet the needs of students are implemented across the district. Information is analyzed and used to prevent student failure. Root causes are known through analyses. Problems are prevented through the use of data.
Outcome	Only anecdotal and hypothetical information are available about student performance, behavior, and satisfaction. Problems are solved individually with short-term results.	Little data are available. Change is limited to some areas of the district and dependent upon individual administrators and their efforts.	Information collected about school needs, effective assessment, and instructional practices are shared with all school and district staff and used to plan for school and district improvement. Information helps staff understand pressing issues, analyze information for "root causes," and track results for improvement.	An information system is in place. Positive trends begin to appear in many schools and districtwide. There is evidence that these results are caused by understanding and effectively using the data collected.	Schools are delighted with their instructional processes and proud of their own capabilities to learn and assess their own growth. Good to excellent achievement is the result for all schools. Schools use data to predict and prevent potential problems. No student falls through the cracks.

© Education for the Future Initiative, Chico, CA (*http://eff.csuchico.edu*)

District Continuous Improvement Continuums
STUDENT ACHIEVEMENT

	One	Two	Three	Four	Five
Approach	Instructional and organizational processes critical to student success are not identified. Little distinction of student learning differences is made. Some schools believe that not all students can achieve.	Some data are collected on student background and performance trends. Learning gaps are noted to direct improvement of instruction. It is known that student learning standards must be identified.	Student learning standards are identified, and a continuum of learning is created across the district. Student performance data are collected and compared to the standards in order to analyze how to improve learning for all students.	Data on student achievement are used throughout the district to pursue the improvement of student learning. The district ensures that teachers collaborate to implement appropriate instruction and assessment strategies for meeting student learning standards articulated across grade levels. All teachers believe that all students can learn.	The district makes an effort to exceed student achievement expectations. Innovative instructional changes are made to anticipate learning needs and improve student achievement. District makes sure that teachers are able to predict characteristics impacting student achievement and to know how to perform from a small set of internal quality measures.
Implementation	All students are taught the same way. There is no communication between the district and schools about students' academic needs or learning styles. There are no analyses of how to improve instruction.	Some effort is made to track and analyze student achievement trends on a districtwide basis. District begins to understand the needs and learning gaps within the schools.	Teachers across the district study effective instruction and assessment strategies to implement standards and to increase students' learning. Student feedback and analysis of achievement data are used in conjunction with implementation support strategies.	There is a systematic focus on implementing student learning standards and on the improvement of student learning districtwide. Effective instruction and assessment strategies are implemented in each school. District supports teachers supporting one another with peer coaching and/or action research focused on implementing strategies that lead to increased achievement.	All teachers correlate critical instructional and assessment strategies with objective indicators of quality student achievement. A comparative analysis of actual individual student performance to student learning standards is utilized to adjust teaching strategies to ensure a progression of learning for all students.
Outcome	There is wide variation in student attitudes and achievement with undesirable results. There is high dissatisfaction among students with learning. Student background is used as an excuse for low student achievement.	There is some evidence that student achievement trends are available to schools and are being used. There is much effort, but minimal observable results in improving student achievement.	There is an increase in communication among district and schools, students, and teachers regarding student learning. Teachers learn about effective instructional strategies that will implement the shared vision, student learning standards, and how to meet the needs of students. The schools make some gains.	Increased student achievement is evident districtwide. Student morale, attendance, and behavior are good. Teachers converse often with each other about preventing student failure. Areas for further attention are clear.	Schools and teachers conduct self-assessments to continuously improve performance. Improvements in student achievement are evident and clearly caused by teachers' and students' understandings of individual student learning standards, linked to appropriate and effective instructional and assessment strategies. A continuum of learning results. No students fall through the cracks.

District Continuous Improvement Continuums
QUALITY PLANNING

	One	Two	Three	Four	Five
Approach	No quality plan or process exists. Data are neither used nor considered important in planning.	The district realizes the importance of a mission, vision, and one comprehensive action plan. Teams develop goals and timelines, and dollars are allocated to begin the process.	A comprehensive plan to achieve the district vision is developed. Plan includes evaluation and continuous improvement.	One focused and integrated districtwide plan for implementing a continuous improvement process is put into action. All district efforts are focused on the implementation of this plan that represents the achievement of the vision.	A plan for the continuous improvement of the district, with a focus on students, is put into place. There is excellent articulation and integration of all elements in the district due to quality planning. Leadership team ensures all elements are implemented by all appropriate parties.
Implementation	There is no knowledge of or direction for quality planning. Budget is allocated on an as-needed basis. Many plans exist.	School district community begins continuous improvement planning efforts by laying out major steps to a shared vision, by identifying values and beliefs, the purpose of the district, a mission, vision, and student learning standards.	Implementation goals, responsibilities, due dates, and timelines are spelled out. Support structures for implementing the plan are set in place.	The quality management plan is implemented through effective procedures in all areas of the district. Everyone commits to implementing the plan aligned to the vision, mission, and values and beliefs. All share responsibility for accomplishing district goals.	Districtwide goals, mission, vision, and student learning standards are shared and articulated throughout the district and with feeder schools. The attainment of identified student learning standards is linked to planning and implementation of effective instruction that meets students' needs. Leaders at all levels are developing expertise because planning is the norm.
Outcome	There is no evidence of comprehensive planning. Staff work is carried out in isolation. A continuum of learning for students is absent.	The school district community understands the benefits of working together to implement a comprehensive continuous improvement plan.	There is evidence that the district plan is being implemented in some areas of the district. Improvements are neither systematic nor integrated districtwide.	A districtwide plan is known to all. Results from working toward the quality improvement goals are evident throughout the district. Planning is ongoing and inclusive of all stakeholders.	Evidence of effective teaching and learning results in significant improvement of student achievement attributed to quality planning at all levels of the district organization. Teachers and administrators understand and share the district mission and vision. Quality planning is seamless and all demonstrate evidence of accountability.

© Education for the Future Initiative, Chico, CA *(http://eff.csuchico.edu)*

District Continuous Improvement Continuums
LEADERSHIP

	One	Two	Three	Four	Five
Approach	The School Board is decision maker. Decisions are reactive to state, district, and federal mandates. There is no knowledge of continuous improvement.	A shared decision-making structure is put into place and discussions begin on how to achieve a district vision. Most decisions are focused on solving problems and are reactive.	District leadership team is committed to continuous improvement. Leadership seeks inclusion of all school sectors and supports study teams by making time provisions for their work.	District leadership team represents a true shared decision-making structure. Study teams are reconstructed for the implementation of a comprehensive continuous improvement plan.	A strong continuous improvement structure is set into place that allows for input from all sectors of the district, school, and community, ensuring strong communication, flexibility, and refinement of approach and beliefs. The district vision is student focused, based on data and appropriate for district/school/community values, and meeting student needs.
Implementation	The School Board makes all decisions, with little or no input from administrators, teachers, the community, or students. Leadership inspects for mistakes.	District values and beliefs are identified; the purpose of district is defined; a district mission and student learning standards are developed with representative input. A structure for studying approaches to achieving student learning standards is established.	The district leadership team is active on study teams and integrates recommendations from the teams' research and analyses to form a comprehensive plan for continuous improvement within the context of the district mission. Everyone is kept informed.	Decisions about budget and implementation of the vision are made within teams, by the school board, by the leadership team, by the individual schools, and by the full staff, as appropriate. All decisions are communicated to the leadership team and to the full staff.	The vision is implemented and articulated across all grade levels and into feeder schools. Quality standards are reinforced throughout the district. All members of the district community understand and apply the quality standards. Leadership team has systematic interactions and involvement with district administrators, teachers, parents, community, and students about the district's direction. Necessary resources are available to implement and measure staff learning related to student learning standards.
Outcome	Although the decision-making process is clearly known, decisions are reactive and lack focus and consistency. There is no evidence of staff commitment to a shared vision. Students and parents do not feel they are being heard.	The mission provides a focus for all district and school improvement and guides the action to the vision. The school community is committed to continuous improvement. Quality leadership techniques are used sporadically.	The district leadership team is seen as committed to planning and quality improvement. Critical areas for improvement are identified. Faculty feel included in shared decision making.	There is evidence that the district leadership team listens to all levels of the organization. Implementation of the continuous improvement plan is linked to student learning standards and the guiding principles of the school. Leadership capacity for implementing the vision throughout the district is evident.	Site-based management and shared decision making truly exists. Teachers understand and display an intimate knowledge of how the school and district operate. Schools support and communicate with each other in the implementation of quality strategies. Teachers implement the vision in their classrooms and can determine how their new approaches meet student needs and lead to the attainment of student learning standards. Leaders are standards-driven at all levels.

© Education for the Future Initiative, Chico, CA *(http://eff.csuchico.edu)*

District Continuous Improvement Continuums
PROFESSIONAL LEARNING

	One	Two	Three	Four	Five
Approach	There is no professional development. Teachers, principals, and staff are seen as interchangeable parts that can be replaced. Professional development is external and usually equated to attending a conference alone. Hierarchy determines "haves" and "have-nots."	The "cafeteria" approach to professional development is used, whereby individual teachers and administrators choose what they want to take, without regard to an overall district plan.	The shared vision, district plan and student needs are used to target focused professional development for all employees. Staff is inserviced on relevant instructional and leadership strategies.	Professional development and data-gathering methods are used by all teachers and administrators, and are directed toward the goals of the shared vision and the continuous improvement of the district and schools. Teachers have ongoing conversations about student achievement data. All staff members receive training in their content areas. Systems thinking is considered in all decisions.	Leadership and staff continuously improve all aspects of the learning organization through an innovative, data-driven, and comprehensive continuous improvement process that prevents student failures. Effective job-embedded professional development is ongoing for implementing the vision for student success. Traditional teacher evaluations are replaced by collegial coaching and action research focused on student learning standards. Policies set professional development as a priority budget line-item. Professional development is planned, aligned, and leads to the achievement of student learning standards.
Implementation	District staff, principals, teachers, and school staff performance is controlled and inspected. Performance evaluations are used to detect mistakes.	Teacher professional development is sporadic and unfocused, lacking an approach for implementing new procedures and processes. Some leadership training begins to take place.	The district ensures that teachers are involved in year-round quality professional development. The school community is trained in shared decision making, team building concepts, effective communication strategies, and data analysis.	Teachers, in teams, continuously set and implement student achievement goals. Leadership considers these goals and provides necessary support structures for collaboration. Teachers utilize effective support approaches as they implement new instruction and assessment strategies. Coaching and feedback structures are in place. Use of new knowledge and skills is evident.	Teams passionately support each other in the pursuit of quality improvement at all levels. Teachers make bold changes in instruction and assessment strategies focused on student learning standards and student learning styles. A *teacher as action researcher* model is implemented. Staffwide conversations focus on systemic reflection and improvement. Teachers are strong leaders.
Outcome	No professional growth and no staff or student performance improvement. There exists a high turnover rate of employees, especially administrators. Attitudes and approaches filter down to students.	The effectiveness of professional development is not known or analyzed. Teachers feel helpless and unsupported in making schoolwide changes.	Teachers, working in teams, feel supported by the district and begin to feel they can make changes. Evidence shows that shared decision making works.	A collegial school district is evident. Effective classroom strategies are practiced, articulated schoolwide. These strategies, focused on student learning standards, are reflective of professional development aimed at ensuring student learning and the implementation of the shared vision.	True systemic change and improved student achievement result because teachers are knowledgeable of and implement effective, differentiated teaching strategies for individual student learning gains. Teachers' repertoire of skills is enhanced and students are achieving. Professional development is driving learning at all levels.

© Education for the Future Initiative, Chico, CA *(http://eff.csuchico.edu)*

District Continuous Improvement Continuums
PARTNERSHIP DEVELOPMENT

	One	Two	Three	Four	Five
Approach	There is no system for input from parents, business, or community. Status quo is desired for managing the school district.	Partnerships are sought, but mostly for money and things.	School district has knowledge of why partnerships are important and seeks to include businesses and parents in a strategic fashion related to student learning standards for increased student achievement.	School district seeks effective win-win business and community partnerships and parent involvement to implement the vision. Desired outcomes are clearly identified. A solid plan for partnership development exists.	Community, parent, and business partnerships become integrated across all student groupings. The benefits of outside involvement are known by all. Parent and business involvement in student learning is refined. Student learning regularly takes place beyond the school and district walls.
Implementation	Barriers are erected to close out involvement of outsiders. Outsiders are managed for least impact on status quo.	A team is assigned to get partners and to receive input from parents, the community, and business in the school district.	Involvement of business, community, and parents begins to take place in some schools and after school hours related to the vision. Partners begin to realize how they can support each other in achieving district goals. District staff understand what partners need from the partnership.	There is systematic utilization of parents, community, and businesses districtwide. Areas in which the active use of these partnerships benefit student learning are clear.	Partnership development is articulated across all district groupings. Parents, community, business, and educators work together in an innovative fashion to increase student learning and to prepare students for the Twenty-first Century. Partnerships are evaluated for continuous improvement.
Outcome	There is little or no involvement of parents, business, or community at-large. The district is a closed, isolated system.	Much effort is given to establishing partnerships. Some spotty trends emerge, such as receiving donated equipment.	Some substantial gains are achieved in implementing partnerships. Some student achievement increases can be attributed to this involvement.	Gains in student satisfaction with learning and school are clearly related to partnerships. All partners benefit.	Previously non-achieving students enjoy learning with excellent achievement. Community, business, and home become common places for student learning, while school becomes a place where parents come for further education. Partnerships enhance what the school district does for students.

© Education for the Future Initiative, Chico, CA (http://eff.csuchico.edu)

District Continuous Improvement Continuums

CONTINUOUS IMPROVEMENT AND EVALUATION

	One	Two	Three	Four	Five
Approach	Neither goals nor strategies exist for the evaluation and continuous improvement of the district organization or for elements of the organization.	The approach to continuous improvement and evaluation is problem-solving. If there are no problems, or if solutions can be made quickly, there is no need for improvement or analyses. Changes in parts of the system are not coordinated with all other parts.	Some elements of the district organization are evaluated for effectiveness. Some elements are improved on the basis of the evaluation findings.	All elements of the district's operations are evaluated for improvement. Efforts are consistently made to ensure congruence of the elements with respect to the continuum of learning that students experience.	All aspects of the district organization are rigorously evaluated and improved on a continuous basis. Students, and the maintenance of a comprehensive learning continuum for students, become the focus of all aspects of the school district improvement process.
Implementation	With no overall plan for evaluation and continuous improvement, strategies are changed by individual schools, teachers, and/or administrators only when something sparks the need to improve. Reactive decisions and activities are a daily mode of operation.	Isolated changes are made in some areas of the district organization in response to problem incidents. Changes are not preceded by comprehensive analyses, such as an understanding of the root causes of problems. The effectiveness of the elements of the district organization is not known.	Elements of the district organization are improved on the basis of comprehensive analyses of root causes of problems, client perceptions, and operational effectiveness of processes.	Continuous improvement analyses of student achievement and instructional strategies are rigorously reinforced within each classroom and across learning levels to develop a comprehensive learning continuum for students and to prevent student failure.	Comprehensive continuous improvement becomes the way of doing business throughout the district. Teachers continuously improve the appropriateness and effectiveness of instructional strategies based on student feedback and performance. All aspects of the district organization are improved to support teachers' efforts.
Outcome	Individuals struggle with system failure. Finger pointing and blaming others for failure occur. The effectiveness of strategies is not known. Mistakes are repeated.	Problems are solved only temporarily and few positive changes result. Additionally, unintended and undesirable consequences often appear in other parts of the system. Many aspects of the school district are incongruent, keeping the district from reaching its vision.	Evidence of effective improvement strategies is observable. Positive changes are made and maintained due to comprehensive analyses and evaluation.	Teachers become astute at assessing and in predicting the impact of their instructional strategies on individual student achievement. Sustainable improvements in student achievement are evident at all grade levels due to continuous improvement supported by the district.	The district becomes a congruent and effective learning organization. Only instruction and assessment strategies that produce quality student achievement are used. A true continuum of learning results for all students and staff. The impact of improvements is increasingly measurable.

Appendix B

MARYLIN AVENUE DATA PROFILE

Marylin Avenue Elementary School, our example school, created a data profile to answer the question, *Where are we now?* The majority of that data profile follows.

The data profile, the manifestation of the four circles described in Chapter 3, summarizes Marylin Avenue's longitudinal schoolwide data, including demographics, perceptions, student learning, and school processes.

Use this data profile with staff as a case study to experience and practice looking at comprehensive schoolwide data. You can also use this data profile to model how to set up your own school's data profile. *Look fors* and *planning implications* have been included for each graph and data table to assist with your analysis.

As you study the data, it is suggested that you take notes as you go so you can answer the questions that appear at the end of each data section: *What are the strengths, challenges, and implications for the school improvement plan?*

DEMOGRAPHIC DATA

1. What are Marylin Avenue Elementary School's demographic *strengths* and *challenges?*	
Strengths	**Challenges**
2. What are some *implications* for the Marylin Avenue continuous improvement plan?	
3. Looking at the data presented, what other Marylin Avenue demographic data would you want to answer the question *Who are we?*	

Your analysis of the data will be much more complete if you answer the questions as you review the data, as opposed to reviewing the data and then answering the questions. After identifying strengths, challenges, and implications for the school improvement plan, review the implications for the school improvement plan across the four types of data, synthesize the major implications for the school improvement plan, and then determine what the data are telling you should be in the plan, with respect to curriculum, instruction, assessment, data, vision, leadership, etc. An activity that describes instructions for analyzing data for school improvement planning appears in Appendix D.

What we saw in the Marylin Avenue data profile is shown in Appendix C.

MARYLIN AVENUE ELEMENTARY SCHOOL PROFILE

DEMOGRAPHICS

Marylin Avenue Elementary School is a Kindergarten through grade five school located in Livermore, California. As of 2010, Livermore had an estimated population of 83,800. The estimated median household income in 2008 was $94,259, compared to the median household income in California of $61,021. The 2008 cost of living index in Livermore was 154.1 (the U.S. average is 100). Lawrence Livermore National Laboratory, Sandia National Laboratory, and Kaiser Permanente are the major stable employers in Livermore.

Marylin Avenue Elementary School is part of the Livermore Valley Joint Unified School District *(http://www.livermoreschools.com),* which in 2009-10, served 13,225 students in 19 schools: 9 elementary (K-5), 2 K-8 schools, 3 middle (6-8), 2 comprehensive high (9-12), and 3 alternative schools. In 2000-01, the district served 13,935 students. This decrease (after a few years of increases) in overall district enrollment is shown in Figure B1.

Look Fors: **Increasing, steady, or decreasing enrollment.**

Planning Implications: **Is there a need to expand or decrease district/school facilities, services, and/or staff? Are enrollment changes congruent with community population changes?**

Figure B1

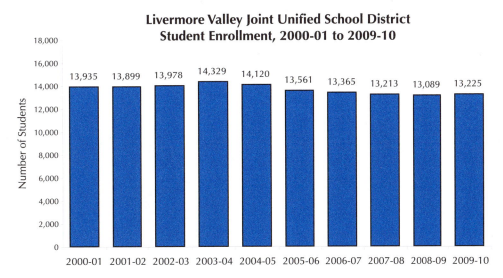

Livermore Valley Joint Unified School District Student Enrollment, 2000-01 to 2009-10

Marylin Avenue Elementary School served 458 students in 2009-10, down 18 students from the previous year (Figure B2). The lowest enrollment was 445 students in 2001-02; the highest was 529 in 2004-05.

Look Fors: **Increasing, steady, or decreasing enrollment.**

Planning Implications: **Is there a need to expand or decrease facilities, services, and/or staff? Why is enrollment increasing or decreasing?**

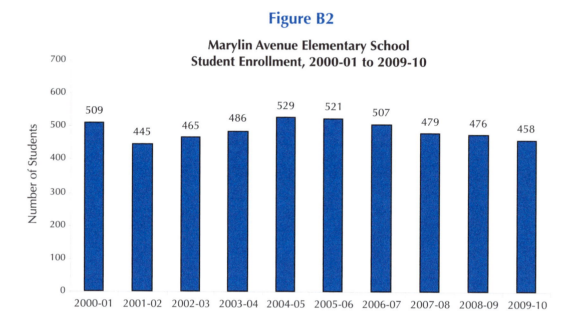

Figure B2

The district student enrollment is shown in Figure B3 by percent ethnicity. Figure B4 shows the enrollment by percent ethnicity for the elementary schools in Livermore (excluding Marylin Avenue). Figure B5 shows enrollment by percent ethnicity for Marylin Avenue.

Look Fors: **Degree of diversity in the school/district population.**

Planning Implications: **Are teachers prepared to meet the needs of students from all backgrounds? Are instructional materials geared for all students? Is there a need for diversity programs?**

Figure B3

Livermore Valley Joint Unified School District Student Enrollment by Percent Ethnicity 2009-10 (*N*=13,225)

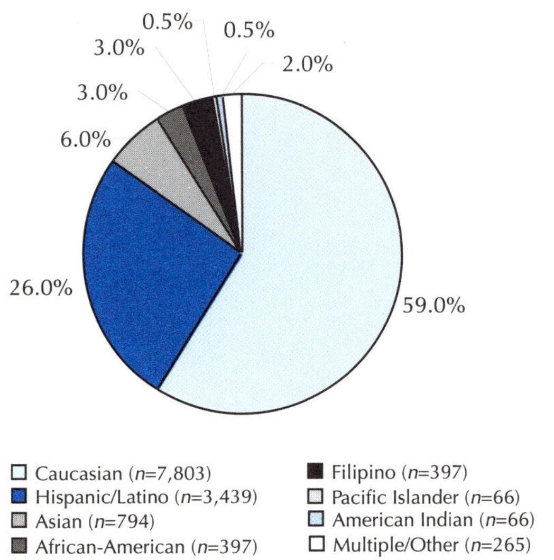
0.5%
0.5%
3.0%
2.0%
3.0%
6.0%
26.0%
59.0%
Caucasian (n=7,803)
Hispanic/Latino (n=3,439)
Asian (n=794)
African-American (n=397)
Filipino (n=397)
Pacific Islander (n=66)
American Indian (n=66)
Multiple/Other (n=265)

Figure B4

Livermore Valley Joint Unified School District Elementary Student Enrollment by Percent Ethnicity 2009-10 (*N*=5,586)

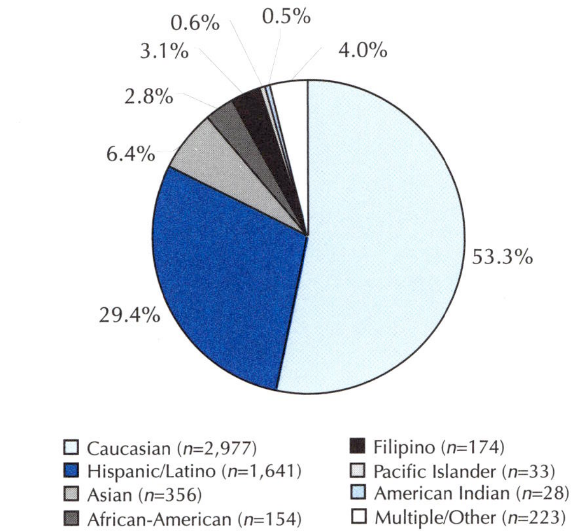
0.6%
0.5%
3.1%
4.0%
2.8%
6.4%
53.3%
29.4%
Caucasian (n=2,977)
Hispanic/Latino (n=1,641)
Asian (n=356)
African-American (n=154)
Filipino (n=174)
Pacific Islander (n=33)
American Indian (n=28)
Multiple/Other (n=223)

Figure B5

Marylin Avenue Elementary School Student Enrollment by Percent Ethnicity 2009-10 (*N*=458)

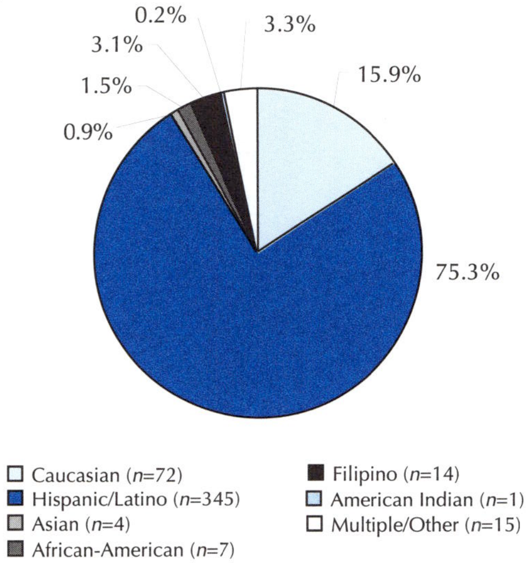
0.2%
3.3%
3.1%
15.9%
1.5%
0.9%
75.3%
Caucasian (n=72)
Hispanic/Latino (n=345)
Asian (n=4)
African-American (n=7)
Filipino (n=14)
American Indian (n=1)
Multiple/Other (n=15)

The Livermore District student enrollment by percent ethnicity since 2004-05 is shown in Figure B6. The graph shows the diversity of students has changed very little over time, except the percentage of Hispanic/Latino students is increasing while the percentage of Caucasian students is decreasing.

Figure B6

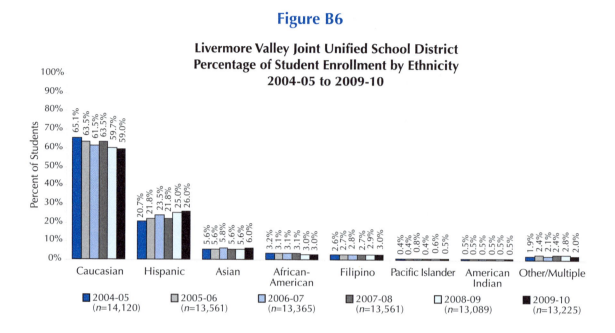

Livermore Valley Joint Unified School District
Percentage of Student Enrollment by Ethnicity
2004-05 to 2009-10

Over the past six years, as shown in Figure B7, the percentage of Marylin Avenue Hispanic/Latino students increased from 58.0% to 75.3%, increasing each year. The percentage of Caucasian students decreased from 27.6% to 15.9%, while the percentage of Asian students decreased from 3.4% to 0.9%, African-Americans from 3.4% to 1.5%, and Filipino students from 6.4% to 3.1%. The changes in the other groups were relatively minor.

Look Fors: **Changes in diversity over time.**

Planning Implications: **Is staff equipped to meet the needs of a changing population? What do staff need to know about diversity? Do instructional materials meet the needs of all the students?**

Figure B7

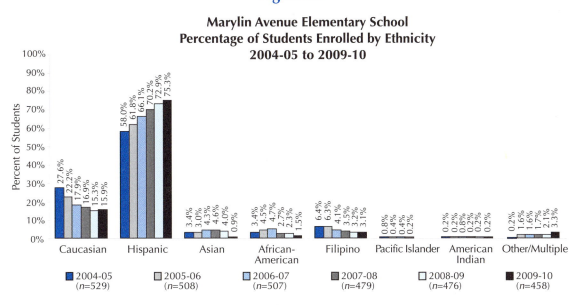

Marylin Avenue Elementary School
Percentage of Students Enrolled by Ethnicity
2004-05 to 2009-10

Figure B8 shows the Marylin Avenue Elementary School enrollment by ethnicity numbers.

Figure B8

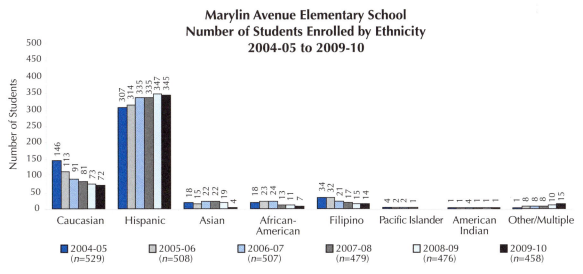

Marylin Avenue Elementary School
Number of Students Enrolled by Ethnicity
2004-05 to 2009-10

One can see the fluctuations and differences in the numbers across grade levels over time (Figure B9). Looking at the same grade level over time is called *grade level analysis.*

Look Fors: Consistency of numbers within and across grade levels.

Planning Implications: Is there mobility within the school? Are enrollment fluctuations indicators of satisfaction with the services provided? What is the impact of grade-level enrollment on class size?

Figure B9

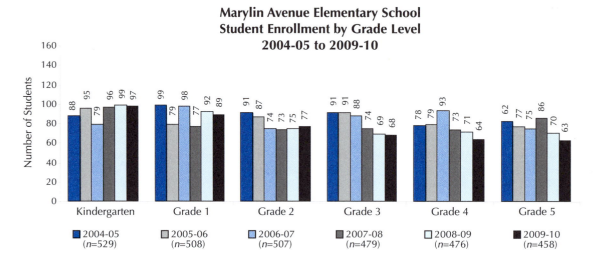

Reorganizing the data (Figure B10) to look at the groups of students progressing through the grades together over time is called a *cohort analysis.* If we were looking at the same students (as opposed to the groups of students), the analysis would be called *matched cohorts.*

Cohort A	Kindergarten 2003-04, grade one 2004-05, grade two 2005-06, grade three 2006-07, grade four 2007-08, grade five 2008-09.
Cohort B	Grade one 2003-04, grade two 2004-05, grade three 2005-06, grade four 2006-07, grade five 2007-08.
Cohort C	Grade two 2003-04, grade three 2004-05, grade four 2005-06, grade five 2006-07.
Cohort D	Grade three 2003-04, grade four 2004-05, grade five 2005-06.
Cohort E	Grade four 2004-05, grade five 2005-06.

Look Fors: Consistency of numbers within cohorts. The degree of mobility and stability.

Planning Implications: Do cohort sizes differ greatly from year-to-year? Are additional programs needed, including services to welcome new students to, or to keep them in, the school system? Does the school understand the mobility, particularly why students leave?

Figure B10

**Marylin Avenue Elementary School
Student Cohorts by Grade Level
Kindergarten to Grade Four**

By analyzing grade level and gender, one can also see the fluctuations and the differences in the numbers and percentages of males and females over time, within any grade level (Figure B11).

Look Fors: Fluctuations in enrollment across grade levels and gender over time.

Planning Implications: What are the enrollment fluctuations over time? Do instructional services and programs meet the needs by gender?

Figure B11

Marylin Avenue Elementary School Enrollment
Number and Percentage of Students by Grade Level and Gender, 2004-05 to 2009-10

Grade Level	Gender	2004-05 (N=529)		2005-06 (N=508)		2006-07 (N=507)		2007-08 (N=479)		2008-09 (N=476)		2009-10 (N=458)	
Kindergarten	Male	43	49%	43	45%	43	54%	47	49%	48	49%	52	54%
	Female	45	51%	52	55%	36	46%	49	51%	51	52%	45	46%
Grade One	Male	46	47%	39	49%	49	50%	37	48%	42	46%	41	46%
	Female	53	54%	40	51%	49	50%	40	52%	50	54%	48	54%
Grade Two	Male	40	44%	35	40%	39	53%	35	48%	33	44%	33	43%
	Female	51	56%	52	60%	35	47%	38	52%	42	56%	44	57%
Grade Three	Male	46	51%	33	36%	35	40%	35	47%	33	48%	31	46%
	Female	45	50%	58	64%	53	60%	39	53%	36	52%	37	54%
Grade Four	Male	40	51%	36	46%	40	43%	34	47%	33	47%	30	47%
	Female	38	49%	43	54%	53	57%	39	53%	38	54%	34	53%
Grade Five	Male	45	55%	44	57%	31	41%	37	43%	27	39%	27	43%
	Female	37	45%	33	43%	44	59%	49	57%	43	61%	36	57%
Totals	Male	**260**	**49%**	**230**	**45%**	**237**	**47%**	**225**	**47%**	**216**	**45%**	**214**	**47%**
	Female	**269**	**51%**	**278**	**55%**	**270**	**53%**	**254**	**53%**	**260**	**55%**	**244**	**53%**

Mobility

Figure B12 shows the number of students who moved to or from the school zero, one, two, and more than three times between 2004-05 and 2009-10. Marylin Avenue has a mobility rate of 28% for 2009-10—down from previous years (Figure B13). School mergers are reflected in the high mobility in 2005-06.

Note: Student mobility is defined as students changing schools other than when they are promoted from one school level to the other, such as when students are promoted from elementary school to middle school, or middle school to high school.

Look Fors: **Fluctuations in mobility over time. Differences in mobility percentages over time.**

Planning Implications: **Does the school need additional support or special services for students moving in and out? Does the school understand its mobility? Where do the students go? Does the school need a common curriculum? Are there effective transfer policies in place?**

Figure B12

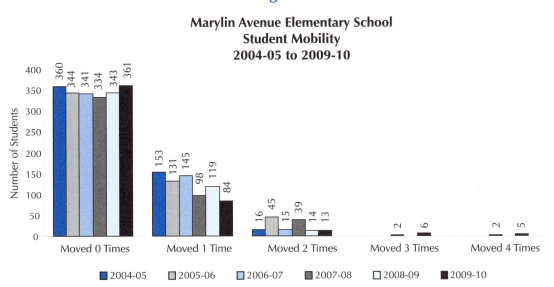

Marylin Avenue Elementary School
Student Mobility
2004-05 to 2009-10

Figure B13

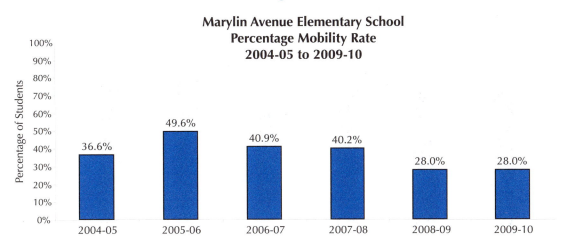

Marylin Avenue Elementary School
Percentage Mobility Rate
2004-05 to 2009-10

Open Enrollment Policy Change

It is easy to see the changes in the Marylin Avenue student population over time. There are dramatic increases in the numbers and percentages of English Learners, Hispanic students, and students who qualify for free/reduced lunches (indicating an increased level of poverty at this school). Some of the changes in population may be due to a district open-enrollment policy that permits families to transfer to any school in the district. Some of the changes took place in 2004-05 when one elementary school was closed and two schools were merged.

Attendance

Marylin Avenue students have maintained an average yearly attendance rate of about 95% over the last six years. The data in Figure B14 show the 2009-10 school attendance rate to have decreased, compared to the previous years. (*Note:* The school noted a large number of students were absent in the winter of 2009-10, because of a flu virus.) In 2009-10, Marylin Avenue had a total of 3,062 absences and 2,759 tardies. In the same year, the total number of absences for the District was 110,796, with 96,814 tardies. Marylin Avenue is working on an approach to display this information meaningfully.

Look Fors: **High or low average student attendance. Decreasing or increasing attendance rates over time.**

Planning Implications: **Why is student attendance *low* or *high?* Why are students missing school? When are students missing school? What can be done to improve attendance?**

Figure B14

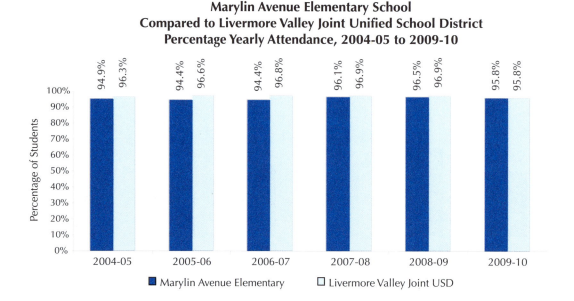

Marylin Avenue Elementary School
Compared to Livermore Valley Joint Unified School District
Percentage Yearly Attendance, 2004-05 to 2009-10

English Learners

The number of English Learners (EL) by grade level has increased over time, as shown in Figure B15. Compared to the district, Marylin Avenue's student population of English Learners is nearly 4.5 times as many. Ninety percent of English Learners speak Spanish. Other languages in small percentages include Filipino, Vietnamese, Farsi, Gujarati, Punjabi, Mandarin, Indonesian, and Hindi. There is no English Language Development Program at Marylin Avenue Elementary School.

Look Fors: **The increases/decreases in the number of English Learner populations.**

*Planning
Implications:*   **Are additional materials/programs needed to provide services to these students? Do staff need professional learning to meet these students' needs? What are the implications for home school communications? What instructional strategies and approaches should staff use for this population?**

Figure B15

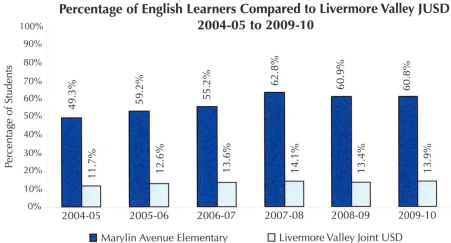

Marylin Avenue Elementary School
Percentage of English Learners Compared to Livermore Valley JUSD
2004-05 to 2009-10

Free/Reduced Lunch Status

Figure B16 compares the percentage of Marylin Avenue students qualifying for free/reduced lunch to the overall district and to the other district elementary schools. (*Note:* there are 8 other elementary schools in Livermore Valley Joint Unified School District, including two K-8 schools.) The Marylin Avenue data show that over a six-year period, the total percentage of students qualifying for Free/Reduced Lunch has almost doubled from 54% of the school population in 2004-05, to 82% in 2009-10, an indicator of the increased number of families of low socioeconomic levels. Marylin Avenue's free/reduced lunch student percentage is more than 3.5 times that of the district and the other elementary schools, on average. The majority of Marylin Avenue parents do not have high school educations.

Look Fors: **Increases/decreases in the percentage of free/reduced lunch students.**

Planning Implications: **Free/reduced lunch count is an indicator of poverty—or an indicator of the degree to which the school is tracking paperwork to get all qualified students signed up to take advantage of free/reduced lunch. Have all students who qualify for free/reduced lunch returned their forms? Do staff need professional learning to meet these students' needs? How do staff best prepare instruction and environment for this population?**

Figure B16

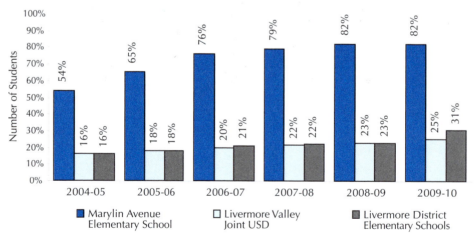

**Marylin Avenue Elementary School
Percentage of Students Receiving Free/Reduced Lunch
Compared to Livermore Valley Joint Unified School District
2004-05 to 2009-10**

Retentions

The number of Marylin Avenue Elementary School students retained in a grade level has fluctuated over the past eight years, but has remained low (Figure B17). No students at any grade level were retained in 2004-05. In 2005-06, 10 students were retained; 13 students in 2006-07; 6 students retained in 2007-08; and four students were retained in 2008-09. Two students (Kindergarten) were retained in 2009-10.

Look Fors: Changes in numbers of retentions by grade level over time.

Planning   Who are the students that are retained and why? Is retaining helpful/
Implications: effective? When do we retain?

Figure B17

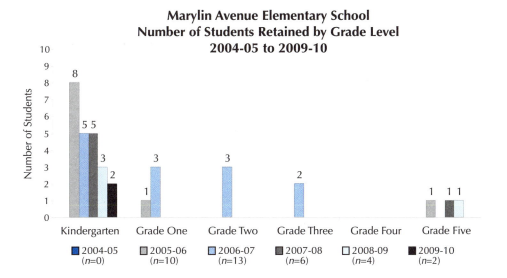

Marylin Avenue Elementary School
Number of Students Retained by Grade Level
2004-05 to 2009-10

Special Education

Up to 2009-10, Marylin Avenue Elementary School had been serving an increasing number of students classified as needing special education (SE) services. Not all identified students from Marylin Avenue receive services at the school. Some receive services at other schools in the district. The majority of students receiving special education assistance were speech and language impaired, followed by specific learning disabilities. Sixty-four students (12% of the school enrollment) were classified as requiring special education services in 2009-10. Figure B18 shows the numbers and percentages of students receiving special education services by primary disability for Marylin Avenue, the District and state. In 2009-10, Marylin Avenue staff began implementing a comprehensive RtI system in English Language Arts (ELA).

Look Fors: Changes in the number and percentage of students qualifying for special
                 education services over time in the school, district, and state.

Planning   Are the numbers increasing or decreasing? Are the services provided meeting
Implications: the needs of students with learning disabilities? Do teachers have the
                 professional learning required to work with these students?

Figure B18

Marylin Avenue Elementary School Compared to the District and State Special Education Numbers by Primary Disability, 2007-08 to 2009-10

Primary Disability	2007-08 MAS (N=59) Percent	Number	District (N=1,603) Percent	Number	State (N=677,875) Percent	Number	2008-09 MAS (N=57) Percent	Number	District (N=1,610) Percent	Number	State (N=677,875) Percent	Number	2009-10 MAS (N=54) Percent	Number	District (N=1,984) Percent	Number
Intellectual disability			3.0%	48	6.4%	43,113			3.0%	48	6.3%	42,646	1.9%	1	2.9%	58
Hard of hearing	1.7%	1	1.1%	18	1.3%	8,481	3.5%	2	1.2%	19	1.3%	9,016	1.9%	1	1.0%	19
Deaf			0.1%	1	0.6%	4,185			0.1%	1	0.6%	4,162		0	0.2%	4
Speech/language impairment	55.9%	33	39.6%	635	26.0%	176,256	50.9%	29	39.9%	643	25.5%	172,669	57.4%	31	40.1%	795
Visual impairment	1.7%	1	0.7%	12	0.7%	4,530	1.8%	1	0.8%	13	0.7%	4,588			0.7%	13
Emotional disturbance			3.8%	61	4.0	27,199			4.3%	70	4.0%	27,124			4.4%	88
Orthopedic impairment	1.7%	1	1.3%	21	2.3%	15,294	1.8%	1	1.4%	22	2.3%	15,404	1.9%	1	1.2%	23
Other health impairment	3.4%	2	12.5%	200	7.0%	47,232	8.8%	5	12.7%	204	7.5%	50,614	13.0%	7	13.1%	259
Specific learning disability	35.6%	21	31.4%	504	44.0%	297,933	33.3%	19	29.9%	482	43.0%	291,456	25.9%	14	29.8%	592
Deaf-blindness					0.03%	204					0.03%	182				
Multiple disability			1.1%	18	0.8%	5,476			1.1%	18	0.8%	5,210			0.9%	17
Autism			5.1%	18	6.8%	49,196			5.3%	85	7.8%	53,183			5.6%	112
Traumatic brain injury (TBI)			0.2%	4	0.3%	1,776			0.3%	5	0.3%	1,851			0.2%	4

Figure B19 compares the percentage of total student enrollment by ethnicity and special education, by ethnicity, for the district and school.

Look Fors: **The percentage of students qualifying for special education services by ethnicity, compared to the overall enrollment by ethnicity.**

Planning Implications: **Are the percentages in special education disability numbers across ethnicities congruent with the ethnicity percentages for the district/school?**

Figure B19

Livermore Valley JUSD Enrollment and Special Education Enrollment by Ethnicity

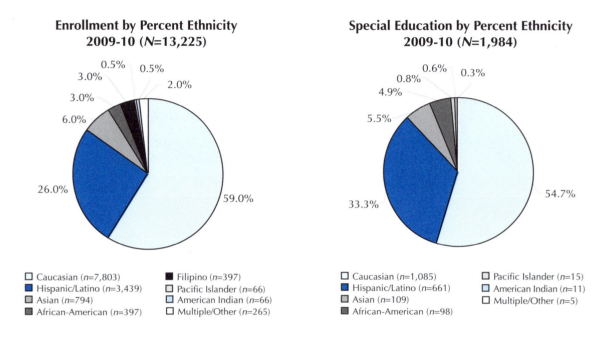

Enrollment by Percent Ethnicity 2009-10 (N=13,225)

0.5% 0.5%
3.0%
2.0%
3.0%
6.0%
26.0%
59.0%

☐ Caucasian (n=7,803)   ■ Filipino (n=397)
■ Hispanic/Latino (n=3,439)   ☐ Pacific Islander (n=66)
☐ Asian (n=794)   ☐ American Indian (n=66)
■ African-American (n=397)   ☐ Multiple/Other (n=265)

Special Education by Percent Ethnicity 2009-10 (N=1,984)

0.6% 0.3%
0.8%
4.9%
5.5%
33.3%
54.7%

☐ Caucasian (n=1,085)   ☐ Pacific Islander (n=15)
■ Hispanic/Latino (n=661)   ☐ American Indian (n=11)
☐ Asian (n=109)   ☐ Multiple/Other (n=5)
■ African-American (n=98)

Marylin Avenue Elementary School Enrollment and Special Education by Ethnicity

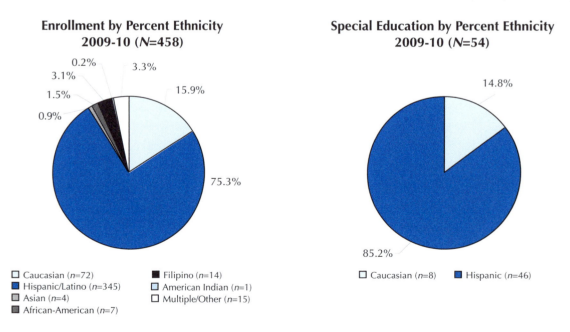

Enrollment by Percent Ethnicity 2009-10 (N=458)

0.2% 3.3%
3.1%
1.5%   15.9%
0.9%
75.3%

☐ Caucasian (n=72)   ■ Filipino (n=14)
■ Hispanic/Latino (n=345)   ☐ American Indian (n=1)
☐ Asian (n=4)   ☐ Multiple/Other (n=15)
■ African-American (n=7)

Special Education by Percent Ethnicity 2009-10 (N=54)

14.8%
85.2%

☐ Caucasian (n=8)   ■ Hispanic (n=46)

Figure B20 shows the number of district special education students by primary disability and ethnicity, over time, while Figure B21 shows the same data for Marylin Avenue Elementary School.

Look Fors: **Changes in the number of students qualifying for special education services, by type, by ethnicity, over time.**

Planning Implications: **Is the number and percentage identified per ethnicity consistent with overall student population and, if so, how and why are students being identified for special education services? Are assessments used for eligibility determinations appropriate for the populations being assessed? Could there be some testing bias?**

Figure B20

Livermore Valley Joint Unified School District
Special Education Numbers by Primary Disability and Ethnicity, 2004-05 to 2008-09

Primary Disability	Ethnicity	2004-05 (N=1,622)	2005-06 (N=1,581)	2006-07 (N=1,637)	2007-08 (N=1,603)	2008-09 (N=1,610)
Intellectual Disability	Asian	3	2	5	1	1
	Filipino	1	0	0	0	0
	Hispanic	18	17	15	12	18
	African-American	4	2	1	1	2
	Caucasian	35	41	37	34	27
	Total	**61**	**62**	**58**	**48**	**48**
Hard of Hearing	Asian	1	1	2	1	1
	Filipino	1	0	0	1	1
	Hispanic	0	0	1	5	7
	African-American	2	1	1	1	1
	Caucasian	6	8	7	10	9
	Total	**10**	**10**	**11**	**18**	**19**
Deaf	Hispanic	0	1	0	0	0
	Caucasian	1	2	1	1	1
	Total	**1**	**3**	**1**	**1**	**1**
Speech or Language Impairment	American Indian	0	0	1	2	4
	Asian	25	24	29	30	30
	Pacific Islander	0	1	5	4	3
	Filipino	17	18	21	21	19
	Hispanic	148	162	200	209	223
	African-American	29	24	20	26	18
	Caucasian	404	380	400	343	346
	Total	**623**	**609**	**676**	**635**	**643**
Visual Impairment	Hispanic	4	6	6	6	5
	African-American	1	1	1	1	1
	Caucasian	5	6	4	5	7
	Total	**10**	**13**	**11**	**12**	**13**
Emotional Disturbance	American Indian	0	0	0	1	2
	Hispanic	10	11	10	10	9
	African-American	8	4	4	4	3
	Caucasian	50	49	53	46	56
	Total	**68**	**64**	**67**	**61**	**70**
Orthopedic Impairment	Asian	2	3	2	2	2
	Filipino	1	0	0	0	0
	Hispanic	0	1	2	2	2
	African-American	1	1	1	0	0
	Caucasian	18	19	18	17	18
	Total	**22**	**24**	**23**	**21**	**22**

Figure B20 *(Continued)*

Livermore Valley Joint Unified School District
Special Education Numbers by Primary Disability and Ethnicity, 2004-05 to 2008-09

Primary Disability	Ethnicity	2004-05 (N=1,622)	2005-06 (N=1,581)	2006-07 (N=1,637)	2007-08 (N=1,603)	2008-09 (N=1,610)
Other Health Impairment	American Indian	1	1	0	1	2
	Asian	3	3	5	7	5
	Pacific Islander	0	0	0	0	1
	Filipino	2	1	3	2	1
	Hispanic	18	23	28	23	40
	African-American	1	1	1	0	0
	Caucasian	18	19	18	17	18
	Total	**22**	**24**	**23**	**21**	**22**
Specific Learning Disability	American Indian	1	2	2	4	5
	Asian	9	8	7	7	9
	Pacific Islander	1	1	2	2	1
	Filipino	5	7	3	6	3
	Hispanic	123	133	134	138	168
	African-American	38	32	40	34	34
	Caucasian	385	337	310	313	262
	Total	**562**	**520**	**498**	**504**	**482**
Multiple Disability	Asian	0	0	0	1	2
	Pacific Islander	0	0	1	1	0
	Filipino	0	0	0	0	1
	Hispanic	4	3	4	4	6
	African-American	1	1	1	2	0
	Caucasian	18	13	14	10	9
	Total	**23**	**17**	**20**	**18**	**18**
Autism	Asian	7	2	5	9	11
	Filipino	3	2	2	1	1
	Hispanic	4	2	5	7	13
	African-American	1	1	1	2	2
	Caucasian	45	55	54	62	58
	Total	**60**	**62**	**67**	**81**	**85**
Traumatic Brain Injury (TBI)	Asian	0	1	1	0	0
	Hispanic	0	0	1	2	3
	Caucasian	6	7	4	2	2
	Total	**6**	**8**	**6**	**4**	**5**

Figure B21

Marylin Avenue Elementary School Special Education
By Primary Disability and Ethnicity, 2009-10

Primary Disability	Ethnicity		2009-10 (N=54)
Hard of Hearing	Hispanic		1
		Total	1
Speech or Language Impairment	Hispanic		28
	Caucasian		3
		Total	31
Orthopedic Impairment	Caucasian		1
		Total	1
Other Health Impairment	Hispanic		4
	Caucasian		3
		Total	7
Specific Learning Disability	Hispanic		13
	Caucasian		1
		Total	14

Figure 22 shows the number of Marylin Avenue students qualifying for special education by primary disability and grade level, over time. The majority of students qualifying for Special Education services are speech and language impaired. Most disabilities are fairly evenly distributed across grade levels.

Look Fors: Changes in the number of students qualifying for special education services, by primary disability and grade level, over time.

Planning Implications: Is there one grade level that has more students identified than the others? Is there an increase or decrease in special education disability numbers across grade levels, over time? Is there a large group of students with IEPs in any grade level that may influence teacher ability to address needs or allocation of resources?

Figure B22

Marylin Avenue Elementary School
Special Education Numbers by Primary Disability and Grade Level, 2004-05 to 2009-10

Primary Disability	Grade Level	2004-05 (N=55)	2005-06 (N=60)	2006-07 (N=54)	2007-08 (N=59)	2008-09 (N=57)	2009-10 (N=54)
Speech or Language Impaired	Kindergarten	4	5	1	7	7	3
	Grade One	3	3	5	4	7	7
	Grade Two	4	2	3	5	2	8
	Grade Three	11	9	3	5	5	6
	Grade Four	8	10	11	2	6	5
	Grade Five	5	5	6	10	2	2
	Total	**35**	**34**	**29**	**33**	**29**	**31**
Specific Learning Disabilities	Kindergarten	0	0	0	1	1	
	Grade One	2	1	0	0	0	1
	Grade Two	2	3	2	3	2	0
	Grade Three	2	7	4	6	4	1
	Grade Four	2	4	7	5	4	5
	Grade Five	6	4	4	6	8	7
	Total	**14**	**19**	**17**	**21**	**19**	**14**
Visually Impaired	Grade One	0	1	1	0	0	0
	Grade Two	0	0	1	0	0	0
	Grade Three	1	0	0	1	0	0
	Grade Four	0	1	0	0	1	0
	Grade Five	0	0	1	0	0	0
	Total	**1**	**2**	**3**	**1**	**1**	**0**
Hearing Impaired	Grade Three	0	2	0	0	0	0
	Grade Four	1	0	2	0	1	0
	Grade Five	0	0	0	1	1	1
	Total	**1**	**2**	**2**	**1**	**2**	**1**
Behavior	Grade Five	1	0	0	0	0	0
	Total	**1**	**0**	**0**	**0**	**0**	**0**
Orthopedic Impairment	Grade One	0	0	0	0	1	1
	Total	**0**	**0**	**0**	**0**	**1**	**1**
Other Health Impairment	Kindergarten	1	0	0	0	1	1
	Grade One	0	1	1	0	1	0
	Grade Two	1	0	1	0	0	1
	Grade Three	0	1	0	1	2	0
	Grade Four	0	1	1	0	1	2
	Grade Five	1	0	2	1	0	3
	Total	**4**	**5**	**5**	**3**	**7**	**6**

Pre-Referral Team (PRT)

As a part of their RtI system, Marylin Avenue created a Pre-Referral Team (PRT) and process. When children are identified as at risk for failure, a Pre-Referral Team of teachers and other professionals determine appropriate interventions, communicate with a child's parent(s)/guardian(s), and encourage ongoing participation in the pre-referral process.

The Special Education Referral Team (SpERT) is the team of professionals that reviews the interventions used and progress made with an individual student to see if there is support to suspect that this could be a student with a disability; therefore, requiring a complete evaluation. If this is the case, permission to evaluate is sought from the parents, and a Multi-Disciplinary Team (MDT) conducts the evaluation to determine if a disability exists. If the SpERT determines there is not sufficient information to suspect a disability, they will not seek permission to conduct the evaluation, or if permission for an evaluation is denied, then the SpERT generates additional recommendations for the classroom teacher, grade-level team and multi-level-intervention providers to use with the student. Likewise, if the student is not found to have a disability and is not eligible for special education services, the MDT will generate additional recommendations for the classroom teacher, grade-level team, and multi-level-intervention providers to use with the student.

The table in Figure B23 reflects the number of students reviewed by the PRT at Marylin Avenue to discuss strategies and interventions for addressing student need for the spring semester of the 2009-10 school year. Following implementation of these strategies and progress monitoring of student performance, some students were referred for consideration of special education evaluation, reflected in the number of referrals to SpERT. Out of 64 students reviewed by the PRT across grades, only 15 (23%) of the students were referred for consideration of special education evaluation. Of those students referred, 11 were evaluated (17%) and all but one was found eligible. This means the pre-referral teams were able to effectively plan and implement interventions for the majority (83%) of the students for whom there were significant concerns about performance and learning.

Look Fors: **How many students are referred to Special Education by grade level? How many students are evaluated for Special Education? How many students are determined eligible?**

Planning Implications: **How effective is the pre-referral process? Are students referred found eligible (means the team is accurate in referrals)?**

Are teachers providing appropriate instruction and intervention to effectively intervene for students who do not have a disability so only students who do are referred for evaluation? If not, what professional learning do staff need to better identify and address the needs of students?

Figure B23

Marylin Avenue Elementary School
Pre-Referral Effectiveness: January to May 2010
Number of Students Reviewed, Referred for Evaluation, and Found Eligible

Grade Level	K	One	Two	Three	Four	Five	Total
Number reviewed by PRT	27	12	10	14	1	0	**64**
Number of Referrals to SpERT	4	2	1	2	2	4	**15**
Number of Students Evaluated for SE	3	1	1	1	1	4	**11**
Number Determined Eligible	3	1	0	1	1	4	**10**

Behavior

Figures B24, B25, and B26 show suspension data from 2004-05 to 2009-10. A new principal joined the staff at the beginning of the 2005-06 school year. Marylin Avenue began collecting data differently in 2009-10, so some graphs and table have incomplete or only one year of data. (*Note:* Empty graphs are included for modeling purposes.)

Look Fors: **Increase/decrease in the number of suspensions over time.**

Planning Implications: **Who are the students being suspended? Why and when are the students being suspended? How are the students treated by adults and each other? Are there policy implications?**

Figure B24

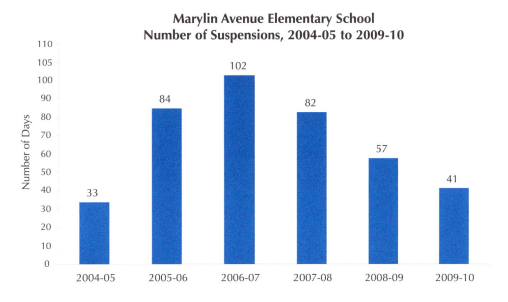

Marylin Avenue Elementary School
Number of Suspensions, 2004-05 to 2009-10

Figure B25

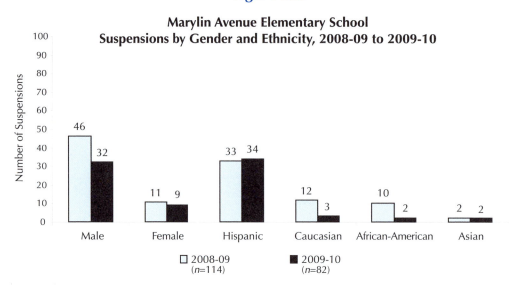

Marylin Avenue Elementary School
Suspensions by Gender and Ethnicity, 2008-09 to 2009-10

Look Fors:	Increase/decrease in suspensions, by reason.
Planning Implications:	What are the reasons students are being suspended?

Figure B26

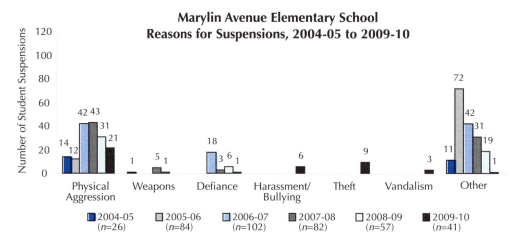

Marylin Avenue Elementary School
Reasons for Suspensions, 2004-05 to 2009-10

Figure B27 shows the number of students referred for behavior, by grade level and demographics available. Placeholders are shown for the way the school will gather data in 2010-11.

Look Fors: Behavioral referrals by gender, ethnicity, poverty indicator, special education, and number of years in the school and country.

Planning Implications: Who is being referred most often? Do teachers need professional learning to address specific populations? Do students or groups of students need direct instruction on behavioral expectations? Does the school need to refine a behavior plan?

Figure B27

Marylin Avenue Elementary School
Number of Behavior Referrals by Student Group and Grade Level, 2009-10

Grade Level	Gender		Ethnicity				Free/ Reduced Lunch		IEP		# Years in the School	# Years in the Country
	Female	Male	African-American	Hispanic/ Latino	Caucasian	Other/ Multiple	Yes	No	Yes	No		
Kindergarten	6	12		13	5							
Grade One	2	14		15	1							
Grade Two	12	23		13	11	6						
Grade Three	6	6	1	11								
Grade Four	2	12	1	13								
Grade Five	0	10		8	2							
Total	28	73	2	78	19	6						

Figure B28 shows the number of behavior events by demographic.

Look Fors: Increase/decrease in number of behavior events, over time, by gender, ethnicity, socio-economic status, English learners and fluent English proficient, and IEP and non-IEP. How many students are contributing to the number of events? How many days of instruction do these students miss?

Planning Implications: How many students (and who) are contributing to behavior events? Is this pervasive across many students or a select few? Does the school need a system for addressing repeat offenders that involve teaching/reteaching expectations?

Figure B28

Marylin Avenue Elementary School
School Behavior Events by Student Group, 2009-10

Student Group		Number of Events				
		0	1	2 to 5	6 to 10	10 or More
By Gender	Female					28
	Male					77
By Ethnicity	African-American			2		
	Hispanic					78
	Caucasian					19
	Other				6	
By Socio-Economic Status	Free					
	Paid					
By English Learners						
By Fluent English Proficient/English Only						
IEP						
Non-IEP						

Figure B29 shows the number of school behavior referrals by reason and student group for 2009-10.

Look Fors: Number of behavior referrals by reason, grade level, gender, ethnicity, free/reduced lunch, IEP and non-IEP.

Planning Implications: How many referrals does each subgroup receive? Do teachers need professional learning to address behaviors in diverse populations?

Figure B29

Marylin Avenue Elementary School
Behavior Referrals by Reason and Student Group, 2009-10

Reason for Referral	Grade Level						Gender		Ethnicity				Free/Reduced Lunch		IEP	Non-IEP	# Years in the School	Totals
	Kindergarten	Grade 1	Grade 2	Grade 3	Grade 4	Grade 5	Female	Male	African-American	Hispanic/Latino	Caucasian	Other/Multiple	Yes	No				
Forgery/theft			6	2	2		7	3	2	6	2							30
Minor: property misuse			1					1		1								3
Property damage/vandalism					1	2	3		3									9
Fighting/physical aggression	6	12	15	5	7	5	14	36		8	10	2						120
Harassment/bullying	3	1	4		3	1		12		11		1						36
Abusive language	2	1	2	4			1	9		6	4	2						31
Defiance/disrespect/insubordination/non-compliance	2	1	3				3	3		4	2							18

Figure B30 shows the location of behavior referrals in 2009-10, while Figure B31 shows the number of referrals by month.

Look Fors: **Where are students when they get behavior referrals?**

Planning Implications: **What is going on during high referral times and what can be changed?**

Figure B30

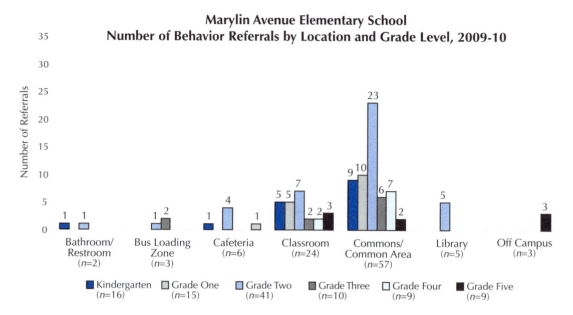

Marylin Avenue Elementary School
Number of Behavior Referrals by Location and Grade Level, 2009-10

Look Fors: Are there specific months with more behavior referrals than others?

Planning Implications: What is staff doing for behavior throughout the year?

Figure B31

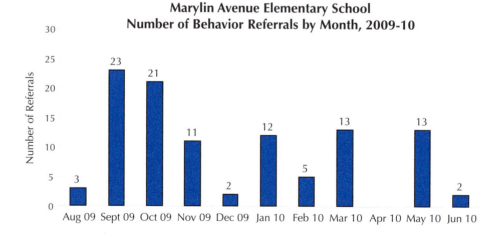

Marylin Avenue Elementary School
Number of Behavior Referrals by Month, 2009-10

Figure B32 shows the number of school referrals by time of day for 2009-10. The table that follows displays the school day time schedule.

Look Fors: **What time of day are most students referred?**

Planning Implications: **What is going on during high behavior times and what can be changed?**

Figure B32

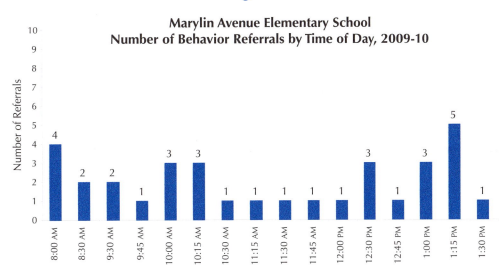

Marylin Avenue Elementary School Daily Time Schedule, 2009-10

Daily Schedule

Kindergarten	8:30 AM to 1:45 PM
Grades 1 – 3	8:30 AM to 2:40 PM
Grades 4 – 5	8:30 AM to 2:50 PM

Note: Wednesdays are early release for all grades: 8:30 AM to 1:30 PM

Recess Schedule

Grades K – 2	10:00 AM to 10:15 AM
Grades 3 – 5	10:30 AM to 10:45 AM

Lunch Schedule

Kindergarten	11:30 AM to 12:10 PM
Grade 1	11:50 AM to 12:30 PM
Grade 2	12:00 PM to 12:40 PM
Grades 3/4	12:35 PM to 1:15 PM
Grade 5	12:20 PM to 1:00 PM

Figure B33 shows who referred the students in 2009-10.

Look Fors: Who refers students, by grade level?

Planning Implications: What is going on during high referral times, by grade levels, and what can be changed?

Figure B33

Marylin Avenue Elementary School
Pre-Referral Effectiveness: January to May 2010
Number of Students Reviewed, Referred for Evaluation, and Found Eligible

Referred By	Kindergarten	Grade One	Grade Two	Grade Three	Grade Four	Grade Five	Total
Classroom Teacher	16	14	24	7	5	6	72
Special Education Teacher							
School Psychologist							
Instructional Specialist							
Principal	1		2	3	1	3	10
Playground Supervisor	1	1	3	1	4	1	10
Instructional Assistant							
District Administrator							
Other		1	4				5
Totals	18	16	33	11	10	10	97

The Staff

During the 2007-08 to 2009-10 school years, the total number of teachers increased at Marylin Avenue Elementary School, up slightly over recent years because of the addition of specialists. The majority of classroom teachers are both female and Caucasian. The 2009-10 pupil/teacher ratio for grades K-3 was 18.5, and for grades 4-5 was 21.5. The maximum class enrollment for K-3 was 20 students, and 25 students for grades 4-5. The number of classroom teachers and specialists is shown below in Figure B34.

Look Fors: **Increases/decreases in number of teachers over time, commensurate with student population.**

Planning Implications: **Are there enough teachers to keep class sizes low?**

Figure B34

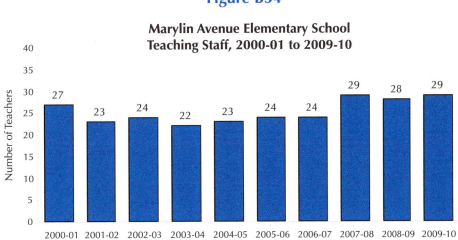

**Marylin Avenue Elementary School
Teaching Staff, 2000-01 to 2009-10**

Figure B35 shows the average number of years of teaching experience for Marylin Avenue teachers, compared to the district average, for the past six years for the school and district.

Look Fors: **Number of years teaching experience within and across grade levels.**

Planning Implications: **How is the average number of years of teaching experience changing, over time, for the school and district?**

Figure B35

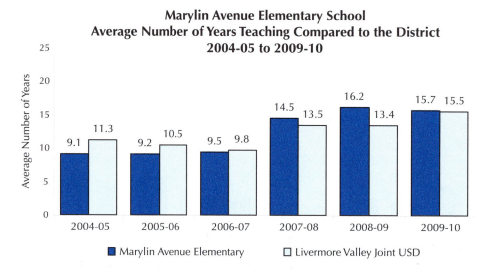

Marylin Avenue Elementary School
Average Number of Years Teaching Compared to the District
2004-05 to 2009-10

Figure B36 shows the total number of years of teaching experience, by grade taught, for each of the classroom teachers at Marylin Avenue Elementary School for 2009-10. The overall average number of years of teaching experience is just under 16 years. The principal has been the leader of this school since 2005-06.

Look Fors: Number of years of teaching experience within and across grade levels.

Planning Implications: Is a teacher mentoring program required within specific grade levels? Is teaching expertise even across grade levels?

Figure B36

Marylin Avenue Elementary School
Teaching Experience by Grade Level and Teacher, 2009-10

Grade Level	Teacher	Years of Experience	Grade Level	Teacher	Years of Experience
Kindergarten	Teacher A	11	Grade Three	Teacher A	24
	Teacher B	21		Teacher B	15
	Teacher C	5		Teacher C	15
	Teacher D	18		Teacher D	35
	Teacher E	13	Grade Four	Teacher A	11
Grade One	Teacher A	31		Teacher B	18
	Teacher B	8		Teacher C	15
	Teacher C	16	Grade Five	Teacher A	41
	Teacher D	2		Teacher B	3
	Teacher E	5		Teacher C	10
Grade Two	Teacher A	15	Specialists	Science	7
	Teacher B	26		Science	12
	Teacher C	6		Resource	8
	Teacher D	14		Psychologist PT	20
	Teacher E	19		Title 1	32
				Speech PT	18

PERCEPTIONS

To get a better understanding of the learning environment at Marylin Avenue Elementary School, students, staff, and parents completed *Education for the Future* questionnaires five years in a row in 2006, 2007, 2008, 2009, and 2010. Staff also assessed where they felt the school ranked on the *Education for the Future Continuous Improvement Continuums* (CICs). Summaries of the results follow, starting with the questionnaires.

Student Questionnaire Results

Students in kindergarten through grade five at Marylin Avenue Elementary School responded to an online *Education for the Future* questionnaire designed to measure how they feel about their learning environment in June 2006 (n=490), May 2007 (n=479), June 2008 (n=455), April 2009 (n=446), and May 2010 (n=451). Students in kindergarten and grade one were asked to respond to items using a three-point scale: 1 = disagree; 2 = neutral; and, 3 = agree. Students in grades two through five were asked to respond to items using a five-point scale: 1 = strongly disagree; 2 = disagree; 3 = neutral; 4 = agree; and 5 = strongly agree.

Average responses to each item on the questionnaire were graphed by the totals for the five years and disaggregated by gender, grade level, and ethnicity.

The icons in the figures that follow show the average responses to each item by the disaggregation indicated in the legend. The lines join the icons to help the reader know the distribution results for each disaggregation. The lines have no other meaning.

Look Fors: **Items which students are in agreement or disagreement.**

Planning Implications: **Where can/should the school provide leadership with respect to school environment?**

Kindergarten and Grade One Student Responses

Total Student Responses for Five Years

Overall, the average responses to the items in the student questionnaire were in agreement all five years (June 2006, n=165; May 2007, n=166; June 2008, n=170; April 2009, n=180; and May 2010, n=184), as shown in Figure B37.

Figure B37

**Marylin Avenue Elementary School Students (Kindergarten–Grade One)
Responses by Year, June 2006, May 2007, June 2008, April 2009, and May 2010**

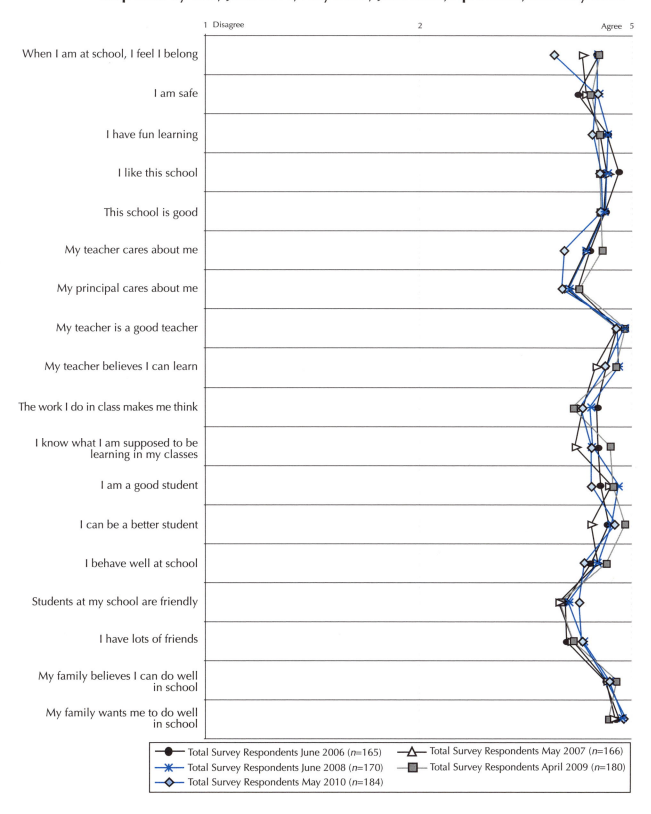

Student Responses by Gender

When the K-1 data were disaggregated by gender (91 female; 93 male), the data revealed that responses were in agreement and clustered around the overall average (graph not shown here).

Student Responses by Grade Level

The questionnaire results were also disaggregated by grade level. In 2010, there were 95 kindergartners and 89 first graders responding. All students were in agreement with the items on the questionnaire (graph not shown here).

Student Responses by Ethnicity

When K-1 student questionnaire data were disaggregated by ethnicity: 128 Hispanic/Latino students (70% of the responding population); 39 Caucasian students (21%); 8 Asians (4%); and 8 "Others" (4%) responded. (*Note*: Ethnicity numbers add up to more than the total number of respondents because some students identified themselves by more than one ethnicity.)

While there were slight differences between ethnicities, all students responded in agreement (graph not shown here).

Student Open-ended K-1 Responses

Marylin Elementary School K-1 students were asked to respond to two open-ended questions: *What do you like about your school?* and *What do you wish was different at your school?* Below are the top ten written-in responses for the two questions. (*Note:* When analyzing open-ended results, one must keep in mind the number of responses that were optionally written-in. Open-ended responses often help us understand the multiple choice responses, although caution must be exercised with small numbers of respondents.)

Look Fors: The most often written-in responses to what students like about school and wish was different.

Planning Implications: Perhaps issues regarding how students are treated?

Student Open-Ended Responses (Kindergarten to Grade One)

What do you like about your school?

May 2007 (*N*=165)	May 2008 (*N*=170)
♦ Learning/classroom activities (66) ♦ Friends (36) ♦ Teachers (33) ♦ Playground (25) ♦ Recess (20) ♦ Computers (15) ♦ Feeling safe (10) ♦ Library (8) ♦ Food/snacks (7) ♦ Principal (4)	♦ Learning (54) ♦ Recess/playing (50) ♦ Friends (49) ♦ Teachers (41) ♦ School (20) ♦ Classroom (10) ♦ Decision time (10) ♦ Computers (9) ♦ All (8) ♦ Library (6)

April 2009 (*N*=180)	May 2010 (*N*=184)
♦ I like to play (47) ♦ Good friends (44) ♦ Good teachers (29) ♦ Reading (29) ♦ Learning (24) ♦ Recess (18) ♦ Writing (11) ♦ Math (11) ♦ I like the playground (11) ♦ Self-directed learning time/choice time (9)	♦ Reading/books (32) ♦ Playing with my friends (27) ♦ Learning (to draw pictures, write name, work with other kids) (27) ♦ I like to play (20) ♦ My teacher (19) ♦ Self-directed learning time (16) ♦ Math timed tests (16) ♦ Computers, computer lab (12) ♦ I like recess (11) ♦ Going to lunch; school is fun (9)

What do you wish was different at your school?

May 2007 (*N*=165)	May 2008 (*N*=170)
♦ Playground/swings (38) ♦ Nothing (36) ♦ Food (14) ♦ Friends (11) ♦ Less classroom time (10) ♦ Teachers (5) ♦ Prettier school (4) ♦ More computers (4) ♦ More respect (3) ♦ Classroom (4)	♦ Playground (25) ♦ Nothing (24) ♦ Free time (11) ♦ Friends (10) ♦ Toys (10) ♦ More recess (9) ♦ Classroom (8) ♦ Curriculum (7) ♦ Lunch/food (7) ♦ Be nice to me (6)

April 2009 (*N*=180)	May 2010 (*N*=184)
♦ Nothing (28) ♦ Better/more lunch (17) ♦ New/better equipment on the playground (17) ♦ A swimming pool (11) ♦ My friends were nicer to me (9) ♦ More computers/time 8) ♦ We could play more (7) ♦ More nice people (5) ♦ More recess (5) ♦ More books (4)	♦ Nothing/I like it the way it is (22) ♦ Everybody was nice to each other, no mean people (10) ♦ That the school had more toys/games (10) ♦ We had more time to learn more things/read aloud/ more school (9) ♦ More recess/longer (8) ♦ That school had more books (7) ♦ I wish there was swings (6) ♦ More books (5) ♦ I wish I had more friends ♦ Allow pets at school (5)

Grades Two through Five Student Responses

Total Student Responses for Five Years

Overall, the average responses to the items in the student questionnaire were in agreement all five years (June 2006, n=325; May 2007, n=313; June 2008, n=285; April 2009, n=266; and May 2010, n=267), as shown in Figure B38. Students strongly agreed with all items in 2010, with the following exceptions which were in agreement:

- I have freedom at school.

- I have choices in what I learn.

- Students are treated fairly by the people on recess duty.

- Students at my school treat me with respect.

- Students at my school are friendly.

Figure B38

Marylin Avenue Elementary School Students (Grades 2 to 5)
Responses by Year, June 2006, May 2007, June 2008, April 2009, and May 2010

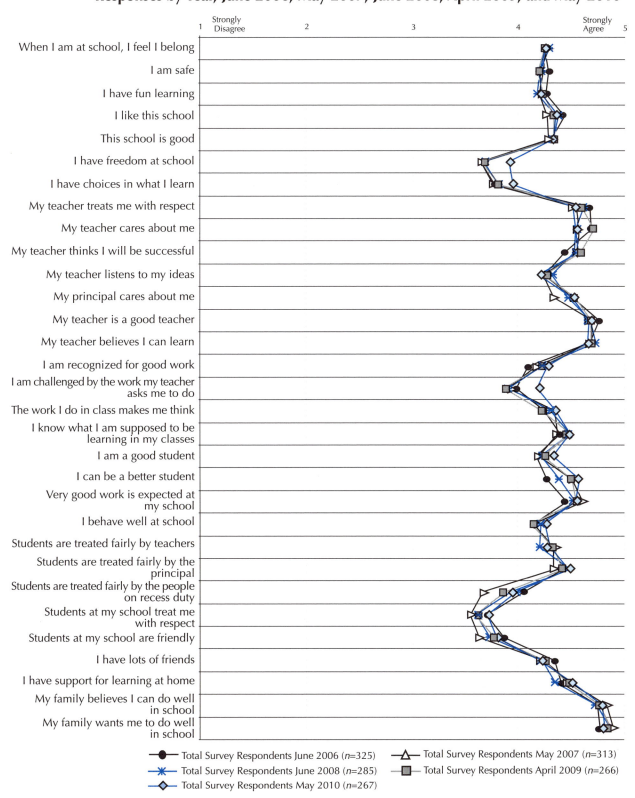

Total Survey Respondents June 2006 (*n*=325)
Total Survey Respondents May 2007 (*n*=313)
Total Survey Respondents June 2008 (*n*=285)
Total Survey Respondents April 2009 (*n*=266)
Total Survey Respondents May 2010 (*n*=267)

Student Responses by Gender

When disaggregated by gender (140 female; 120 male), the data revealed that disaggregated responses were very similar and clustered around the overall average (graph not shown here). (*Note:* Gender numbers do not add up to the total number of respondents because some students did not identify themselves by this demographic.)

Student Responses by Grade Level

The 2010 questionnaire results were also disaggregated by grade level (72 second graders, 67 third graders, 62 fourth graders, and 61 fifth graders), as shown in Figure B39. (*Note:* Grade-level numbers do not add up to the total number of respondents because some students did not identify themselves by this demographic.) All grade levels were in agreement—however, compared to grades two and three, grades four and five students were less positive in their responses.

Figure B39

**Marylin Avenue Elementary School Students (Grades 2 to 5)
Responses by Grade Level, May 2010**

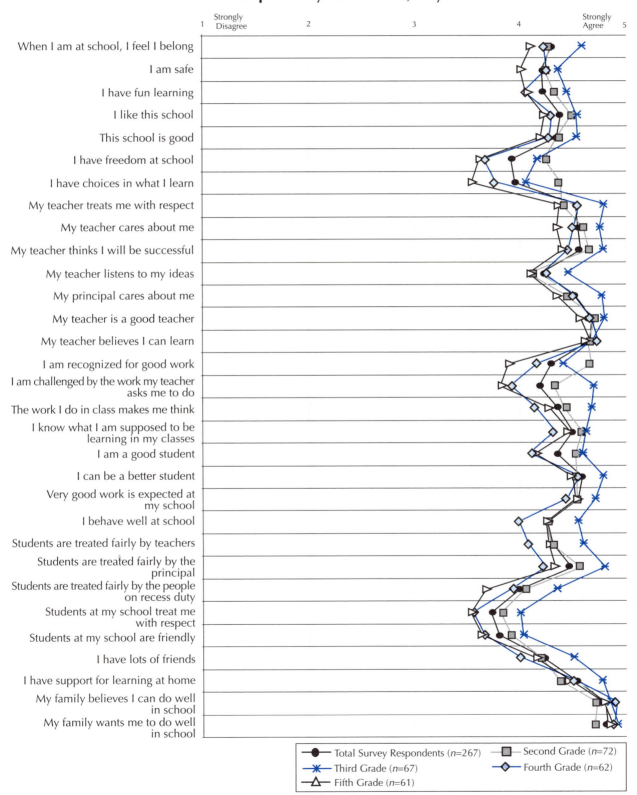

Student Responses by Ethnicity

When 2010 student questionnaire data were disaggregated by ethnicity: 183 Hispanic/Latino students (62% of the responding population); 44 Caucasians (15%); 19 Asians (6%); 7 African-Americans (2%); 8 American Indians (3%); and 32 "Others" (12%) responded. (*Note:* Ethnicity numbers add up to more than the total number of respondents because some students identified themselves by more than one ethnicity.)

While there were a few differences between ethnicities (graph not shown here), students mostly responded in agreement, with some exceptions. African-American and American Indian students were the least positive with their responses, in comparison to the other students.

African-American students (n=7) were in disagreement with average responses falling between two and three on the five-point scale, about the items:

- I have fun learning.
- I like this school.
- The school is good.
- I have freedom at school.
- I have choices in what I learn.
- My teacher treats me with respect.
- Students are treated fairly by teachers.
- Students at my school treat me with respect.
- Students at my school are friendly.
- I have lots of friends.

American Indian students (n=8) responded in disagreement to the items:

- Students at my school treat me with respect.
- Students at my school are friendly.

Student Open-ended Grades Two through Five Responses

Marylin Elementary School students, grades two through five, were asked to respond to two open-ended questions: *What do you like about your school?* and *What do you wish was different at your school?* Below are the top ten written-in responses for the two questions.

Look Fors: **The most often written-in responses to what students like about school and wish was different.**

Planning Implications: **Perhaps issues regarding how students are treated?.**

Student Open-Ended Responses (Grades Two to Five)

What do you like about your school?

May 2007 (*N*=313)	May 2008 (*N*=285)
◆ Teachers (121) ◆ Friends (79) ◆ Classroom (60) ◆ Recess/playground (48) ◆ Computers (33) ◆ Library (24) ◆ P.E. (22) ◆ Everything (20) ◆ Principal (19) ◆ Science (13)	◆ Teachers (97) ◆ Friends (56) ◆ Recess (55) ◆ Curriculum (37) ◆ Computer (34) ◆ PE (24) ◆ Learning (23) ◆ Library (21) ◆ People (18) ◆ Principal (18)

April 2009 (*N*=266)	May 2010 (*N*=267)
◆ The teachers (101) ◆ Friends/Making new friends (48) ◆ Computers (34) ◆ Recess (31) ◆ Everyone is treated with respect/ very nice people/ kids/teachers (27) ◆ The playground/playing outside (25) ◆ I like math (25) ◆ I like to learn (23) ◆ School library (21) ◆ P.E. (20)	◆ Teachers (73) ◆ Math (53) ◆ Recess (42) ◆ Reading (39) ◆ Computer lab (34) ◆ Friends (32) ◆ Lunch (27) ◆ Friendly atmosphere/respectful/trusting (19) ◆ Learning (17) ◆ Our principal; P.E. (16)

What do you wish was different at your school?

May 2007 (*N*=313)	May 2008 (*N*=285)
◆ Better playground/swings (53) ◆ More recess (48) ◆ More respect (43) ◆ Better food (42) ◆ Nothing (27) ◆ Better teachers (13) ◆ Better learning (13) ◆ More fun (9) ◆ Principal (8) ◆ More math (7)	◆ Nothing (41) ◆ Playground equipment (35) ◆ More recess (35) ◆ Lunch (26) ◆ More respect (24) ◆ Homework (17) ◆ More PE (12) ◆ Curriculum (9) ◆ Freedom (9) ◆ Computers (7)

April 2009 (*N*=266)	May 2010 (*N*=267)
◆ The food was better (42) ◆ Bigger playground with more equipment (seesaws, sand, swings) (40) ◆ Nothing, I like it the way it is (38) ◆ Kids/people treated everyone with respect (28) ◆ We had more/longer recess (25) ◆ Nice yard duties (12) ◆ We could have laptops at school (9) ◆ Shorter school time (9) ◆ That there were more books in the library/check-out more at one time (10) ◆ There was a swimming pool (8)	◆ Better lunch food/snacks (46) ◆ Nothing/everything is good (31) ◆ Longer recess (21) ◆ Bigger/playground slide/swings (16) ◆ Respectful/more friendly/nicer people (15) ◆ Get new soccer goals/bigger field/better soccer balls (14) ◆ We could have brownies/ice cream at lunch (9) ◆ Cleaner bathrooms/dry floors (8) ◆ I wish I could bring my skateboard (8) ◆ Ride our bikes (7)

Staff Questionnaire Results

Marylin Avenue Elementary School staff responded to a questionnaire designed to measure their perceptions of the school environment in June 2006 ($n=36$), May 2007 ($n=38$), June 2008 ($n=45$), May 2009 ($n=48$), and May 2010 ($n=43$). Staff members were asked to respond to items using a five-point scale: 1 = strongly disagree; 2 = disagree; 3 = neutral; 4 = agree; and 5 = strongly agree.

Average responses to each item on the questionnaire were graphed by year, and disaggregated by ethnicity, job title, and number of years teaching experience, revealing some differences. The two-page graphs are shown in Figures B43 and B45.

The icons in the figures that follow show the average responses to each item by disaggregation indicated in the legend. The lines join the icons to help the reader know the distribution results for each disaggregation. The lines have no other meaning.

Look Fors:	**Items which staff members are in agreement or disagreement.**
Planning Implications:	**Where can/should the school provide leadership with respect to school environment?**

Total Staff Responses for Five Years

Overall, the average responses to the items in the staff questionnaire were mostly in agreement all five years, except for one item: *This school has a good public image* (Figure B40). Staff responding in 2008 and 2009 were in low agreement, while staff in 2006 and 2007 were in strong disagreement, and closer to neutral in 2008. Responses were in agreement in 2009 and 2010.

In addition to items completed by all staff, the questionnaire contained a set of five statements for teachers and instructional assistants only. The respondents were in agreement, and results are shown in Figure B41.

Figure B40

Marylin Avenue Elementary School Staff Responses by Year
June 2006, May 2007, June 2008, May 2009, and May 2010

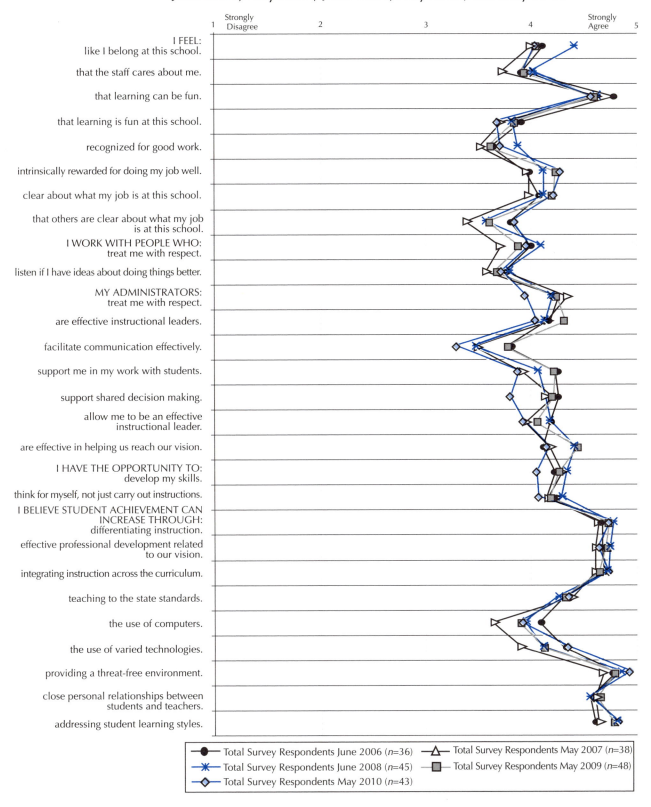

Figure B40 *(Continued)*

Marylin Avenue Elementary School Staff Responses by Year (Continued)
June 2006, May 2007, June 2008, May 2009, and May 2010

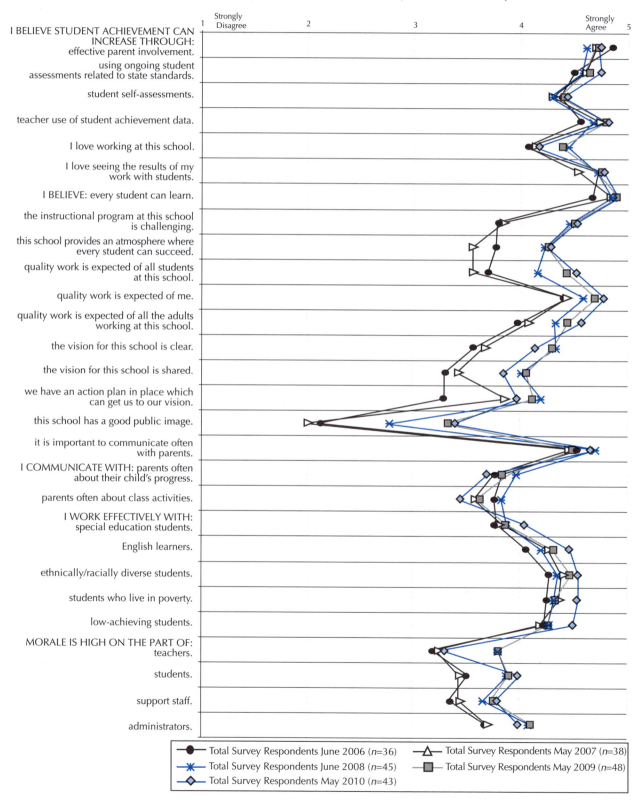

Total Survey Respondents June 2006 (*n*=36)
Total Survey Respondents May 2007 (*n*=38)
Total Survey Respondents June 2008 (*n*=45)
Total Survey Respondents May 2009 (*n*=48)
Total Survey Respondents May 2010 (*n*=43)

Figure B41

Marylin Avenue Elementary School Staff Responses by Year Items for Teachers and Instructional Assistants by Year June 2006, May 2007, June 2008, May 2009, and May 2010

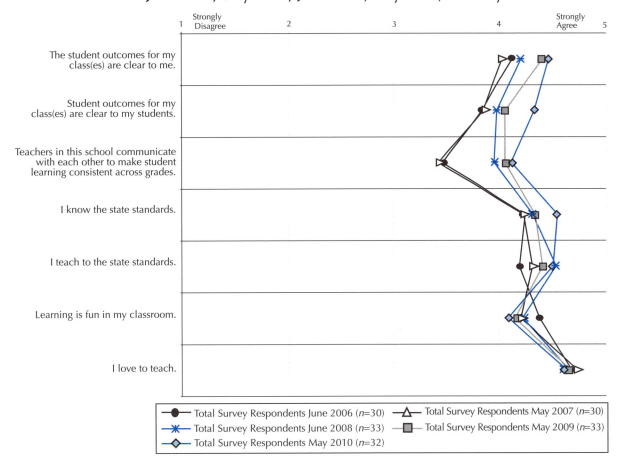

Staff Responses by Ethnicity

When staff questionnaire data were disaggregated by ethnicity: 30 Caucasians (75% of the responding population); 5 Asians (12.5%); and 5 Hispanic/Latino (12.5%), responded (graph not shown here). (*Note:* Ethnicity numbers do not add up to the total number of respondents because some staff did not identify themselves by this demographic.)

While there were a few differences among ethnicities, staff responded mostly in agreement, except that Hispanic/Latino staff were in disagreement with the item: *My administrators support shared decision making.* Hispanic/Latino staff were neutral (at 3.0 on the five-point scale) about: *My administrators facilitate communication effectively.* Caucasian staff also responded near neutral to this statement. Asian staff were neutral about the item: *I communicate with parents often about class activities.*

Staff Responses by Job Title

When staff questionnaire data were disaggregated by job title: 25 classroom teachers, 7 instructional staff, 5 certified staff, and 6 classified staff responded (graph not shown here). Most respondents were in agreement, with some exceptions. Classified staff disagreed with the item: *I feel that others are clear about what my job is at this school.* Some staff responded neutral to the following:

♦ My administrators facilitate communication effectively (certificated staff).

♦ I believe this school has a good public image (classified staff).

♦ I believe I communicate with parents often about class activities (certificated staff).

♦ Morale is high on the part of teachers (classroom teachers).

Staff Responses by Number of Years Teaching

Staff questionnaire data were disaggregated by the number of years teaching experience: four to six years (n=8); seven to ten years (n=7); and eleven or more years (n=21). (*Note:* Numbers do not add up to the total number of respondents because some staff did not identify themselves by this demographic.)

While there were some differences between respondents (Figure B42), staff responded mostly in agreement. Some staff responded neutral (at 3.0 on the five-point scale), or near neutral, to the three items listed below:

♦ My administrators facilitate communication effectively (seven to ten years; eleven or more years).

♦ This school has a good public image (seven to ten years).

♦ I communicate with parents often about class activities (four to six years; seven to ten years).

♦ Morale is high on the part of teachers (eleven or more years).

Figure B42

Marylin Avenue Elementary School Staff
Responses by Number of Years Teaching, May 2010

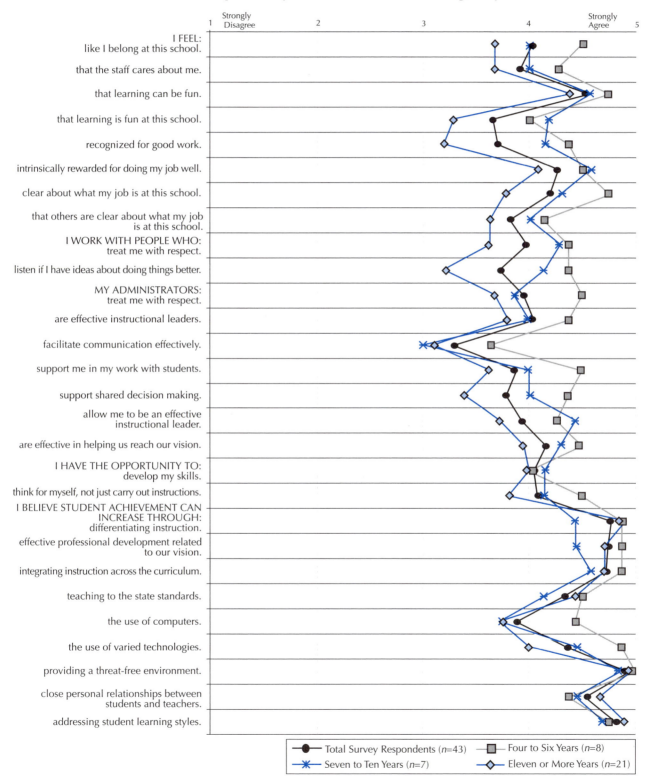

Figure B42 *(Continued)*

Marylin Avenue Elementary School Staff (Continued)
Responses by Number of Years Teaching, May 2010

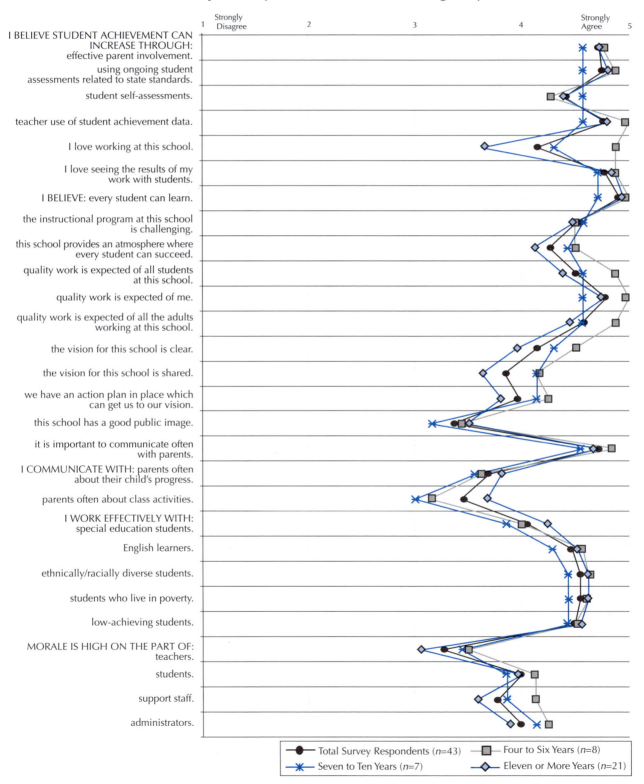

Legend:
- Total Survey Respondents (*n*=43)
- Four to Six Years (*n*=8)
- Seven to Ten Years (*n*=7)
- Eleven or More Years (*n*=21)

Staff Open-ended Responses

Marylin Avenue Elementary School staff completed two open-ended questions: *What are the strengths of this school?* and *What needs to be improved?* The top ten results are shown below.

Look Fors: The most often written-in responses to what staff members like about school and what needs to be improved.

Planning Implications: Perhaps issues regarding communication and climate.

Staff Open-Ended Responses

What are the strengths of this school?	
May 2007 (*N*=38)	**May 2008 (*N*=45)**
◆ Staff (17) ◆ Collaboration (14) ◆ Focus of our work on a vision/goals (11) ◆ Classroom practices (8) ◆ Principal (6) ◆ High expectations (5) ◆ Shared leadership (5) ◆ Common, frequent assessments (4) ◆ Use of standards (3) ◆ Diverse student population (2)	◆ School culture (18) ◆ Collaboration among staff (16) ◆ Administration (9) ◆ Teachers (7) ◆ Instructional practices (6) ◆ Shared leadership (5) ◆ Continuous improvement (5) ◆ Use of data and common formative assessments (4) ◆ Support for bilingual students (2) ◆ Diversity (2)
May 2009 (*N*=34)	**May 2010 (*N*=43)**
◆ The teachers (13) ◆ Shared leadership/supportive principal (12) ◆ The level of teamwork (9) ◆ Wanting to improve/learn (8) ◆ Enthusiastic students (5) ◆ High expectations (5) ◆ Data driven instruction (5) ◆ Shared vision (5) ◆ Goal to be PLC (2) ◆ Moving on the right path-much has improved over the past 3 years	◆ Bilingual staff and support staff/very talented/caring/professional (16) ◆ Teachers have high standards/are well qualified/work closely together/collaborate (13) ◆ Collaboration (9) ◆ We use data to drive instruction/data teams (7) ◆ High expectations of students and teachers/rigor/accountability/growth (6) ◆ Shared vision/leadership (3) ◆ Willingness to try new things like CAFE and RTI (3) ◆ The principal/leadership provides a good vision (3) ◆ Achievement is up, and more kids are thriving (2) ◆ Staff development (2)

Staff Open-Ended Responses *(Continued)*

What needs to be improved?	
May 2007 (*N*=38)	**May 2008 (*N*=45)**
◆ Communication, including staff and parents (15) ◆ Climate including respect and a safe place (9) ◆ Organization (4) ◆ High academic/behavior expectations held by all (4) ◆ Enrichment/fun extras (3) ◆ Vision (2) ◆ Accountability for teachers (2) ◆ Celebrations (2) ◆ Parent participation (2) ◆ More aides (2)	◆ Communication (10) ◆ Timely office communication (9) ◆ Family involvement (5) ◆ Office procedures (4) ◆ Instructional practices (3) ◆ Keep focus (3) ◆ Expand shared vision (2) ◆ Jobs (2) ◆ Job description (2) ◆ Not following protocol (2)
May 2009 (*N*=34)	**May 2010 (*N*=43)**
◆ Better communication with all involved; parents, students, staff (15) ◆ Respect for everyone's opinion (8) ◆ Work-load (3) ◆ Parent involvement (2) ◆ Funding; state budget ◆ Better follow through ◆ There is a sense of isolation for those that are not tied to a specific team ◆ Still need for all students to buy in to school pride ◆ Continue to insure that all students achieve at high levels ◆ Teaching to the whole child not just test scores	◆ Communication/from principal/between grade levels/ between staff (14) ◆ Equity of listening to ideas, respect for, treatment of staff members by administration (9) ◆ A shared leadership with the entire staff-not just a few chosen ones (6) ◆ The fairness/favoritism among staff needs to be figured out (5) ◆ Staff feeling safe to share opinions (4) ◆ Not all voices are heard (3) ◆ Feel pushed beyond means to accommodate decisions/pace of change (3) ◆ Staff development seems to always be given to the same people (2) ◆ More fun/enrichment in the classrooms (2) ◆ Morale (2)

Parent Questionnaire Responses

Parents of students attending Marylin Avenue Elementary School completed a questionnaire designed to measure their perceptions of the school environment in June 2006 (n=290), May 2007 (n=242), June 2008 (n=301), May 2009 (n=295), and May 2010 (n=287). Parents were asked to respond to items using a five-point scale: 1 = strongly disagree; 2 = disagree; 3 = neutral; 4 = agree; and, 5 = strongly agree.

Average responses to each item on the questionnaire were graphed by year and disaggregated by children's grade levels, ethnicity, native language, number of children in the household, number of children in the school, and person completing the questionnaire.

The icons in the figures that follow, show the average responses to each item by disaggregation indicated in the legend. The lines join the icons to help the reader know the distribution results for each disaggregation. The lines have no other meaning.

Look Fors: **Items which are in agreement or disagreement.**

Planning   **Where can/should the school provide leadership with respect to**
Implications: **school environment?**

Total Parent Responses for Five Years

Overall, the average responses to the items in the parent questionnaire were in agreement all five years, as shown in Figure B43. They appear to be "happiest" in 2010.

Figure B43

Marylin Avenue Elementary School Parent Responses by Year
June 2006, June 2007, June 2008, May 2009, and May 2010

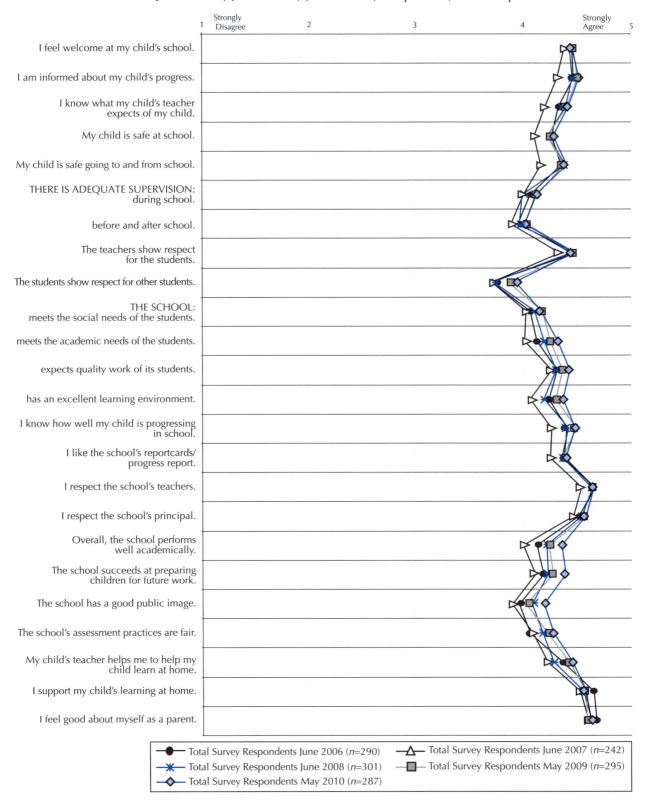

Total Survey Respondents June 2006 (*n*=290)
Total Survey Respondents June 2007 (*n*=242)
Total Survey Respondents June 2008 (*n*=301)
Total Survey Respondents May 2009 (*n*=295)
Total Survey Respondents May 2010 (*n*=287)

Parent Responses by Children's Grade Level

Results graphed by children's grade level (kindergarten, *n*=64; first grade, *n*=78; second grade, *n*=63; third grade, *n*=58; fourth grade, *n*=39; and fifth grade, *n*=43), revealed that average responses were very similar and clustered around the overall average (graph not shown here). All respondents were in agreement with the statements on the questionnaire.

(*Note:* Grade-level numbers add up to more than the total number of respondents because some parents identified themselves by more than one demographic.)

Parent Responses by Ethnicity

Parent questionnaire data were also disaggregated by ethnicity: 203 Hispanic/Latino students (74% of the responding population); 46 Caucasians (17%); 17 Asians (6%); and 9 "Others" (3%) responded. (*Note:* Ethnicity numbers do not add up to the total number of respondents because some parents did not identify themselves by ethnicity.)

While most respondents were in agreement (Figure B44), parents of "Other" ethnicities were neutral in their response to the item: Students show respect for other students. Also, parents of "Other" ethnicities were less positive to most items, compared to other respondents.

Figure B44

Marylin Avenue Elementary School Parent Responses by Ethnicity
May 2010

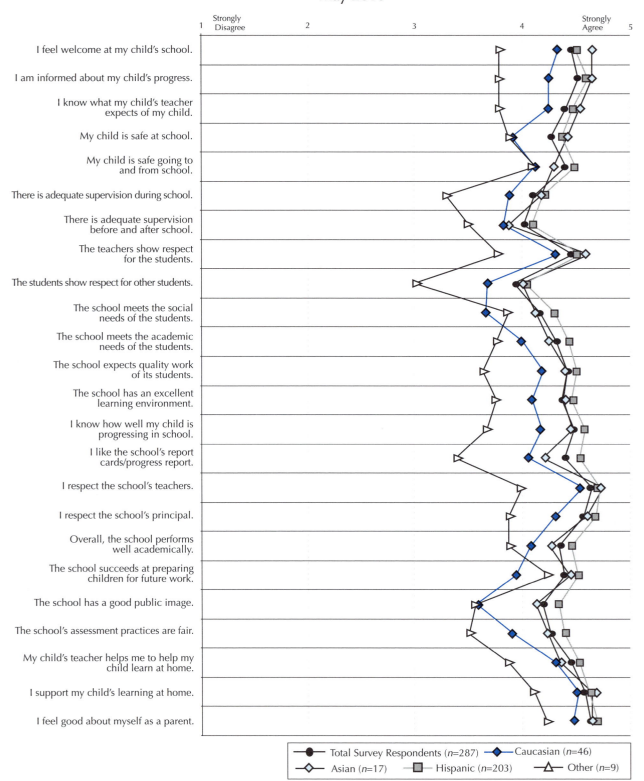

Total Survey Respondents (n=287)   Caucasian (n=46)
Asian (n=17)   Hispanic (n=203)   Other (n=9)

Parent Responses by Native Language

Parent questionnaire data were also graphed by native language: Spanish language, $n=185$ (70% of the responding population); English language, $n=68$ (26%); and other languages, $n=13$ (5%). Data reveal that average responses were very similar and clustered around the overall average (graph not shown here). All respondents were in agreement with the statements on the questionnaire. (*Note:* Native language numbers do not add up to the total number of respondents because some parents did not identify themselves by this demographic.)

Parent Responses by Number of Children in the School

Results graphed by the number of children in the school: one child, $n=148$ (66% of the responding population); two children, $n=67$ (30%); and three children, $n=10$ (4%); reveal that average parent responses were very similar and clustered around the overall average (graph not shown here). All respondents were in agreement with the statements on the questionnaire. (*Note:* Number of children in the school do not add up to the total number of respondents because some parents did not identify themselves by this demographic.)

Parent Responses by Number of Children in the Household

Parent responses were disaggregated by the number of children in the household: one child, $n=40$ (22% of the responding population); two children, $n=76$ (42%); three children, $n=43$ (24%); four children, $n=14$ (8%); and five children, $n=9$ (5%). (*Note:* Numbers do not add up to the total number of respondents because some parents did not identify themselves by this demographic.) Parents were in agreement with all statements on the questionnaire (graph not shown here).

Parent Responses by Person Completing the Questionnaire

Results graphed by the person completing the questionnaire (Mother, $n=223$; and Father, $n=70$), reveal that average responses were very similar and clustered around the overall average (graph not shown here). All respondents were in agreement with the statements on the questionnaire.

Parent Open-ended Responses

Marylin Avenue Elementary School parents completed two open-ended questions: *What are the strengths of this school?* and *What needs to be improved?* The top ten results are shown below.

Look Fors: The most often written-in responses to what parents like about school and what needs to be improved.

Planning Implications: Perhaps issues regarding how students are treated.

Parent Open-Ended Responses

What are the strengths of this school?

May 2007 (*N*=242)	June 2008 (*N*=301)
♦ Teachers (49) ♦ Curriculum (13) ♦ Community support (11) ♦ Principal (9) ♦ Safe (9) ♦ Students (6) ♦ Everything (4) ♦ Bilingual program (3) ♦ Teamwork (3) ♦ Communication (3)	♦ Teachers (84) ♦ Principal (11) ♦ Administration (9) ♦ Climate (10) ♦ Curriculum (9) ♦ Safety (7) ♦ Social skills (6) ♦ Parents (5) ♦ All (4) ♦ Communication (4)

May 2009 (*N*=295)	May 2010 (*N*=287)
♦ The teachers the school has (33) ♦ Education/Academics (7) ♦ The principal is excellent (6) ♦ The students (6) ♦ The team work and communication between parents and teachers (6) ♦ That students keep progressing (6) ♦ The school works together as a team (5) ♦ High expectations (4) ♦ The school's rules and behavior policies (4) ♦ The school shows good communication (4)	♦ Good teachers/caring/supportive/work as a team (39) ♦ We love Marylin Ave/very caring/loving environment/great community (9) ♦ Positive academic environment (6) ♦ Excellent communication between teachers and parents (5) ♦ Multi-cultural environment/diversity (4) ♦ Dedication of staff towards students (3) ♦ Teacher/student ratio (2) ♦ Good education (2) ♦ The principal is a parent in the school ♦ Ability to meet families where they are

What do you wish was different at your school?

May 2007 (*N*=242)	June 2008 (*N*=301)
♦ Academics (16) ♦ Safety (14) ♦ Nothing (12) ♦ Communication (11) ♦ Yard Duty (7) ♦ Teachers (6) ♦ English only (5) ♦ More after school activities (4) ♦ More differentiation (4) ♦ Principal (4)	♦ Nothing (29) ♦ Safety (22) ♦ Curriculum (16) ♦ Communication (10) ♦ Activities/whole child (7) ♦ More homework (5) ♦ Parent involvement (5) ♦ After school programs (4) ♦ Lunch (4) ♦ Physical environment (4)

April 2009 (*N*=295)	May 2010 (*N*=287)
♦ Nothing/Everything is good (27) ♦ School safety and security (6) ♦ Reading (3) ♦ More variety in lunch (3) ♦ More bilingual teachers (3) ♦ More community and social activities (2) ♦ More parent/student activities with the school (2) ♦ More after school programs (2) ♦ Recess supervision (2) ♦ School image to the public (2)	♦ Social skills for the students/manners/no bullying (7) ♦ More supervision before and after school/during lunch recess (7) ♦ Need enrichment-learning beyond what is tested (7) ♦ Breakfast and lunch menus need to be more nutritious (3) ♦ Send more homework (2) ♦ Writing programs and spelling programs (2) ♦ Communication-all aspects (2) ♦ More parent involvement (2) ♦ Nothing - everything is great/Can't think of anything (2) ♦ More teacher/parent conferences

SCHOOL PROCESSES

Marylin Avenue Elementary School Continuous Improvement Continuum Results Over Time

Staff members of the Marylin Elementary School conducted their baseline assessment of where their school is on the *Continuous Improvement Continuums* (CICs) in 2006. Staff conducted subsequent assessments in 2007, 2008, 2009, and 2010. At each assessment, staff members discuss the reasons they select their ratings on the Continuums. Each time, they come to consensus on a number that represents where the school is in terms of *Approach, Implementation,* and *Outcome* for each of the seven Continuums. Staff agree they need to pay special attention to next steps and ensure the next steps are included in the school action plan.

The 2005-06 through 2009-10 ratings and brief discussion for each *Continuous Improvement Continuum* follow.

Look Fors: **Is there a data system in place for use at the school level? Is the school proactive or more reactive? Is there a school vision that is known and shared? Is there a school plan in place aligned to the vision? Does professional learning provided in the school help the school implement its visions? Is the leadership structure known and helpful? Are parents, the community, and business partnerships sought to assist with the learning mission? Does the school evaluate all parts of the learning organization?**

Planning Implications: **How much do all staff members understand where the school is on these Continuums? To what degree are all staff on the same page?**

Information and Analysis

Marylin Avenue Elementary School staff increased their 2009-10 *Information and Analysis* ratings in *Approach, Implementation,* and *Outcome* (Figure B45).

Figure B45

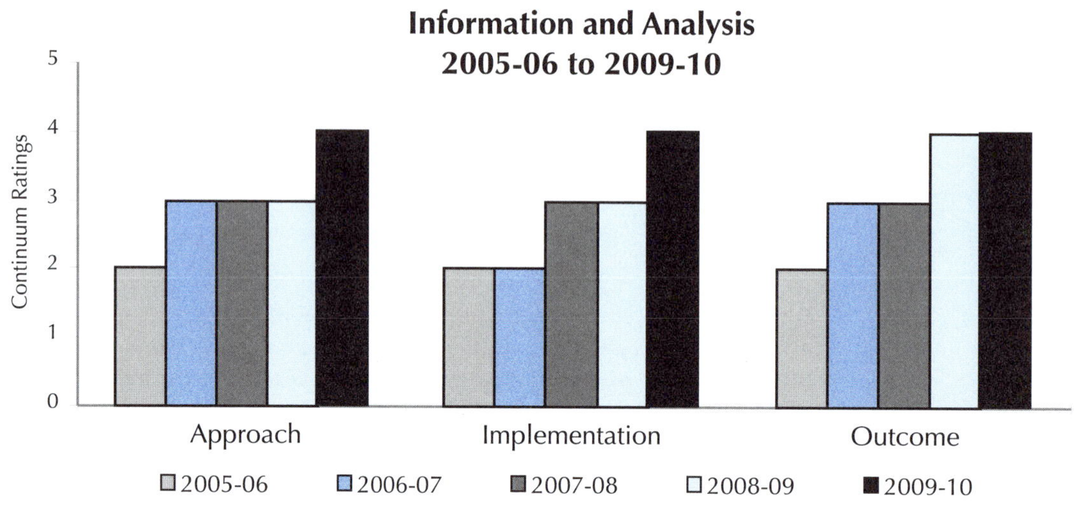

Information and Analysis
2005-06 to 2009-10

Next Steps 2010

- ♦ Systematic reliance on hard data (including data for subgroups).
- ♦ Staff need to set-up systems to record math progress.
- ♦ Staff need to set-up systems to chart and improve behavior.
- ♦ Staff need students to self-assess and track their own progress.
- ♦ Archive data: Since the Marylin Avenue database lost some data, staff need to upload old data so they can get a longitudinal look at their results.
- ♦ Streamline the Pre-Referral Team (PRT) form completion process.

Student Achievement

Marylin Avenue Elementary School staff increased their 2009-10 ratings in all three areas of the *Student Achievement Continuum* (Figure B46).

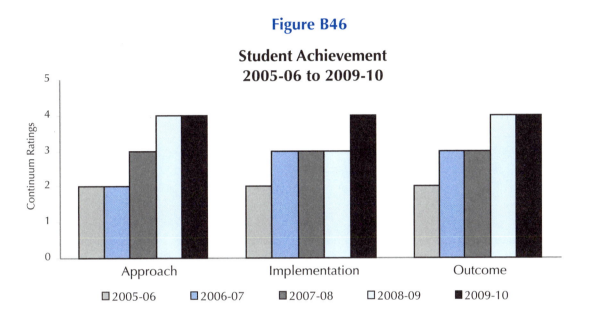

Figure B46

Next Steps 2009-10

♦ Does a level five accurately describe where they want to go? What does it look like to be a five?

♦ Staff need to define terms such as—"internal quality measures."

♦ Staff need to use more student self-assessments.

♦ Staff need more shared knowledge about RtI and what it looks like at Marylin Avenue.

♦ Why does Marylin Avenue have some students with extra interventions who are not moving to proficiency? (Staff need to do a problem-solving cycle.)

♦ Teacher self-assessment and grade-level self-assessment need to be implemented throughout the school.

♦ We need to agree on what we are going to do when students have met benchmark.

♦ We need to explore a balanced assessment system—variety of assessments (performance assessments).

Quality Planning

Marylin Avenue Elementary School staff increased their 2008-09 and 2009-10 ratings in *Approach*, while *Implementation* and *Outcome* remained the same for the past few years (Figure B47).

Figure B47

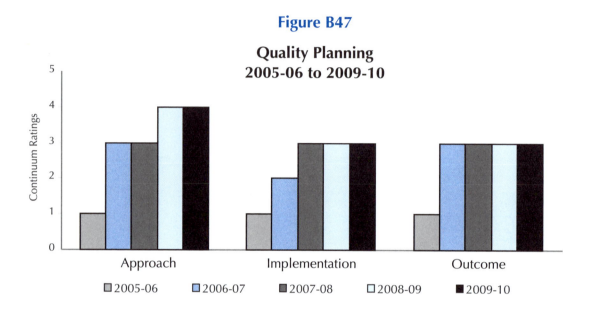

Next Steps 2009-10

- Staff need to stay focused on the school plan.
- Add RtI to the plan.
- Define and revise the word "all"—Marylin Avenue Leadership Team (MALT). Staff think it means everybody. Is that realistic?

Leadership

Marylin Avenue Elementary School staff increased their rating in the areas of *Approach* and *Implementation* for their 2009-10 assessment, while *Outcome* remained the same (Figure B48).

Figure B48

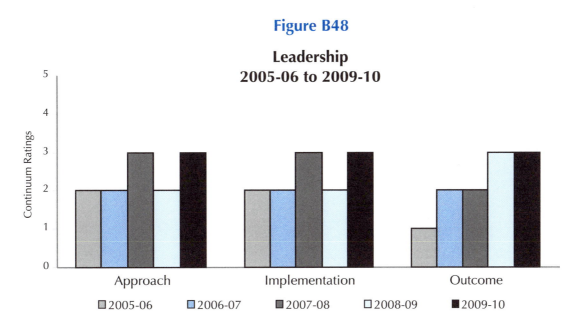

Next Steps 2009-10

♦ Staff need to implement a feeling of inclusion in the shared decision-making process.

♦ Staff need to discover how staff can keep everyone informed of the shared decision-making process.

♦ Staff need to communicate to all staff how decisions are made.

♦ Staff need to define what a true shared decision-making structure looks like with effective lines of communication.

♦ What does "all school" mean?

♦ Get feedback on notes that are taken during meetings.

♦ "All voices are heard" should become part of what the shared decision-making structure looks like.

Professional Learning

Marylin Avenue Elementary School staff increased their rating in the area of *Outcome,* while *Approach* and *Implementation* remained the same for the past couple years (Figure B49).

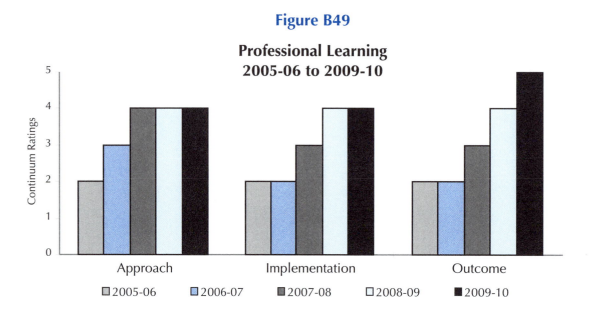

Figure B49

Next Steps 2009-10

♦ Staff need to improve our system with peer coaching—make it systemic.

♦ Clarify how we get coaching/feedback.

♦ Support and provide feedback for new instruction schoolwide for the whole staff.

♦ Create time to develop new skills. Support needs to be provided to strengthen level one RtI.
   Are staff dropping old strategies as they gain new ones or are they combining strategies? Strengthen this as a school.

♦ Think about refinement as staff go deeper into practice.

Partnership Development

In 2009-10, Marylin Avenue Elementary School staff rated themselves a three in *Approach* and *Outcome* on the Continuum (Figure B50).

Figure B50

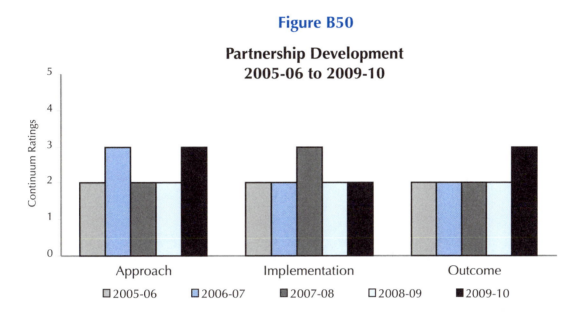

Next Steps 2009-10

We need to—

♦ Clarify what is meant by "school staff understand what partners need from the partnership."

♦ Communicate to staff about the supporting "splinter groups" and assign a "point person" who has the responsibility to inform the rest of the staff.

♦ Ensure all the partnerships know about the Marylin Avenue School Vision.

♦ Observe/look into other schools that may have a four or five rating in Partnership Development and how they communicate their vision.

♦ Make the school mission statement brief and visible to all.

♦ Develop a solid systematic plan for partnerships.

Continuous Improvement and Evaluation

Marylin Avenue Elementary School staff maintained the same ratings in all areas but *Outcome* for their 2009-10 assessment (Figure B51).

Figure B51

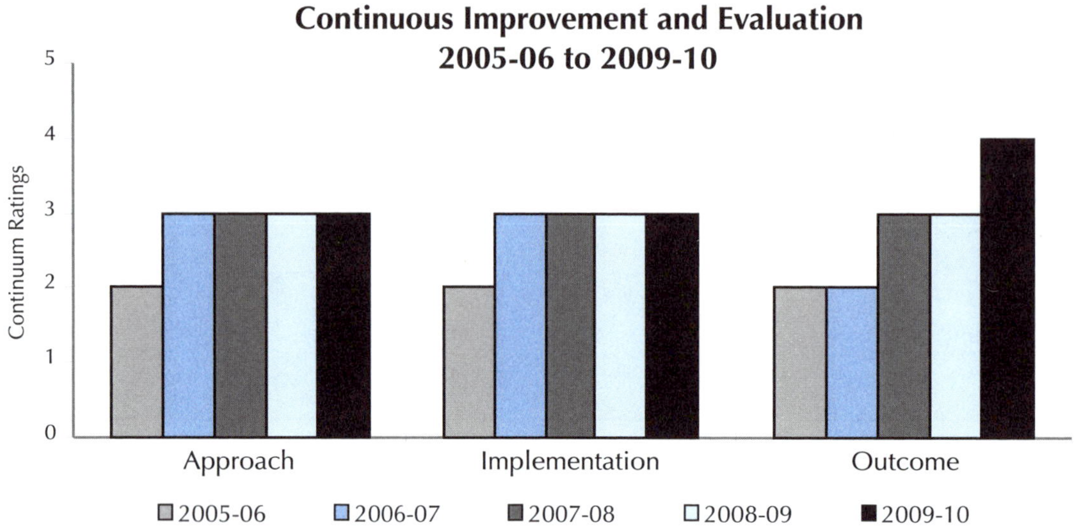

Continuous Improvement and Evaluation
2005-06 to 2009-10

Next Steps 2009-10

We need—

♦ More cross-grade-level meetings to develop the learning continuum—will need to work on the time schedule.

♦ To send more data with students upon entering a new grade (show where students fall out).

♦ To look at what staff can stop doing (what are the steps to accomplishing this?).

STUDENT ACHIEVEMENT

California uses the Standardized Testing and Reporting (STAR) Program as their basis for assessing student performance. The STAR Program is designed primarily to measure how well students are achieving the California content standards and to provide information about how well schools and school districts are meeting state and federal accountability requirements. Through the STAR Program, students in elementary grades two through five are tested each spring in various subject areas.

The California Standards Tests (CST) show how well students are doing in relation to the state content standards. Student scores are reported as performance levels. The five performance levels are *Advanced* (exceeds state standards), *Proficient* (meets standards), *Basic* (approaching standards), *Below Basic* (below standards), and *Far Below Basic* (well below standards). Students scoring at the *Proficient* or *Advanced* level have met state standards in that content area. Students are considered "proficient" when they score in the *Proficient* or *Advanced* levels of each test.

The STAR test results by grade level are shown in Figures B52 through B55 (English Language Arts) and B56 through B59 (Mathematics) for Marylin Avenue students. Test results by cohorts, Figures B60 through B64 (English Language Arts) and B65 through B69 (Mathematics) follow.

Other data analyzed, but not shown here, included:

♦ Individual teacher student growth on CST and CFA, over time, by 2009-10.

♦ Individual teacher results over time.

Look Fors: **Overall student achievement gains/losses. The student groups that have the highest and lowest percentage scoring *Proficient*. The gaps.**

Planning Implications: **Are there professional learning programs that all teachers need in order to meet the needs of all students? What other services can be provided for student groups that are not scoring *Proficient* or *Advanced*, or to move all students to proficiency?**

English Language Arts STAR Proficiency by Grade Level

Figure B52

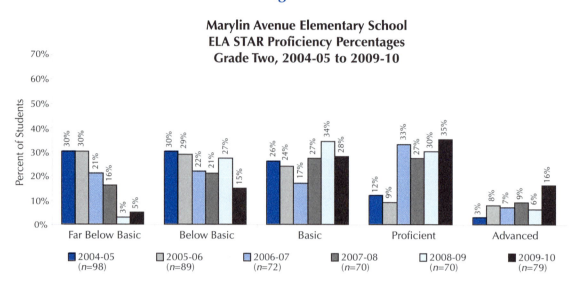

**Marylin Avenue Elementary School
ELA STAR Proficiency Percentages
Grade Two, 2004-05 to 2009-10**

Figure B53

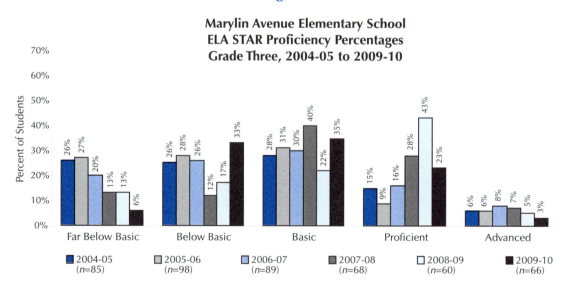

**Marylin Avenue Elementary School
ELA STAR Proficiency Percentages
Grade Three, 2004-05 to 2009-10**

Figure B54

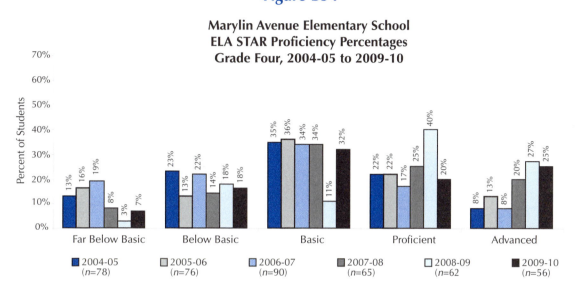

**Marylin Avenue Elementary School
ELA STAR Proficiency Percentages
Grade Four, 2004-05 to 2009-10**

Figure B55

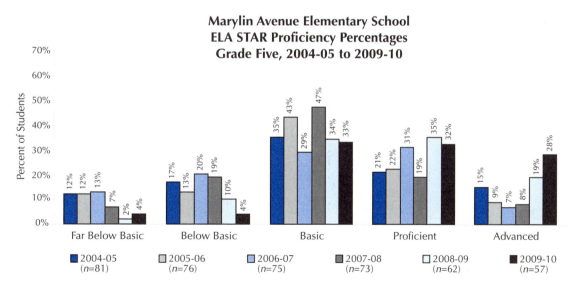

**Marylin Avenue Elementary School
ELA STAR Proficiency Percentages
Grade Five, 2004-05 to 2009-10**

Mathematics STAR Proficiency by Grade Level

Figure B56

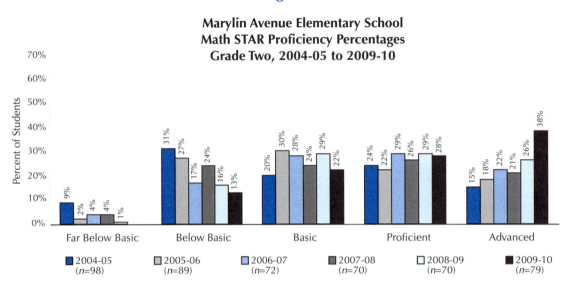

Marylin Avenue Elementary School
Math STAR Proficiency Percentages
Grade Two, 2004-05 to 2009-10

Figure B57

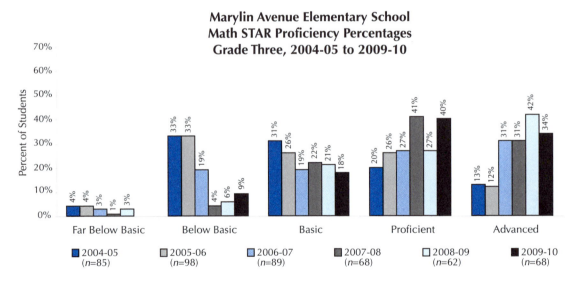

Marylin Avenue Elementary School
Math STAR Proficiency Percentages
Grade Three, 2004-05 to 2009-10

Figure B58

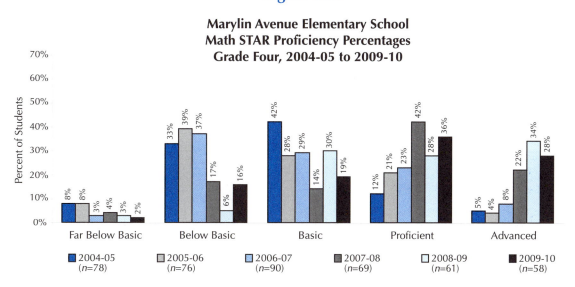

Marylin Avenue Elementary School
Math STAR Proficiency Percentages
Grade Four, 2004-05 to 2009-10

Figure B59

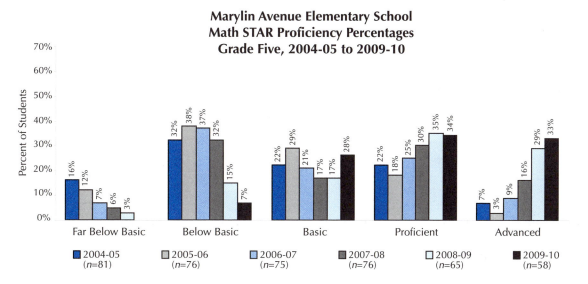

Marylin Avenue Elementary School
Math STAR Proficiency Percentages
Grade Five, 2004-05 to 2009-10

English Language Arts STAR Proficiency by Cohorts

Figure B60

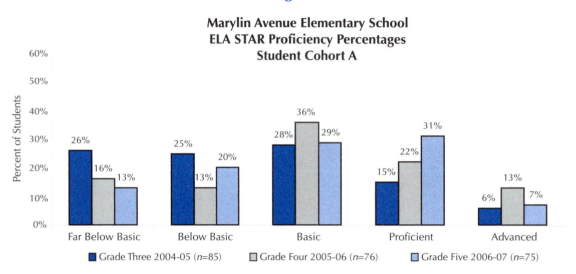

**Marylin Avenue Elementary School
ELA STAR Proficiency Percentages
Student Cohort A**

Figure B61

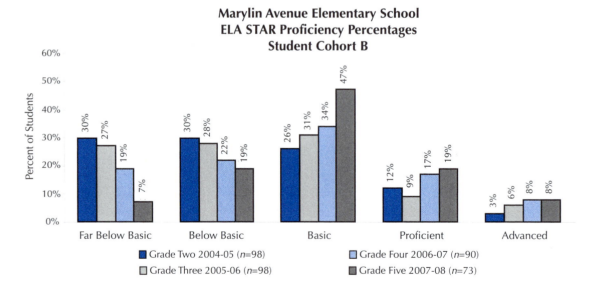

**Marylin Avenue Elementary School
ELA STAR Proficiency Percentages
Student Cohort B**

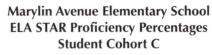

Figure B62

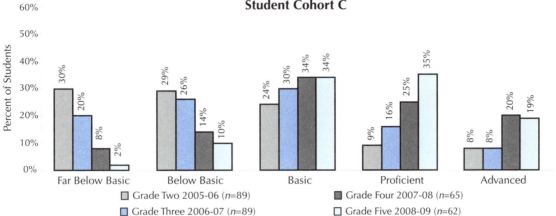

**Marylin Avenue Elementary School
ELA STAR Proficiency Percentages
Student Cohort C**

Figure B63

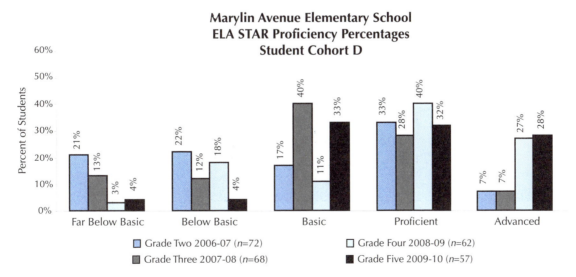

**Marylin Avenue Elementary School
ELA STAR Proficiency Percentages
Student Cohort D**

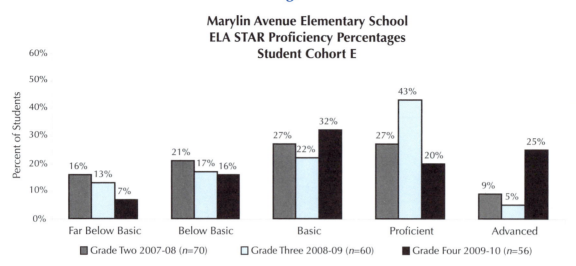

Figure B64

Marylin Avenue Elementary School
ELA STAR Proficiency Percentages
Student Cohort E

Mathematics STAR Proficiency by Cohorts

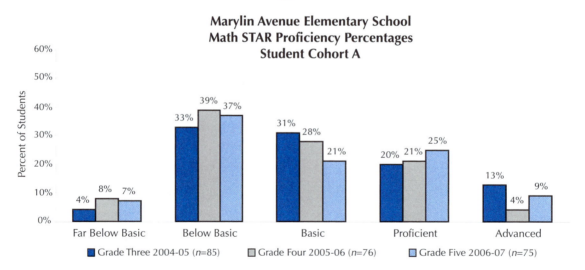

Figure B65

Marylin Avenue Elementary School
Math STAR Proficiency Percentages
Student Cohort A

Figure B66

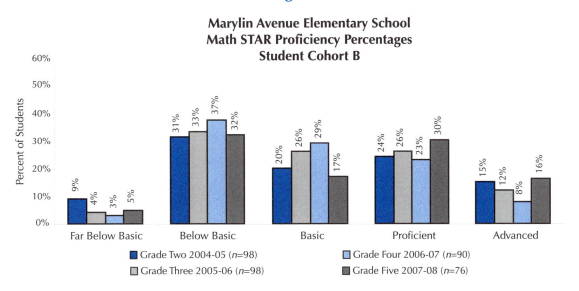

Marylin Avenue Elementary School
Math STAR Proficiency Percentages
Student Cohort B

Figure B67

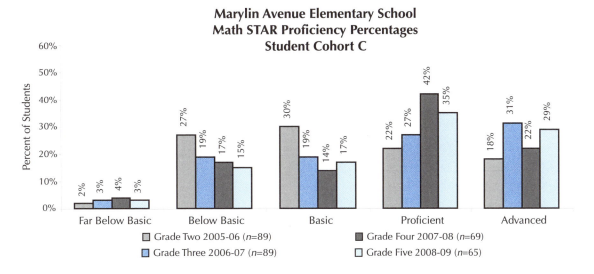

Marylin Avenue Elementary School
Math STAR Proficiency Percentages
Student Cohort C

Figure B68

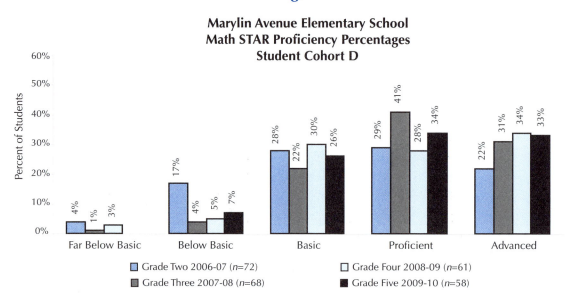

Marylin Avenue Elementary School
Math STAR Proficiency Percentages
Student Cohort D

Figure B69

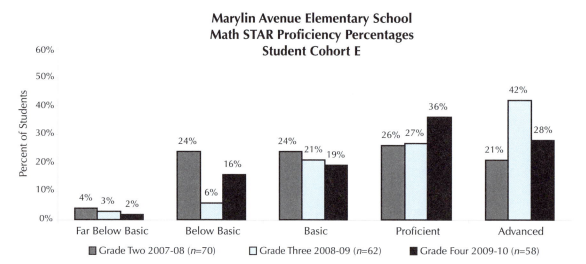

Marylin Avenue Elementary School
Math STAR Proficiency Percentages
Student Cohort E

The STAR summary test results by grade level and school total in Figures 70 (English Language Arts) and 71 (Mathematics) show the number and percentage of Marylin Avenue students scoring *Proficient* or *Advanced*.

Figure B70

Marylin Avenue Elementary School STAR Results for English Language Arts
Number and Percentage Proficient, 2004-05 to 2009-10

			Reading Proficiency									
			Grade 2		Grade 3		Grade 4		Grade 5		School	
			Number	Percent	Number	Percent	Number	Percent	Number	Percent	Number	Percent
Overall	All Students	2004-05	15	15%	18	21%	23	30%	29	36%	85	24%
		2005-06	15	17%	15	15%	27	35%	24	31%	81	24%
		2006-07	29	40%	21	24%	23	25%	29	38%	102	27%
		2007-08	25	36%	24	35%	29	45%	20	27%	98	36%
		2008-09	25	36%	29	48%	42	67%	33	54%	129	51%
		2009-10	40	51%	17	26%	25	45%	34	60%	117	45%
By Gender	Female	2004-05	8	14%	9	20%	14	39%	13	35%	44	25%
		2005-06	9	16%	9	16%	14	33%	12	33%	44	23%
		2006-07	18	50%	12	23%	14	29%	15	33%	59	32%
		2007-08	14	40%	14	37%	16	40%	13	30%	57	36%
		2008-09	14	35%	15	45%	27	75%	20	48%	76	50%
		2009-10	25	57%	10	27%	14	48%	19	59%	68	48%
	Male	2004-05	7	17%	9	23%	9	21%	16	36%	41	25%
		2005-06	6	18%	6	15%	13	38%	12	30%	37	25%
		2006-07	11	31%	9	24%	8	20%	13	43%	41	28%
		2007-08	11	31%	10	33%	13	52%	7	24%	41	34%
		2008-09	11	37%	14	52%	15	58%	14	70%	54	52%
		2009-10	16	46%	7	24%	11	41%	15	60%	49	42%
By Ethnicity	Hispanic/Latino	2004-05	5	9%	7	13%	7	16%	6	15%	25	13%
		2005-06	2	4%	5	8%	16	31%	9	20%	32	15%
		2006-07	17	34%	6	11%	11	18%	14	28%	48	22%
		2007-08	14	29%	14	30%	12	30%	13	27%	53	29%
		2008-09	16	28%	14	37%	29	64%	16	43%	75	43%
		2009-10	29	50%	9	18%	15	39%	23	58%	76	41%
	Caucasian	2004-05	8	36%	7	50%	11	52%	19	61%	45	51%
		2005-06	9	43%	5	33%	8	57%	8	53%	30	46%
		2006-07	11	69%	11	55%	5	45%	10	71%	37	61%
		2007-08	9	82%	10	77%	11	85%	3	25%	33	67%
		2008-09	6	85%	8	80%	10	83%	10	72%	34	81%
		2009-10	9	64%	3	43%	4	67%	9	69%	25	63%
By Free/ Reduced Lunch		2004-05	4	9%	3	6%	13	28%	7	16%	27	14%
		2005-06	20	32%	19	28%	13	25%	8	16%	60	26%
		2006-07	22	39%	6	11%	13	20%	16	32%	56	24%
		2007-08	16	29%	14	27%	14	33%	15	29%	59	29%
		2008-09	17	29%	21	43%	30	60%	19	45%	87	44%
		2009-10	32	50%	12	21%	19	40%	22	50%	85	40%

Note: Number Tested = the number of students in that student group and grade level who took the test.
　Number Proficient = the number of students who scored *Proficient* or *Advanced* on the test.
　Percent Proficient = the number of students who scored *Proficient* or *Advanced* on the test, divided by the number taking the test.
　Shaded cells represent the student groups and grade levels with 50% or fewer students scoring *Proficient*.

Figure B70 *(Continued)*

Marylin Avenue Elementary School STAR Results for English Language Arts
Number and Percentage Proficient, 2004-05 to 2009-10

			Reading Proficiency									
			Grade 2		Grade 3		Grade 4		Grade 5		School	
			Number	Percent	Number	Percent	Number	Percent	Number	Percent	Number	Percent
By English Language Learners	English Learners	2004-05	19	4%	7	14%	6	16%	4	13%	36	21%
		2005-06	3	6%	2	4%	9	23%	8	21%	22	12%
		2006-07	6	19%	4	8%	7	13%	5	15%	22	13%
		2007-08	8	20%	7	20%	9	24%	8	18%	32	21%
		2008-09	16	31%	9	26%	15	55%	12	38%	145	36%
		2009-10	24	47%	11	23%	7	23%	10	41%	52	34%
Fluent English Proficient/ English Only		2004-05	13	26%	11	32%	17	41%	25	51%	66	38%
		2005-06	12	34%	13	32%	18	50%	16	42%	59	39%
		2006-07	23	58%	17	44%	15	41%	23	56%	78	50%
		2007-08	17	57%	17	53%	20	74%	12	41%	66	56%
		2008-09	9	50%	19	79%	27	77%	22	70%	108	71%
		2009-10	17	61%	6	34%	18	69%	24	70%	65	61%

Figure B71

Marylin Avenue Elementary School STAR Results for Math
Number and Percentage Proficient, 2004-05 to 2009-10

			Reading Proficiency									
			Grade 2		Grade 3		Grade 4		Grade 5		School	
			Number	Percent	Number	Percent	Number	Percent	Number	Percent	Number	Percent
Overall	All Students	2004-05	39	39%	28	33%	13	17%	23	29%	102	30%
		2005-06	36	40%	37	38%	19	25%	16	21%	108	32%
		2006-07	37	51%	52	58%	28	31%	26	34%	143	39%
		2007-08	33	47%	50	72%	44	64%	35	46%	162	57%
		2008-09	39	55%	43	69%	38	62%	42	64%	162	63%
		2009-10	52	66%	50	74%	37	64%	39	67%	178	68%
By Gender	Female	2004-05	18	32%	14	30%	7	19%	9	24%	48	27%
		2005-06	20	36%	21	36%	9	21%	8	22%	58	30%
		2006-07	20	56%	29	56%	14	29%	13	29%	76	42%
		2007-08	18	51%	31	81%	23	56%	21	48%	93	59%
		2008-09	19	58%	24	72%	22	63%	25	58%	90	64%
		2009-10	33	75%	22	58%	19	66%	24	76%	99	69%
	Male	2004-05	21	51%	14	36%	6	14%	15	34%	56	34%
		2005-06	16	47%	16	40%	10	29%	8	20%	50	34%
		2006-07	17	47%	23	62%	14	34%	13	43%	67	47%
		2007-08	15	43%	19	61%	21	75%	14	44%	69	55%
		2008-09	19	66%	19	68%	16	62%	17	77%	71	66%
		2009-10	19	54%	28	93%	18	62%	15	58%	80	67%
By Ethnicity	Hispanic/Latino	2004-05	16	28%	14	25%	6	13%	8	21%	44	22%
		2005-06	16	29%	14	22%	11	21%	5	11%	46	21%
		2006-07	21	42%	25	46%	13	21%	15	30%	74	34%
		2007-08	19	40%	31	66%	24	55%	20	40%	94	50%
		2008-09	26	46%	26	66%	27	61%	22	55%	101	56%
		2009-10	36	62%	39	75%	25	61%	28	69%	128	67%
	Caucasian	2004-05	15	68%	6	43%	5	24%	12	39%	38	43%
		2005-06	13	62%	10	67%	6	43%	5	33%	34	52%
		2006-07	12	75%	16	80%	6	55%	8	57%	42	69%
		2007-08	11	100%	11	79%	12	92%	7	58%	41	82%
		2008-09	6	85%	8	80%	7	58%	11	79%	32	74%
		2009-10	11	79%	3	41%	4	67%	8	62%	26	65%
By Free/ Reduced Lunch		2004-05	13	28%	9	18%	6	13%	4	9%	32	17%
		2005-06	5	8%	6	9%	16	31%	13	27%	40	17%
		2006-07	26	46%	31	51%	16	24%	17	32%	90	38%
		2007-08	24	43%	34	64%	26	55%	21	38%	105	50%
		2008-09	28	50%	35	68%	29	60%	26	57%	118	59%
		2009-10	42	66%	44	75%	31	63%	30	67%	148	68%

Note: Number Tested = the number of students in that student group and grade level who took the test.
Number Proficient = the number of students who scored *Proficient* or *Advanced* on the test.
Percent Proficient = the number of students who scored *Proficient* or *Advanced* on the test, divided by the number taking the test.
Shaded cells represent the student groups and grade levels with 50% or fewer students scoring *Proficient*.

Figure B71 *(Continued)*

Marylin Avenue Elementary School STAR Results for Math
Number and Percentage Proficient, 2004-05 to 2009-10

			Reading Proficiency									
			Grade 2		Grade 3		Grade 4		Grade 5		School	
			Number	Percent	Number	Percent	Number	Percent	Number	Percent	Number	Percent
By English Language Learners	English Learners	2004-05	12	25%	16	31%	4	11%	4	13%	36	21%
		2005-06	17	31%	15	27%	6	15%	5	13%	22	12%
		2006-07	10	31%	25	50%	12	23%	7	21%	54	32%
		2007-08	12	30%	22	63%	20	49%	17	36%	71	44%
		2008-09	27	52%	23	64%	14	52%	18	54%	148	55%
		2009-10	31	61%	38	78%	21	66%	13	57%	104	67%
Fluent English Proficient/ English Only		2004-05	27	54%	12	35%	9	22%	20	41%	68	39%
		2005-06	19	54%	22	54%	13	36%	11	29%	65	43%
		2006-07	27	68%	27	69%	16	43%	19	46%	89	57%
		2007-08	21	70%	27	82%	24	89%	18	62%	90	76%
		2008-09	11	61%	19	76%	24	70%	24	75%	109	72%
		2009-10	21	75%	12	63%	16	62%	26	74%	75	69%

The Academic Performance Index (API) is a measure of academic achievement based on a combination of test results from the *State Standardized Testing and Reporting* (STAR) program. The API is a numeric scale from 200-1000; the statewide performance target is 800. Schools are given growth targets to meet each year, overall, and for each statistically significant subgroup. These growth targets are based on the previous year's growth; a school's progress is measured by whether it meets or exceeds growth targets overall, and for each statistically significant subgroup. Figure 72, below, shows the school's API growth overall, and for each of the statistically significant subgroups. (*Note:* White student subgroup too small to "count" in 2009-10.)

Figure B72

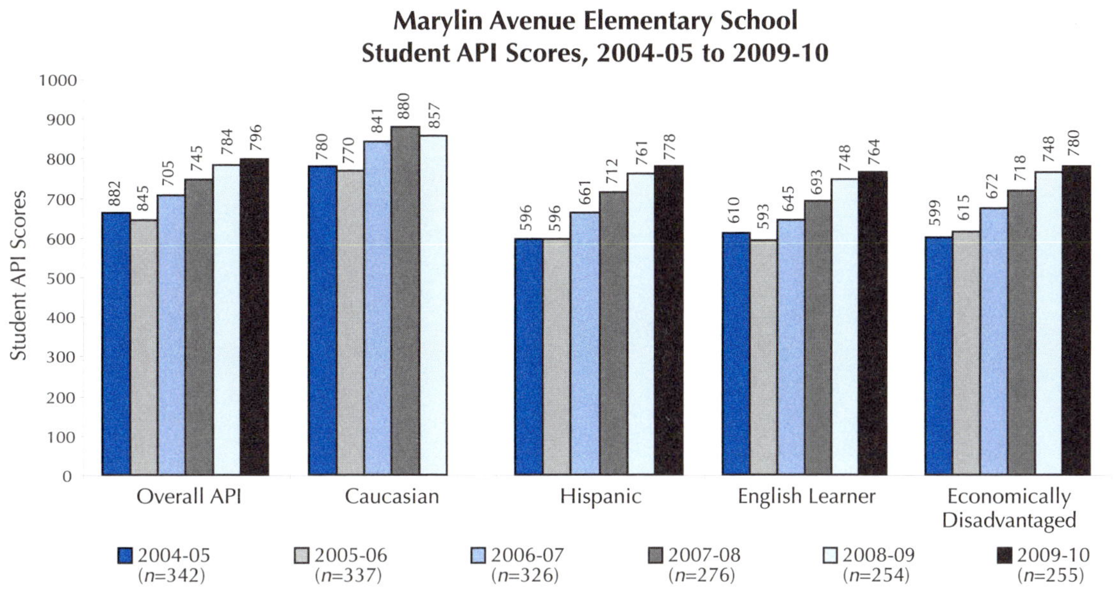

**Marylin Avenue Elementary School
Student API Scores, 2004-05 to 2009-10**

	Overall API	Caucasian	Hispanic	English Learner	Economically Disadvantaged
2004-05 (n=342)	882	780	596	610	599
2005-06 (n=337)	845	770	596	593	615
2006-07 (n=326)	705	841	661	645	672
2007-08 (n=276)	745	880	712	693	718
2008-09 (n=254)	784	857	761	748	748
2009-10 (n=255)	796		778	764	780

Appendix C

WHAT WE SAW IN THE
MARYLIN AVENUE DATA PROFILE

In this Appendix, we model how to analyze a data profile by showing you what we saw in the Marylin Avenue Elementary School data profile (Appendix B). We recommend this approach for looking at your school's data profile. Following is what is shown in this Appendix:

- For each type of *data—demographics, perceptions, student learning,* and *school processes—*we listed *strengths, challenges,* and *implications for the school improvement plan.* We also indicated *other data* we wish the school had—for future data profile updates (Figure C1).

- We lined up the *implications* for each type of data (Figure C2) and highlighted *commonalities* (Figure C3). This helps us paint with a broad brush, so the school can make improvements that impact all subject areas. It also helps staff understand how the school is getting its results and what it has to change to get different results. Knowing the big picture enables staffs to see that there are some things in demographic and perceptions data that need attention or there will not be student learning increases. The reverse is not true: looking at student learning data will not tell staffs what needs to change in other parts of the school.

- After looking at the *implication commonalities,* we stood back and determined what needed to be in the school improvement plan with respect to *instruction, assessment, curriculum, standards,* etc. (Figure C4)

Figure C1
MARYLIN AVENUE ELEMENTARY SCHOOL
DEMOGRAPHIC STRENGTHS, CHALLENGES, IMPLICATIONS, OTHER DATA

DEMOGRAPHIC DATA

1. What are Marylin Avenue's demographic *strengths* and *challenges?*

Strengths	Challenges
• The median income in the town is higher than the state's.	• There is declining districtwide enrollment in the last few years—up slightly in 2009-10.
• Marylin Avenue is a diverse, medium-size school serving grades K-5.	• Marylin Avenue is experiencing declining enrollment.
• Grade-level enrollments seem to be relatively steady, although decreasing in upper grades.	• There are many different ethnicities that are increasing as the Caucasian student population is decreasing. In the school, the Hispanic population has increased from 58% to about 75%, and the Caucasian population decreased from 27% to just under 16%. The Hispanic student population of the district increased from 20% to 26%, while its Caucasian population decreased from 65% to 59%.
• The mobility rate is down from a couple of years ago.	
• Student attendance is high, although down this year.	
• There is a decrease in the number of students retained—only 2 kindergarteners were retained in 2009-10.	• Mobility rate is high at about 28%.
	• Almost 61% of the students are English Learners; this percentage has steadily increased over the years. Marylin Avenue has about 4.5 times more English Learners than the district, with no English Language Development Program.
• The percentage of students by ethnicity identified for special education for the district is compatible with the overall percent enrollment for the district, as well as for the school.	• There has been a steady increase of students qualifying for Free/Reduced Lunch—much higher than the district—82% versus 23%—and over twice as many than in 2001-02.
• Pre-referral team (PRT) and SpERT (special education referral team) seem to be working well.	• The majority of Marylin Avenue parents do not have high school educations.
• There has been a sharp decrease in the number of students suspended over time.	• The district open enrollment policy could be setting up Marylin Avenue for a more challenging share of the student population.
• The class size is low.	• The percentage of students qualifying for special education is about 12%. The majority are male and Hispanic.
• The average number of years of teaching has increased in the last years, as have the number of teachers.	• The highest percentage of special education students are identified for speech/language (57.4%).
• The grades are pretty balanced by number of years of teaching experience.	• There are a lot of suspensions, but the number is about one-half of two years ago.
• The average number of years of teaching was less than the district, then greater than, and now almost equal for Marylin Avenue.	• The greatest number of behavior referrals are Hispanic and males. The referrals happened mostly in September and October, and at the beginning and end of the day, in 2009-10. Second grade has the largest number of behavior referrals, by grade level.
	• We need a stronger Level 3 structure for the students who need it.

---

2. What are some *implications* for the Marylin Avenue school improvement plan?

• Are teachers prepared to teach the changing population? Do teachers know how to teach students with English as a second language, and those who live in poverty? What are the implications of teaching students living in poverty? (Perhaps more male and minority teachers need to be recruited?)

• How are class-size issues dealt with?

• Does the school know why the mobility rate is high, and where students go? Do students stay in the district?

• How are new students and their parents welcomed to the school? How do teachers know what the new students know and are able to do?

• Are materials, programs, and library books appropriate for the student population (e.g., EL, poverty, mobile, special education)? Are there appropriate extra curricular activities, clubs?

• How does the school help parents know how to help their children learn?

• How are the needs of students who speak English as a second language met?

• Why are so many males identified for special education? What is the implemented intention of special education? How effective is the RtI process? Why are so many students identified for Speech and Language?

• A positive, consistent behavior system is needed.

---

3. Looking at the data presented, what other demographic data would you want to answer the question *Who are we?* for Marylin Avenue Elementary School?

• What is the household income of the Marylin Avenue neighborhood?

• How does the district open enrollment policy impact Marylin Avenue Elementary School—and in comparison to the other elementary schools?

• What is the intent of Special Education and how does RtI work?

• More data on behavior—especially following individual students over time.

Figure C1 *(Continued)*

MARYLIN AVENUE ELEMENTARY SCHOOL CONTINUOUS IMPROVEMENT CONTINUUM STRENGTHS, CHALLENGES, IMPLICATIONS, OTHER DATA

CONTINUOUS IMPROVEMENT CONTINUUM DATA
What are some *implications* for the Marylin Avenue school continuous improvement plan?

Marylin Avenue staff needs to—

- Continue using schoolwide data as they have in the past to help them know how the system is doing. Get and keep the database up-to-date so staff can gauge progress.
- Clarify the assessment system:
  - ⋆ Balance it with variety, including performance assessments and student self-assessments.
  - ⋆ Make sure the assessments that are used are telling them what they need to hear to know how to ensure student proficiency.
  - ⋆ For math and behavior.
  - ⋆ Streamline the Pre-referral process, especially the form completion process.
  - ⋆ What staff does when students are proficient on Benchmarks.
- Improve RtI.
  - ⋆ Understand why students who have been through interventions are not proficient. Do a problem-solving cycle to better understand.
  - ⋆ Continue to provide professional development for all staff so everyone can understand it and implement it in the same way.
  - ⋆ Implement a teacher self-assessment and grade level self assessment system to help implement the vision and the RtI system with integrity and fidelity throughout the school. Identify internal quality measures.
  - ⋆ Clarify what the vision and RtI would look like when implemented.
  - ⋆ Improve our peer coaching system: support and provide guidance for new instruction and assessment strategies. Provide time to develop new skills and improve level 1.
- Update, improve, and follow the school improvement plan.
- Improve shared decision making and leadership: Define, implement, and communicate.
- Clarify win-win partnerships with parents. Make sure partners know the vision and mission of the school.
- Ensure cross-grade-level work improves to implement the vision and RtI consistently, and to also ensure that a continuum of learning is in place and makes sense for the students.

3. Looking at the data presented, what other Continuous Improvement Continuum data would you want to answer the question *How do we do business?* for Marylin Avenue Elementary School?

- Has the spread of dots changed over time?

Figure C1 *(Continued)*

MARYLIN AVENUE ELEMENTARY SCHOOL
PERCEPTIONS STRENGTHS, CHALLENGES, IMPLICATIONS, OTHER DATA

PERCEPTUAL DATA

1. What are Marylin Avenue's perceptual *strengths* and *challenges*?

Strengths	Challenges
• The staff has done a wonderful job of getting student responses each year (98.5% in 2010). • It is great to see five years of data. • On the aggregate, all K-1 student responses were in agreement. Not much has changed for them over time. • Overall, the students in grades 2 through 5 are in strong agreement with the items on the questionnaire. • Students in grades 2 to 5 named *teachers* as what they like most about their school in the past 4 years. • Four years ago, students talked about wishing *the playground* and *learning* were different. In 2009-10, *learning* is not mentioned as something they wished was different. • Staff questionnaire results show that staff, for the most part, continue to be very positive about the school. All items were in agreement or strong agreement. Staff now feel that the school has a good public image. They also feel that their school culture and staff collaboration are the biggest strengths of the school. One can see progress over time. • Staff indicate the talented school staff and staff collaboration are their greatest strengths. • Overall, parents continue to be very positive about the school. • Parents, the caring loving staff, and environment are the strengths of Marylin Avenue Elementary School, according to parents.	• Someone should follow-up on the lowest scoring items (K-1)— *I feel like I belong* and *I know what I am supposed to be learning in my classes.* • The lowest items on the grades 2-5 questionnaire are related to students treating each other with respect and being friendly, and having freedom and choices at school. • American Indian students (*n*=8), grades 2-5, were in disagreement with the items, *Students at my school are friendly, Students at my school treat me with respect,* and *I am safe.* • There were 8 American Indian students who marked low on several items; however, there is only 1 American Indian student, according to the demographic data. We don't know who these other students are. They may have thought they marked "American." • Seven (7) African-American students were in disagreement to: *I have fun learning, I like this school, This school is good, I have freedom at school, I have choices in what I learn, Students are treated fairly by teachers, Students at my school treat me with respect, Students at my school are friendly,* and *I have lots of friends.* • *Communication* continues to be the most written in comment of what needs to improve, from the perspective of staff. Equity in ideas and favorites needs to be reviewed. • Parents want more social skills for students and more supervision before/after school and during recess.

2. What are some *implications* for the Marylin Avenue school improvement plan?

• The school personnel might need professional development in behavior/respect and diversity issues, and how they give students freedom and choices.
• Communication and shared leadership need to improve.

Figure C1 *(Continued)*

MARYLIN AVENUE ELEMENTARY SCHOOL STUDENT LEARNING STRENGTHS, CHALLENGES, IMPLICATIONS, OTHER DATA

STUDENT LEARNING DATA

1. What are Marylin Avenue's student learning *strengths* and *challenges*?

Strengths	*Challenges*
English Language Arts (ELA) • Grades two and five showed increases in the percentages of students *Proficient* or *Advanced* overall and for every student group, with the exception of Caucasians in both grade levels and males in grade five. **Math** • Overall, 2009-10 math scores improved over 2008-09 scores, except with grades two and five males; grade three females; Caucasians, except at grade four; and English only students, except at grade two. **API** • The overall API scores have been going up since 2005-06. • The API scores increased for all student groups .	**English Language Arts (ELA)** • 2009-10 was a challenging year for Marylin Avenue. The percentages of students *Proficient* or *Advanced* decreased overall, and for every student group in grades three and four. **Math** • Caucasian student scores were down for all grades, except grade four. • English only scores were down for all but grade two. • Males were down in grades two and five; females in grade three.

2. What are some *implications* for the Marylin Avenue school improvement plan?

• How is ELA being taught? How is ELA being measured on an ongoing basis?

• How is Math being taught? How is Math being measured on an ongoing basis?

• Did teachers focus too much on the students not proficient? Do all teachers know what to do when students are proficient?

• We need a stronger Level 3 structure for the students who need it.

3. Looking at the data presented, what other perceptual data would you want to answer the question *How are our students doing?* **for Marylin Avenue Elementary School?**

• Individual student growth data—are students growing over time?

• Correlation of formative assessments to the California Standards Test (CST).

Figure C2
REVIEW IMPLICATIONS ACROSS DATA

MARYLIN AVENUE ELEMENTARY SCHOOL

DEMOGRAPHICS	STUDENT, STAFF, PARENT QUESTIONNAIRES	STUDENT LEARNING	PROCESS DATA

◆ Are teachers prepared to teach the changing population? Do teachers know how to teach students with English as a second language, those who live in poverty? What are the implications of teaching students living in poverty? (Perhaps more male and minority teachers need to be recruited?)
◆ Does the school know why the mobility rate is high, and where students go? Do they stay in the district?
◆ How are new students and their parents welcomed to the school? How do teachers know what the new students know and are able to do?
◆ Are materials, programs, and library books appropriate for the student population (e.g., EL, poverty, mobile, special education)?
◆ Why are there so many males identified for special education?
◆ Is a new discipline system called for?
	◆ The school personnel might need professional development in behavior/respect and diversity issues and how they give students freedom and choices. Staff might also need to look into the issues of students being challenged.
	◆ Communication and shared leadership needs to improve.
		◆ How is ELA being taught? How is ELA being measured on an ongoing basis?.
		◆ How is Math being taught? How is Math being measured on an ongoing basis?
		◆ Did teachers focus too much on the students not proficient? Do all teachers know what to do when students are proficient?
		◆ We need a stronger Level 3 structure for the students who need it.
			Marylin Avenue staff needs to—
			◆ Continue using schoolwide data as they have in the past to help them know how the system is doing. Get and keep the database up-to-date so staff can gauge progress.
			◆ Clarify the assessment system:
			  ★ Balance it with variety, including performance assessments and student self-assessments.
			  ★ Make sure the assessments that are used are telling them what they need to hear to know how to ensure student proficiency.
			  ★ For math and behavior.
			  ★ Streamline the pre-referral process, especially the form completion process.
			  ★ What staff does when students are proficient on benchmarks.
			◆ Improve RtI:
			  ★ Understand why students who have been through interventions are not proficient. Do a problem-solving cycle to better understand.
			  ★ Continue to provide professional development for all staff so everyone can understand it and implement it in the same way.
			  ★ Implement a teacher self-assessment and grade level self assessment system to help implement the vision and the RtI system with integrity and fidelity throughout the school. Identify internal quality measures.
			  ★ Clarify what the vision and RtI would look like when implemented.
			  ★ Improve our peer coaching system: support and provide guidance for new instruction and assessment strategies. Provide time to develop new skills and improve level 1.
			◆ Update, improve, and follow the school improvement plan.
			◆ Improve shared decision making and leadership: Define, implement, and communicate.
			◆ Clarify win-win partnerships with parents. Make sure partners know the vision and mission of the school.
			◆ Ensure cross-grade-level work improves to implement the vision and RtI consistently; and to also ensure that a continuum of learning makes sense for the students.

Figure C3
LOOK FOR IMPLICATION COMMONALITIES

MARYLIN AVENUE ELEMENTARY SCHOOL

DEMOGRAPHICS	STUDENT, STAFF, PARENT QUESTIONNAIRES	STUDENT LEARNING	PROCESS DATA
◆ Are teachers prepared to teach the changing population? Do teachers know how to teach students with English as a second language, those who live in poverty? What are the implications of teaching students living in poverty? (Perhaps more male and minority teachers need to be recruited?) ◆ Does the school know why the mobility rate is high, and where students go? Do they stay in the district? ◆ How are new students and their parents welcomed to the school? How do teachers know what the new students know and are able to do? ◆ Are materials, programs, and library books appropriate for the student population (e.g., EL, poverty, mobile, special education)? ◆ Why are there so many males identifed for special education? ◆ Is a new discipline system called for?	◆ The school personnel might need professional development in behavior/respect and diversity issues and how they give students freedom and choices. Staff might also need to look into the issues of students being challenged. ◆ Communication and shared leadership need to improve.	◆ How is ELA being taught? How is ELA being measured on an ongoing basis?. ◆ How is Math being taught? How is Math being measured on an ongoing basis? ◆ Did teachers focus too much on the students not proficient? Do all teachers know what to do when students are proficient? ◆ We need a stronger Level 3 structure for the students who need it.	*Marylin Avenue staff needs to—* ◆ Continue using schoolwide data as they have in the past to help them know how the system is doing. Get and keep the database up-to-date so staff can gauge progress. ◆ Clarify the assessment system: ★ Balance it with variety, including performance assessments and student self-assessments. ★ Make sure the assessments that are used are telling them what they need to hear to know how to ensure student proficiency. ★ For math and behavior. ★ Streamline the pre-referral process, especially the form completion process. ★ What staff does when students are proficient on benchmarks. ◆ Improve RtI: ★ Understand why students who have been through interventions are not proficient. Do a problem-solving cycle to better understand. ★ Continue to provide professional development for all staff so everyone can understand it and implement it in the same way. ★ Implement a teacher self-assessment and grade level self assessment system to help implement the vision and the RtI system with integrity and fidelity throughout the school. Identify internal quality measures. ★ Clarify what the vision and RtI would look like when implemented. ★ Improve our peer coaching system: support and provide guidance for new instruction and assessment strategies. Provide time to develop new skills and improve level 1. ◆ Update, improve, and follow the school improvement plan. ◆ Improve shared decision making and leadership: Define, implement, and communicate. ◆ Clarify win-win partnerships with parents. Make sure partners know the vision and mission of the school. ◆ Ensure cross-grade-level work improves to implement the vision and RtI consistently; and to also ensure that a continuum of learning makes sense for the students.

Figure C4
AGGREGATED IMPLICATIONS FOR THE CONTINUOUS SCHOOL IMPROVEMENT PLAN

MARYLIN AVENUE ELEMENTARY SCHOOL

INSTRUCTION	ASSESSMENT	CURRICULUM	BEHAVIOR	VISION / PLAN	PROFESSIONAL LEARNING
• Teachers need to strengthen their instructional strategies in ELA and Math. • There needs to be deeper implementation of RtI. • Continue to ensure that all teachers are teaching to standards and all students are meeting standards in all subject areas. • Clarify what staff does when students are proficient.	• Clarify a balanced assessment system. • We need to make sure teachers know what the new students know and are able to do when they arrive, so we do not lose instructional time. • We need to collect more systematic formative data in writing and math.	• Are materials, programs, and library books appropriate for the student population? (EL, poverty, mobile, special education) • We need to document and continue to improve RtI implementation.	• We need a positive, consistent behavior system schoolwide.	• The vision needs to be fully implemented. • Staff needs to narrow the focus of the plan and stay focused on it; always have next steps in front of them; create and post a graphic organizer to help us stay focused. • We need to systematically include our parents in quality planning.	• Continue our professional learning in meeting the needs of our students, especially students with English as a second language, those who live in poverty, and males, specifically in ELA and Math learning, and for RtI. • School personnel need consistent training and implementation of behavior and motivation strategies.

COLLABORATION	LEADERSHIP	PARTNERSHIPS	DATA	CLIMATE	RtI / SPECIAL EDUCATION
• Staff need to strengthen peer coaching and make it and the feedback structure more systematic and defined. • We need to schedule schoolwide articulation more often and make cross-grade-level articulation meetings more systematic. • Staff need to continue cross-grade-level articulation, including agreements about student behavior in terms of motivation, attitude, and effort—also as related to *Students Committed to Excellence*.	• Communication needs to improve among staff and with parents. • Everyone needs to be a part of professional learning and leadership. • We need to improve shared leadership.	• We need to connect student achievement data to partnerships, and look into relationships that might affect student achievement, based on our mission/vision/ plan. • We need to document different ways the community is contributing to the school, and how parent involvement affects student achievement. • We need to make sure parents know how to help meet the learning needs of their children.	• Where do our mobile students go? Do they stay in the district? • We need to continue using schoolwide data teams. • Staff need to become astute in knowing what works so they can predict and ensure successes. • Staff accessibility to data tools needs to be improved.	• We need a system to welcome new students and their parents to the school. • Staff need to continue cross-grade-level articulation, including agreements about student behavior in terms of motivation, attitude, and effort—also as related to *Students Committed to Excellence*. • Staff need to continue to communicate and collaborate.	We need to: • Look into speech and language referrals. • Streamline PRT process. • Get all staff understanding RtI in the same way. • Strengthen level one RtI. • Evaluate and improve RtI implementation.

Appendix D

ANALYZING DATA FOR CONTINUOUS SCHOOL IMPROVEMENT PLANNING ACTIVITY

WHERE ARE WE NOW?

This is the part of continuous improvement planning that takes a comprehensive and honest look at all the school's data—not just student learning results—and helps to reflect on how the data implications intersect. There are four sub-questions to answer with data within this category:

- Who are we?
- How do we do business?
- How are our students doing?
- What are our programs and processes?

Purpose

The purpose of this activity is to guide the analysis of data to inform the school improvement plan.

Target Audience

School staff.

Time

Up to 3 hours, depending upon the number of staff members and the amount of data available.

Materials

Chart paper, markers, tape, or push pins to post the chart paper, if necessary.

Have the school's data profile printed on paper or available via the online *SchoolPortfolio* Application for each person doing the analysis.

Note: The *SchoolPortfolio Application* is a software tool, created by *SchoolCity, Inc.* (*www.schoolcity.com*), that automates the *School Portfolio*—from the data profile to the evaluation of your school's vision and plan.)

Process Protocol

1. **Strengths, Challenges, Implications**

   Print out a *Strengths, Challenges,* and *Implications* worksheet for each staff member (Figures D1 through D4).

DEMOGRAPHIC DATA

1. What are Marylin Avenue Elementary School's demographic *strengths* and *challenges?*	
Strengths	*Challenges*

2. What are some *implications* for the Marylin Avenue continuous improvement plan?

3. Looking at the data presented, what other Marylin Avenue demographic data would you want to answer the question *Who are we?*

As individuals review each type of data (e.g., *demographics, perceptions, student learning,* and *school processes*), have them document what they are seeing as—

♦ *strengths,*

♦ *challenges,*

♦ *implications for the continuous improvement plan,* and

♦ *other data they wished the school had.*

Note: Analyses are much richer if notes about the data are jotted down *as* they are reviewed. **(15-20 minutes)**

In small groups, have staff members share what they see as *strengths, challenges, implications for the school improvement plan,* and *other data they wished the school had.* Record commonalities in each of the four areas. (This makes it easier to combine the small-groups' thinking with full-group thinking in the next step.) **(15 minutes)**

Combine the small group results to get a comprehensive *set of strengths, challenges, implications for the school improvement plan,* and *other data you wished the school had.* This is best done by having a reporter from each small group stand beside her/his group's chart paper ready to mark off items mentioned as each group's reporter indicates what the group saw as *strengths, challenges, implications for the school improvement plan,* and *other data you wished the school had.*

Process Protocol

Start on the left and have the first reporter read all the group's strengths. Other reporters check off commonalities. Going to the right, the next reporter reads only what her/his group had on its "strengths" list that has not been read. Continue until all the "strengths" have been read. Have another group read its list of "challenges." You might want to start on the right this time, and go left. Continue with "implications for the school improvement plan," and then "what other data do you wish you had," until you are finished. The result will be a comprehensive list of *Strengths, Challenges, Implications for the school improvement plan,* and *Other Data You Wished the School Had.* **(20 minutes)**

Repeat the process with the other three types of data.

Process options: The process described above is an excellent way to review and combine thinking with demographic data. It is important that all staff members review all the information in at least one area of data.

With perceptions and student learning data, parts of the data work could be delegated to different members of each small group. For example, when a school has student, staff, and parent questionnaires to analyze, one third of each team could review the student questionnaire; another third, the staff questionnaire; and the last third, the parent questionnaire. The sub-teams could then report what they saw in the data to their team, who then will combine their thinking with the other teams. With student learning, the data could be delegated by subject area, with process data, your school may use the CICs. The summary of next steps could replace the strengths/challenges/implications worksheet for processes. Also, your school might choose to use the process and program worksheets, shown in Appendix Figures H1 and H2, to replace the school process strengths/challenges/implications worksheet.

2. **Implications**

   After staff has documented the school's data strengths, challenges, implications for the continuous improvement plan, and what other data they wished the school had for *demographics, perceptions, student learning, school processes,* review the implications side-by-side. (The *SchoolPortfolio Application* will automatically aggregate the implications, by data element.)

   This alignment is important for seeing commonalities across the different implications (see following partial example).

3. **Implication Commonalities**

   In small groups, look across and highlight commonalities in your *demographics, perceptions, student learning,* and *school process implications.* Share small group thinking with the large group. (Partial example shown on the following page.)

REVIEW IMPLICATIONS ACROSS DATA

Demographics	Student, Staff, Parent Questionnaires	Student Learning	Process Data

◆ Are teachers prepared to teach the changing population? Do teachers know how to teach students with English as a second language, those who live in poverty? What are the implications of teaching students living in poverty? (Perhaps more male and minority teachers need to be recruited?)
◆ Does the school know why the mobility rate is high, and where students go? Do they stay in the district?
◆ How are new students and their parents welcomed to the school? How do teachers know what the new students know and are able to do?
◆ Are materials, programs, and library books appropriate for the student population (e.g., EL, poverty, mobile, special education)?
◆ Why are there so many males identified for special education?
◆ Is a new discipline system called for?
	◆ The school personnel might need professional development in behavior/respect and diversity issues and how they give students freedom and choices. Staff might also need to look into the issues of students being challenged.
	◆ Communication and shared leadership needs to improve.
		◆ Teachers need to keep doing what they are doing to get student achievement increases.
		◆ How are teachers teaching ELA and Math? Processes need to be mapped.
		◆ Are teachers prepared to teach students with backgrounds different from their own?
		◆ It appears the early grades need to get even stronger.
			Marylin Avenue staff needs to—
			◆ Continue using schoolwide data as they have in the past to help them know how the system is doing. Get and keep the database up-to-date so staff can gauge progress.
			◆ Clarify the assessment system:
			  ∗ Balance it with variety, including performance assessments and student self-assessments.
			  ∗ Make sure the assessments that are used are telling them what they need to hear to know how to ensure student proficiency.
			  ∗ For math and behavior.
			  ∗ Streamline the pre-referral process, especially the form completion process.
			  ∗ What staff does when students are proficient on benchmarks.
			◆ Improve RtI:
			  ∗ Understand why students who have been through interventions are not proficient. Do a problem-solving cycle to better understand.
			  ∗ Continue to provide professional development for all staff so everyone can understand it and implement it in the same way.
			  ∗ Implement a teacher self-assessment and grade level self assessment system to help implement the vision and the RtI system with integrity and fidelity throughout the school. Identify internal quality measures.
			  ∗ Clarify what the vision and RtI would look like when implemented.
			  ∗ Improve our peer coaching system: support and provide guidance for new instruction and assessment strategies. Provide time to develop new skills and improve level 1.
			◆ Update, improve, and follow the school improvement plan.
			◆ Improve shared decision making and leadership: Define, implement, and communicate.
			◆ Clarify win-win partnerships with parents. Make sure partners know the vision and mission of the school.

LOOK FOR IMPLICATION COMMONALITIES

Demographics	Student, Staff, Parent Questionnaires	Student Learning	Process Data

◆ Are teachers prepared to teach the changing population? Do teachers know how to teach students with English as a second language, those who live in poverty? What are the implications of teaching students living in poverty? (Perhaps more male and minority teachers need to be recruited?)
◆ Does the school know why the mobility rate is high, and where students go? Do they stay in the district?
◆ How are new students and their parents welcomed to the school? How do teachers know what the new students know and are able to do?
◆ Are materials, programs, and library books appropriate for the student population (e.g., EL, poverty, mobile, special education)?
◆ Why are there so many males identified for special education?
	◆ The school personnel might need professional development in behavior/respect and diversity issues and how they give students freedom and choices. Staff might also need to look into the issues of students being challenged.
	◆ Communication and shared leadership needs to improve.
		◆ Teachers need to keep doing what they are doing to get student achievement increases.
		◆ How are teachers teaching ELA and Math? Processes need to be mapped.
		◆ Are teachers prepared to teach students with backgrounds different from their own?
		◆ It appears the early grades need to get even stronger.
			Marylin Avenue staff needs to—
			◆ Continue using schoolwide data as they have in the past to help them know how the system is doing. Get and keep the database up-to-date so staff can gauge progress.
			◆ Clarify the assessment system:
			  ∗ Balance it with variety, including performance assessments and student self-assessments.
			  ∗ Make sure the assessments that are used are telling them what they need to hear to know how to ensure student proficiency.
			  ∗ For math and behavior.
			  ∗ Streamline the pre-referral process, especially the form completion process.
			  ∗ What staff does when students are proficient on benchmarks.
			◆ Improve RtI:
			  ∗ Understand why students who have been through interventions are not proficient. Do a problem-solving cycle to better understand.
			  ∗ Continue to provide professional development for all staff so everyone can understand it and implement it in the same way.
			  ∗ Implement a teacher self-assessment and grade level self assessment system to help implement the vision and the RtI system with integrity and fidelity throughout the school. Identify internal quality measures.
			  ∗ Clarify what the vision and RtI would look like when implemented.
			  ∗ Improve our peer coaching system: support and provide guidance for new instruction and assessment strategies. Provide time to develop new skills and improve level 1.
			◆ Update, improve, and follow the school improvement plan.
			◆ Improve shared decision making and leadership: Define, implement, and communicate.

Process Protocol

4. **Aggregate Implications for the Continuous School Improvement Plan**

In small groups, or if manageable in the large group, stand back from the *implication commonalities* and begin a bulleted list of *implications for the plan*, with respect to *leadership, curriculum, instruction, assessment, curriculum, standards, vision/plan, etc.* Use the provided worksheets (Figures D5 and D6), which can be adjusted as needed. (Partial "snapshot" example shown below.)

AGGREGATE IMPLICATIONS FOR THE CONTINUOUS SCHOOL IMPROVEMENT PLAN

INSTRUCTION	ASSESSMENT	CURRICULUM	STANDARDS	VISION / PLAN	PROFESSIONAL LEARNING
• Teachers need to keep doing what they are doing instructionally that are getting student achievement increases. • Teachers need to strengthen their instruction and strategies in the early grades in ELA and Math. • We need deeper implementation of RtI.	• Clarify the assessment system. • We need to make sure teachers know what the new students know and are able to do when they arrive, so we do not lose instructional time. • We need to collect more systematic formative data in writing and math.	• Are materials, programs, and library books appropriate for the student population? (EL, poverty, mobile, special education) • We need to document and continue to improve RtI.	• Continue to ensure that all teachers are teaching to standards and all students are meeting standards in all subject areas.	• The vision needs to be fully implemented. • We need to narrow the focus of the plan and stay focused on it; always have our next steps in front of us; create and post a graphic organizer to help us stay focused. • We need to systematically include our parents in quality planning.	• Continue our professional learning in meeting the needs of our students, especially students with English as a second language, those who live in poverty, and males, specifically in ELA and Math learning. • School personnel need consistent training and implementation of behavior and motivation strategies.

COLLABORATION	LEADERSHIP	PARTNERSHIPS	DATA	CLIMATE	CONTINUOUS IMPROVEMENT
• Staff need to strengthen peer coaching and make it and the feedback structure more systematic and defined. • We need to schedule schoolwide articulation more often and make cross-grade-level articulation meetings more systematic.	• Communication needs to improve among staff and with parents. • Staff need to continue cross-grade-level articulation, including agreements about student behavior in terms of motivation, attitude, and effort—also as related to *Students Committed to Excellence.*	• We need to define who our stakeholders are, and establish win-win relationships with parents and the community. • We need to connect student achievement data to partnerships, and look into relationships that might affect student achievement, based on our mission/vision/ plan.	• Where do our mobile students go? Do they stay in the district? • Who are the students who are retained? Are retentions helping these students? • We need to continue using schoolwide data teams. • Staff need to become astute in knowing what works so they can predict and ensure successes.	• We need a system to welcome new students and their parents to the school. • Staff need to continue cross-grade-level articulation, including agreements about student behavior in terms of motivation, attitude, and	• Evaluate and improve RtI. • Work on implementing the vision.

Process Protocol

5. **Create the Plan**

   Use this comprehensive data analysis, along with the vision, to create the school improvement plan.

Comments to the Facilitator

This is an activity to ensure the analysis of all types of comprehensive schoolwide data and to engage all staff members in analyzing the data. The important concepts are to have participants:

♦ Review the data independently.

♦ Write their thoughts as they analyze the data.

♦ Combine thinking of staff members.

♦ Look across the different analyses to paint with a broad brush.

The analysis of comprehensive data, in conjunction with the school vision, will inform a schoolwide plan that will make a difference for all students.

Figure D1

STRENGTHS, CHALLENGES, IMPLICATIONS WORKSHEET

DEMOGRAPHIC DATA	
1. What are the school's demographic *strengths* and *challenges*?	
Strengths	*Challenges*

2. What are some *implications* for the school improvement plan?

3. Looking at the data presented, what other demographic data would you want to answer the question *Who are we?*

Figure D2
STRENGTHS, CHALLENGES, IMPLICATIONS WORKSHEET

SCHOOL PROCESSES DATA

1. What are the *strengths* and *challenges* of the school processes?

Strengths	*Challenges*

2. What are some *implications* for the school improvement plan?

3. Looking at the data presented, what other school process data would you want to answer the question *What are our programs and processes?*

Figure D3
STRENGTHS, CHALLENGES, IMPLICATIONS WORKSHEET

PERCEPTUAL DATA

1. What are the school's perceptual *strengths* and *challenges*?

Strengths	Challenges

2. What are some *implications* for the school improvement plan?

3. Looking at the data presented, what other perceptual data would you want to answer the question *How do we do business?*

Figure D4
STRENGTHS, CHALLENGES, IMPLICATIONS WORKSHEET

STUDENT LEARNING DATA

1. What are the school's student learning *strengths* and *challenges*?

Strengths	*Challenges*

2. What are some *implications* for the school improvement plan?

3. Looking at the data presented, what other student learning data would you want to answer the question *How are our students doing?*

Figure D5
IMPLICATION COMMONALITIES WORKSHEET

LOOK FOR IMPLICATION COMMONALITIES

Demographics	Student, Staff, Parent Questionnaires	School Processes	Student Learning

Figure D6
AGGREGATE IMPLICATIONS WORKSHEET

AGGREGATE IMPLICATIONS FOR THE CONTINUOUS SCHOOL IMPROVEMENT PLAN

INSTRUCTION	ASSESSMENT	CURRICULUM	BEHAVIOR	VISION / PLAN	PROFESSIONAL LEARNING

COLLABORATION	LEADERSHIP	PARTNERSHIPS	DATA	CLIMATE	RtI / SPECIAL EDUCATION

Appendix E

CREATING A SHARED VISION ACTIVITY

Schools and school districts must have a vision that reflects what the learning organization would *look like, sound like,* and *feel like* when it is carrying out its purpose and mission, and to keep everyone's efforts focused on the target.

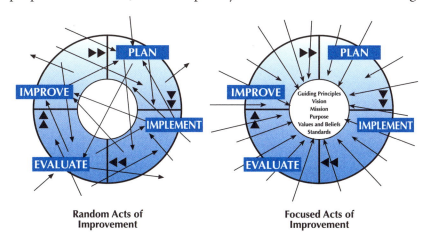

Random Acts of Improvement

Focused Acts of Improvement

From Values & Beliefs to Action

ACTION PLAN

GOALS/OBJECTIVES

SHARED VISION

Mission

PURPOSE

Values and Beliefs

To create a vision that is *truly* shared (i.e., agreed upon unanimously and understood in the same way), we must begin with the values and beliefs of the individuals to create core values and beliefs for the school, and a core purpose and mission for the school. With core values and beliefs, purpose and mission, a vision can be created for the school. *Goals* are the outcomes of the vision.

Prior to the visioning work, it is imperative that staff review the school data and read Best Practices related to areas of need. If staff do not learn new ideas of meeting the needs of their students, all they will do is create the same vision—over and over. The end result will be the same.

Purpose
To help staff create a vision that is truly shared (i.e., committed to unanimously and understood in the same way).

Target Audience
District or school staff.

Time
Approximately 3.5 to 5 hours.

Materials
Chart pad paper, material for posting paper on the wall, markers (for each table), scissors, computer, projector, and vision worksheets, attached.

Number of Facilitators
Preferably two.

Overview
To create a vision that is truly shared—committed to unanimously and understood in the same way—we must build on the values and beliefs of the school staff members to create core values and beliefs, a core purpose, and a mission for the school. With core values and beliefs, purpose and mission, a vision can be created for the school.

We must begin with the personal and move to the collective. Systems thinker Peter Senge (*The Fifth Discipline*, 2006) sums up the rationale:

Shared visions emerge from personal visions.
This is how they derive their energy and
how they foster commitment . . .
If people don't have their own vision,
all they can do is "sign up" for someone else's.
The result is compliance, never commitment.

To create a shared vision, gather all staff members together in a location with tables that seat 5 to 7 people.

Process Protocol
Prior to the session, organize seating arrangements to ensure a mixture (grade level/subjects taught) in the small groups and to ensure that time will be used effectively. Staff members should be well-versed in the literature about what works in schools like theirs.

The steps that follow describe the process in detail. Use the vision worksheet on the day of the vision work to assist with the documentation. Be sure to personalize the worksheet before copying it.

1. **Review Ground Rules**
   - This is a safe room.
   - There is no rank in this room.
   - All ideas are valid.
   - Each person gets a chance to speak.
   - Each person gets a chance to listen.
   - We are here to focus on the future.
   - Our purpose is improvement, not blame.

Process Protocol

2. Determine Core Values and Beliefs

Have the members of the group *individually* brainstorm and document their thoughts about: *What are the curriculum, instruction, assessment, and environmental factors that support effective learning for our students?* **(10 minutes, or longer if needed)**

Compare and merge ideas in *small groups.* Write the ideas on poster paper. It is okay to add or to agree to ideas that were not on an individual's original list. *Stick to the topic.* **(15-20 minutes)**

Reconvene as a *large group.* Someone from each group stands next to the group's posters to note duplicates and to report. Start on one end of the room, for example, and have the reporter for the first group read all of the group's ideas about curriculum. Other groups note duplications on their poster and when it is their turn, report what they have left. Start with a different group for each category and vary the direction so each group gets maximum exposure.

Come to agreement on core values and beliefs for the school. *Recorder types on a laptop so statements are displayed on the screen.* **(30 minutes)**

There is no limit to the number of core values and beliefs. However, after this day, with staff approval, the Leadership Team might merge some ideas if the list is very long and overlapping.

3. Determine the Core Purpose

Have staff members *individually* brainstorm and document personal ideas about the purpose of the school—*do not worry about the wording at this point.* **(5 minutes)**

Share individual purposes in *small groups* and post a common purpose with which everyone in the small group can live. **(10 minutes)**

Look for commonalities across the small group purposes with the *large group.* Come to agreement on a core purpose for the school. *Recorder types the core purpose on the laptop.* **(15-20 minutes)**

PRINT THE CORE VALUES AND BELIEFS AND PURPOSE FOR EACH PARTICIPANT TO USE FOR THE NEXT STEPS.

4. Revisit the Mission

Review the current mission statement. Either agree that the current mission is fine, or that a committee will craft the mission statement at a different time using the core values and beliefs and purpose, and bring it back to the whole staff. As long as the purpose is clear, the process can proceed without the mission statement completely written. It is the purpose that is most important. Determine who will write the mission. *Use the existing mission, update it quickly, or delegate the mission to be rewritten. Move on.* **(5-10 minutes)**

5. Create a Vision

Still assembled in the large group, *individuals* brainstorm and document personal visions for the school in terms of what the school would *look like, sound like, feel like* if we were doing what we

Process Protocol

need to do for our children—if we are living our core values and beliefs, purpose, and mission. Identify curriculum, instruction, assessment, and environmental components. (*Note:* If the core values and beliefs are done well, the individuals will say "The vision should be our core values and beliefs," which is what we would like to see happen.) **(10 minutes)**

Share personal visions in *small groups* and document commonalities. It is okay to add or to agree to ideas that were not on an individual's original list. Post ideas. **(15 minutes—sometimes this step can be skipped if the note about values and beliefs holds true.)**

Come to agreement on the commonalities with the *large group*. Come to agreement on the elements of the vision for the school. *Make sure everyone understands that these agreements become commitments for implementation.* **(30 minutes)**

6. **Determine School Goals—The Outcomes of the Vision**

   There should only be two or three school goals. Again, have *individuals* take time to do their own thinking. **(5 minutes)**

   Share individual ideas in *small groups* and document commonalities. **(10 minutes)**

   Small groups share and merge ideas with the *large group*. **(15 minutes)**

7. **Draft Vision Narrative**

   In addition to the specifics of the vision, it is important to write a narrative (or create a flowchart) about what it would *look like, sound like, feel like* if the vision was being implemented in every classroom. Brainstorm ideas, at a minimum, if this piece must be delegated to the Leadership Team to finish because of time constraints.

   Again, give *individuals* a chance to think. **(5 minutes)**

   Have individuals compare and combine notes in their *small groups*. **(15 minutes)**

   Compare and combine small group notes to *whole group*. **(20 minutes)**

8. **Answer Questions**

   You might ask the staff to answer these questions if you have time after you finish the shared vision and school goals.

   - What professional development is needed and when?
   - What materials are needed to implement the vision?
   - What other things need to be done to implement the vision?
   - How will the implementation of the vision be supported?
   - How can progress be measured?

THIS IS PROBABLY WHERE YOU WILL END AFTER ONE DAY. WHEREVER YOU ARE AT THE END OF THE DAY, THE FOLLOWING WILL HAVE TO BE COMPLETED AT A LATER TIME.

Process Protocol

9. **Document**

   Document the shared vision. Someone can be assigned this task, with review and agreement by the entire staff. Make sure every staff member has a copy of what has been done to this point.

   Suggestion: Develop a rubric, flowchart, or assessment tool of some sort that would describe the logical evolution and implementation of the vision in the classroom and across classrooms. This will support the implementation later on.

10. **Quality Plan**

    Determine a plan to implement the vision. Include the points that follow, especially the professional learning required to implement the vision, materials to purchase, and support mechanisms for implementation, such as peer coaching.

11. **Curriculum and Instruction**

    Grade-level/subject-area teams adapt the vision into real terms for each teacher. Check across grade-level teams to ensure a continuum of learning that makes sense. (Determine a structure and time for grade-level meetings and cross-grade-level meetings.)

12. **Leadership**

    Determine a leadership structure to implement and monitor the vision.

13. **Professional Learning**

    Create time in the work week for teachers to collaborate to implement and maintain the vision. Provide professional learning so everyone understands her/his role in implementing the vision and has the support to do it.

14. **Partnership Development**

    Determine how partnerships can help with the implementation of the vision and build them into the vision and the school plan.

15. **Continuous Improvement and Evaluation**

    Determine an evaluation and monitoring system, specifically to gauge implementation and success.

Comments to the Facilitator

This is a very action-packed time period. If you keep within the time estimates, the task will go fast and be productive. If you feel comfortable doing so, consider interspersing the time with continuous team building activities.

Appendix F

PROBLEM-SOLVING CYCLE ACTIVITY

When schools discover gaps, they naturally want to find solutions immediately to close the gaps. To really eliminate problems, schools must look for root causes, or contributing causes (we believe there is more than one cause for undesirable results).

The problem-solving cycle is a great activity for getting all staff involved in thinking through a problem before jumping to solutions. By starting with brainstorming hunches and hypotheses, all staff can be heard. When voices are expressed, there is a better chance of all staff using the information later. During the brainstorming, staff hears what they believe are the reasons for the undesirable results, or gaps. Next, staff will need to determine what questions must be answered with data (and what data) before the "problem" can be solved. Deeper data analyses result. (The first three steps in the problem-solving cycle are key and the focus of this activity.)

Purpose

To get all staff involved in thinking through a problem before jumping to solutions. This activity can also result in a comprehensive data analysis design. By starting with hunches and hypotheses, all staff can get their voices heard. When voices are expressed, there is a better chance of all staff using the information later. (The first three steps in the problem-solving cycle are *key* and the focus of this activity.)

Target Audience

All staff.

Time

One hour for the first three steps of the cycle.

Materials

Chart pad paper, masking tape/tacks, and markers.
Handouts for each participant: hunches and hypothesis, and questions and data worksheets.

Process Protocol

Make sure each person has a copy of the handout and that you are prepared to help small groups identify their problem(s) in objective terms. You will need about one hour to get through the first three steps, if getting the data analysis design is your focus. Analyzing the data will take another two hours—probably at a different time. Developing the action plan will take days with small groups going back to the larger group (see *Action Planning Activity*). Implementing the action plan is the ongoing work of the learning organization, as is evaluating the implementation of the action plan, and improving the processes.

1. Establish the size of the group(s) that will be going through this activity. Small groups are beneficial in allowing everyone to participate, even if groups are working on the same problem.

2. Start out with guidelines or ground rules of acceptable and unacceptable behavior, and how they will be monitored. Make sure it is a "safe" room for threat-free, honest, open discussion.

3. Have each group clearly identify a problem to be solved, stated in objective terms. For example, *Not all students are reading at grade level by grade three*, as opposed to, *40 percent of our students are not capable of reading by grade three*. The problem should let you find the data.

4. Brainstorm 20 hunches and hypotheses about why the problem exists (takes about ten minutes). This can spell out what teachers are thinking about the problem currently. You could also use a "cause and effect diagram," shown in Figure F4 and F5 (example and blank diagram).

5. Considering the problem, identify questions that need to be answered to find out more about the problem (e.g., *How many students have not been reading on grade level by grade three for the past three years?*) Get at least eight questions.

Process Protocol

6. For each question, determine the data that need to be gathered to answer the question. This list becomes the data analysis. Eye-balling this list, one can see that for the most part, the data will fall into the four categories of *demographics, student learning, perceptions,* and *school processes.* (At this point, you should have uncovered new ways of looking at the problem. This might be as far as you go on this day.)

7. Have the groups share their problem-solving cycle, letting others add to it, if appropriate.

8. Gather and analyze the data. This is often where the schools have the most trouble because they do not have the data readily available. Help them get the data.

9. Continue with the problem-solving cycle through action planning and implementation.

Comments to the Facilitator

This is a very action-packed time period. If teams are working on different "problems," you might want to share.

Some staffs will want to use this activity to evaluate programs and processes. Some may want to use this process before a visioning process. The problem-solving cycle will work wherever it is needed.

Figure F1

STEPS IN SOLVING A PROBLEM

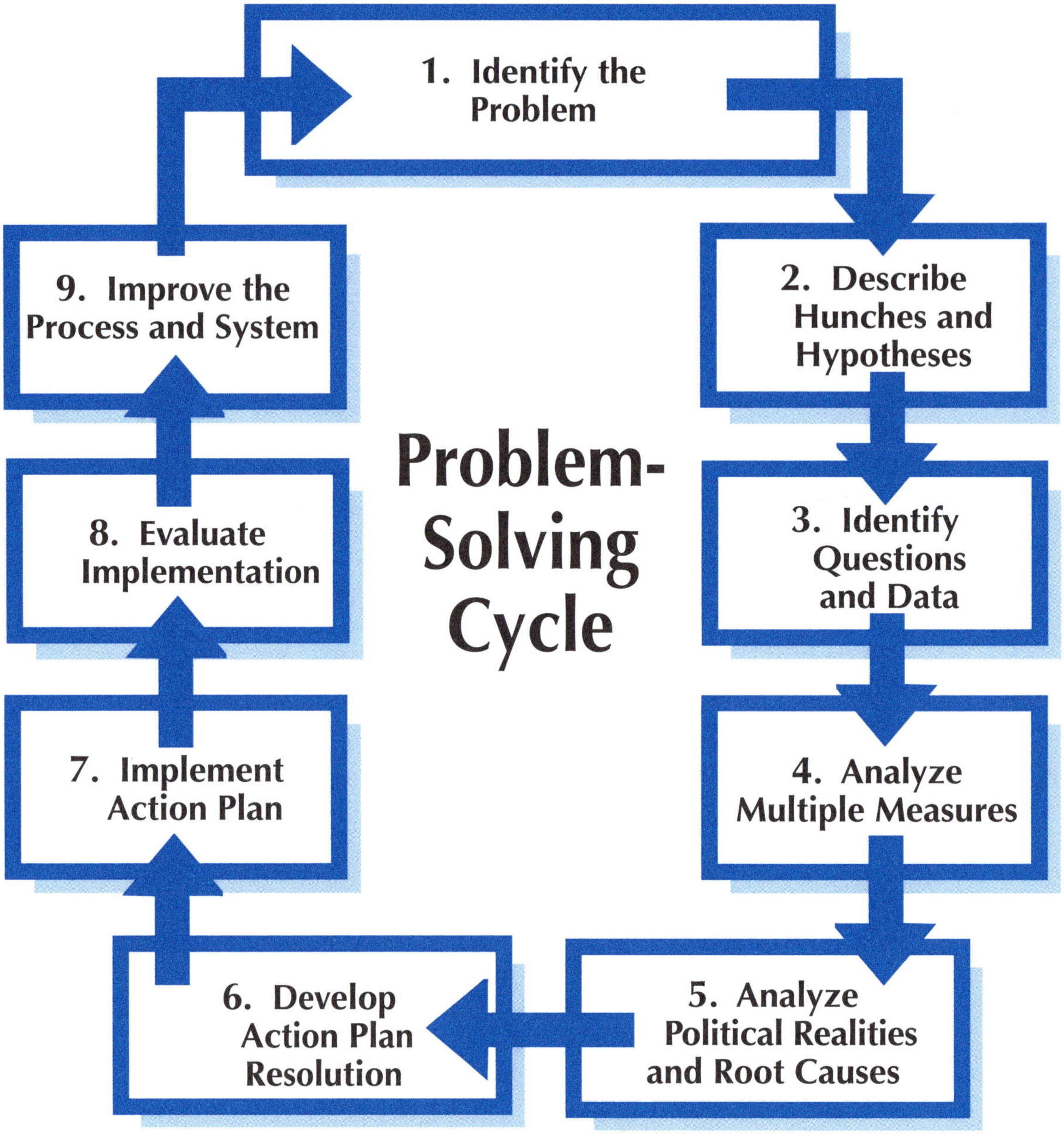

Figure F2
HUNCHES AND HYPOTHESES WORKSHEET

Identify the problem.
List hunches and hypotheses about why the problem exists.
1.
2.
3.
4.
5.
6.
7.
8.
9.
10.
11.
12.
13.
14.
15.
16.
17.
18.
19.
20.

Figure F3
QUESTIONS AND DATA NEEDED WORKSHEET

What questions do you need to answer to know more about the problem, and what data do you need to gather?

Questions	Data Needed

Figure F4
CAUSE AND EFFECT BUILT ON TEACHER BRAINSTORMING

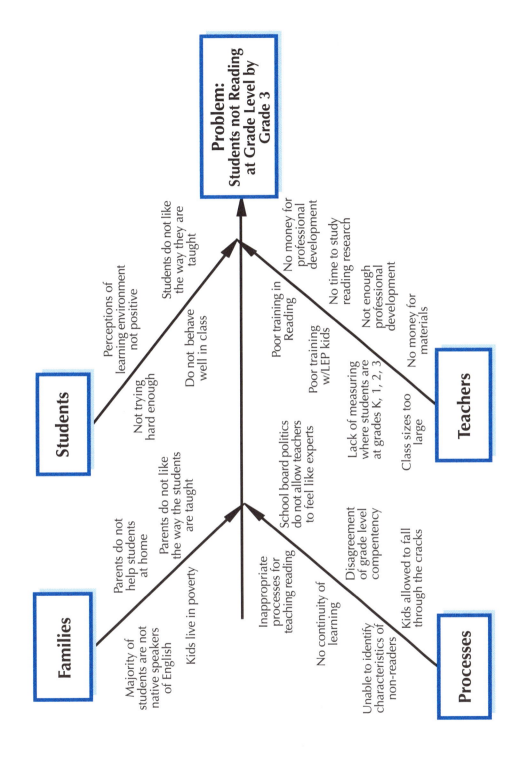

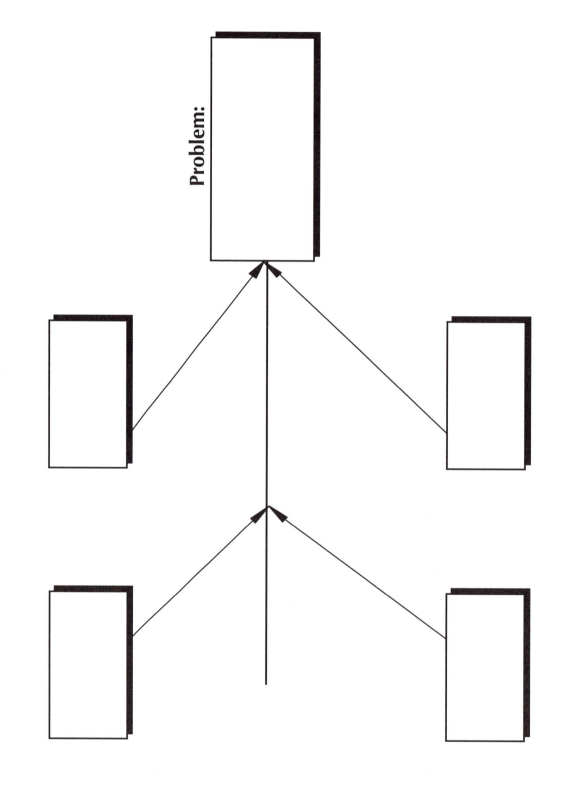

Figure F5
CAUSE AND EFFECT DIAGRAM

Appendix G

DEVELOPING A CONTINUOUS SCHOOL IMPROVEMENT PLAN ACTIVITY

HOW ARE WE GOING TO GET TO WHERE WE WANT TO BE?

The data profile helps us know *where we are now,* so we can create a plan of action that starts where we are, not where we think we are. Our mission, vision, and goal tells us *where we want to be,* and our gap analysis, and problem-solving cycle inform us of *how we got to where we are now.* Our objectives and implication commonalities provide insight into the strategies and activities that will need to take place in order to achieve the vision. All of these pieces are critical for determining *how we are going to get to where we want to be,* as documented in the school improvement plan.

The plan consists of these items:

- Baseline Data
- Goals
- Objectives
- Strategies to implement the vision
- Activities
- Persons responsible for the activities and strategies
- Measurement to know if the activities are being done
- Resources needed
- Due date
- Timeline

Figure G1 shows a flowchart graphic, illustrating the process of *Comprehensive Data Analysis to School Improvement Implementation.*

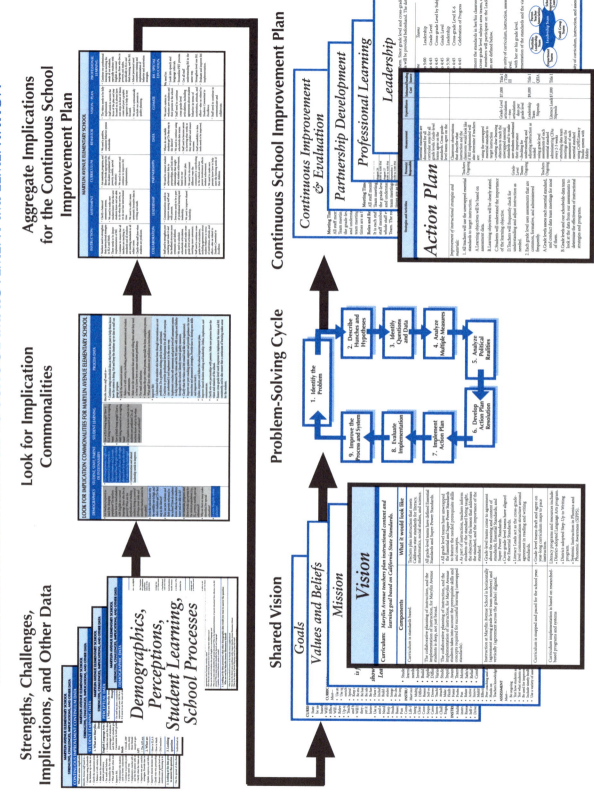

Figure G1
COMPREHENSIVE DATA ANALYSIS TO SCHOOL IMPROVEMENT IMPLEMENTATION

Purpose

The purpose of this activity is to take the shared vision to the action level.

Target Audience

A cross-representative team of school staff and school community.

Time

Overall, this planning activity will stretch over a couple of weeks and will go back and forth to full staff for review and revisions.

Materials

Post-it notes (3x5), chart pad paper, masking tape, markers, and a large amount of wall space.

Process Protocol

1. *Enroll a Planning Team*
   Enroll a representative group of staff members, not just those who think alike, and not just the leadership team. Include stakeholders such as parents, community, and students. This team will lead the development and draft the plan, then bring the plan back to the whole staff to review and suggest changes. Although five to eight people is a good size for a functioning team, the more change required of staff to implement the vision and plan, the more individuals need to be involved at the plan creation level.

2. *Review the Data*
   The action planning team reviews the multiple measures of data analysis (that the entire staff analyzed together) and that answers the question, *Where are we now?*

3. *Consider the School Vision*
   If the vision is done well, it will be very clear what needs to be put in the plan and implemented, with respect to *curriculum, instruction, assessment,* and *environment.*

4. *Perform a Gap Analysis*
   The action team compares the gap between where the school is now (the synthesis of the school results, strengths, challenges, and implications) and where they want the school to be in the future (the vision). This gap leads to a summary of areas needing improvement.

5. *Determine Contributing Causes*
   Analyze the underlying reasons for the problems or needs that emerge from the gap analysis. (See *Problem Solving Activity,* Appendix F.)

6. *Set Goals*
   Schoolwide goals need to be set with the whole staff before the actual writing of the plan commences. Goals are statements of

Process Protocol

the intended outcomes of the vision. They are stated in broad, general, abstract, and largely measurable terms. We should have only two or three school goals. Write each broad goal on the top of a piece of chart pad paper. Example: *All students will demonstrate continuous improvement in the areas of math, reading, and writing.*

6. *Identify Objectives*
Draft objectives that will close the gap for each of the goals. Objectives are goals that are redrafted in clearly tangible terms. Objective statements are narrow, specific, concrete, and measurable. When writing objectives, it is important to describe the intended results, rather than the process or means to accomplish them. Write each objective on a large post-it and place under the appropriate goal that is written on the chart pad paper.

Example: *The percentage of students achieving the reading comprehension standard will increase from 80 to 90 by Spring 2012.*

7. *Determine How the Objectives will be Measured*
Objectives are measurable statements. Determine what assessment tools and strategies will be used to know if the objectives are being met or have been met.

Example: *The percentage of students achieving the reading comprehension standard will increase from 80 to 90 by Spring 2012, as measured by the state reading assessment exam at each grade level.*

8. *Identify and Group Strategies to Achieve the Objectives*
Brainstorm and discuss different strategies to reach the objectives, making sure contributing causes of the gap(s) have been analyzed. Your comprehensive data analysis will provide aggregated commonalities to consider. Group the strategies under the objectives.

Example: *To increase the number of students reading on grade level by 10 percent, the strategies might include:*
   ♦ professional development in teaching reading for all teachers
   ♦ study how reading is successfully taught in other locations
   ♦ coach each other to implement new strategies
   ♦ determine how to implement standards at every grade level

9. *Actions Required to Implement the Strategies*
Below each strategy, list the actions that need to be accomplished to implement the strategy (i.e., *study the learning standards, study the research on reading, and increase reading time*).

10. *Arrange Strategies and Activities*
Begin to arrange the strategies and activities in chronological order. (Keep the version for later reference and fine-tune the plan in chronological summary form, starting with the action to be taken first.)

Process Protocol

11. *Determine How the Actions will be Evaluated*

    For each activity, determine how you will know if the action is being implemented and the impact of its implementation.

12. *Use a Planning Template*

    Using a planning template, label columns—strategy/action, person responsible, measurement, resources, due date, and timeline. Place the reorganized strategies and actions in the action column in a manner that is easiest for staff to utilize later. In the column next to each action, identify the person ultimately responsible for the action. Try not to use team names like Language Arts Action Team in the person responsible column. Accountability is most effective if the responsibility is delegated to an individual. Responsible persons determine how accountability reviews are conducted, and how to talk with one another about fostering and demonstrating accountability (example template is shown in Figure G2).

13. *Establish Due Date*

    In the column next to "person responsible," write in the due date. For each strategy or activity (depends on the topic and structure for implementation) determine when the activity absolutely must be completed. In the columns that represent months, weeks, and sometimes days, make notations that will indicate when each activity will begin and when it will be completed, by showing an "X" in the cell. Indicate the duration by marking a line between the "Xs" across the months.

14. *Determine Resources*

    Using the action plan, determine the resources required of each action and the costs. This budget, developed in conjunction with the action plan, will determine the financial feasibility of the actions for the year. Alterations are made simultaneously and balanced back and forth, while looking for items that can leverage other items. Dollars sometimes limit activities. School staff are often surprised, however, to discover that many times what they have to spend is equivalent to what they can do in a year's time. If the latter does not hold true, the school staff has important and specific information (i.e., the vision, action plan, and budget plan) to utilize in seeking additional support for their efforts. Note that the budget plan is a part of the action plan and that all school funds are used with the one resulting school plan. Everything in the school should be working toward that one plan and the school vision. All school money is a part of this plan. The planning team must have a clear understanding of all budget resources.

    Collapsing funding sources for implementing professional development is also possible. This strategy serves to focus professional development efforts, for example, and reinforces collaboration for design implementation and evaluation, because funds are utilized more wisely to serve a wider sector.

Process Protocol

15. *Evaluate*

    The whole continuous school improvement plan must be evaluated, with the vision as the target. This comprehensive evaluation will evaluate the parts and the whole of the plan to indicate if the goals, objectives, and strategies are leading to the attainment of the vision.

16. *Refine the Plan*

    With the first draft of the plan complete, review the elements and the big picture of the plan. Below are some guiding questions:

    ◆ Will this plan lead to improved student learning?

    ◆ Are the objectives about improved student learning for all students?

    ◆ What evidence do you need to know if the objectives are being met?

    ◆ Will the strategies lead to attainment of the objectives?

    ◆ Do the strategies address contributing causes?

    ◆ Are there strategies/actions that can be further collapsed?

    ◆ Will staff know what is expected of them?

    ◆ Does the plan include new learnings required of staff? If so, has training and support been incorporated for each area?

    ◆ Are the time frames realistic?

    ◆ How will you keep the ultimate goal of improved student learning for all students at the forefront of everything you do?

    ◆ How often will the plan and strategies be monitored?

    ◆ Whose job is it to monitor the implementation of the plan?

    ◆ How will new staff members learn about the plan?

17. *Report*

    Determine how the action plan will be documented, communicated, reported, and updated. Communicate progress toward the attainment of the school improvement goals and objectives in newsletters, staff bulletins, websites, and bulletin boards.

Comments to the Facilitator

This activity will take many iterations, and is done best with a small group, and reviewed by the larger group. Bring copies of the shared vision, values and beliefs, purpose, mission, goals, and aggregated implications of your data analysis work. You may want to post large versions of these items on chart paper around the room.

As groups identify actions, the actions will begin to collapse. For example, actions might include *professional development in integrated instruction, project-based learning,* and *hands-on math and science.* If considered separately, this professional development could stretch out over years. If considered comprehensively, the professional development could end up with one facilitator who could help staff translate these elements into grade-level implementation.

Figure G2
ACTION PLANNING FLOWCHART

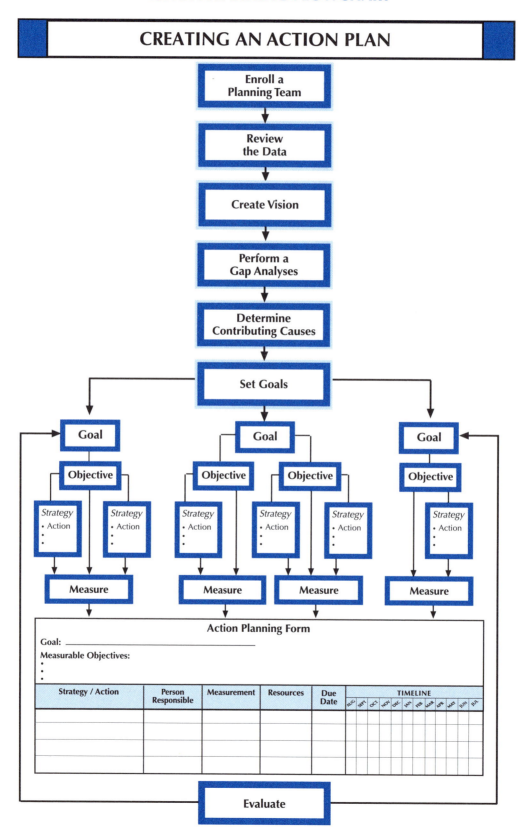

Appendix H

EVALUATING A PROGRAM OR PROCESS ACTIVITY

To measure and improve programs and processes, start by making a list of the programs and processes that are being implemented, or intended to be implemented, at your school. After listing each program or process, determine if there are some programs that need to be merged, improved, added, or deleted, and note implications for the continuous school improvement plan for each program or process intended to be implemented, complete Figure H1 to answer these questions.:

- What is the purpose of the program or process?
- How will you know the intent is being met? (What are the outcomes?)
- Who is the program/process intended to serve?
- Who is being served? Who is not being served?
- What would it look like when the program/process is fully implemented?
- How is implementation being measured? (Should it be measured differently?)
- To what degree is the program being implemented?
- What are the results?

Figure H2 is a completed example for RtI implemented in an elementary school.

To answer the question, *What would the program or process look like if it was fully implemented?*, have your staff create a process flowchart. Process flowcharts show how the program or process is intended to be implemented and/or how it is being implemented now, which is helpful for improving program/process implementation. (see Appendix I).

Purpose

The purpose of this activity is to create an evaluation design to determine the impact of an educational program or process, and to know how to improve the program or process.

Target Audience

School/School District Staff.

Time

A couple of hours.

Materials

Self-stick notes (3x5), chart pad paper, and markers. Reserve a room with big blank walls for this activity.

Process Protocol

1. Layout the intent, desired results, and objectives for the program (see *Measuring Programs and Processes Worksheet*, Figure H1).

2. Brainstorm how you will know the objectives are met.

3. Document whom the program is intended to serve.

4. Review data and document whom the program is serving and whom the program is not serving.

5. As a part of the evaluation, determine to what degree the program is being implemented. The group will need to brainstorm what the program would look like if fully implemented, and how the degree of implementation can be determined.

6. Measure the degree of implementation.

7. Describe how the implementation *is* being measured and how the implementation *should* be measured.

8. Document results of objectives and implementation.

9. You might need to regroup the questions as the group determines the method(s) that will provide this information (e.g., questionnaire, interview, student achievement data analysis).

Comments to the Facilitator

If you can complete the first four steps, you will have a good beginning of an evaluation. Steps 5 through 7, although more difficult, get to the deeper, true evaluation of the program/process.

This activity can be done before or after the program/process is designed. Of course, it would be best if the evaluation design was thought through as the program/process is being developed, so perceptions and implementation data can be captured before, during, and after program participation.

Figure H1
MEASURING PROGRAMS AND PROCESSES

PROGRAM/PROCESS:

PURPOSE		PARTICIPANTS		IMPLEMENTATION			RESULTS
What is the purpose of the program or process?	*How will you know the purpose is being met? (What are the outcomes?)*	*Who is the program/process intended to serve?*	*Who is being served? Who is not being served?*	*What will it look like when the program/process is fully implemented?*	*How is implementation being measured? (Should it be measured differently?)*	*To what degree is the program being implemented?*	*What are the results?*

NEXT STEPS:

Figure H2
MEASURING RtI EFFECTIVENSS AT MARYLIN AVENUE ELEMENTARY SCHOOL

PURPOSE		PARTICIPANTS		IMPLEMENTATION		RESULTS
What is the purpose of the program or process?	*How will you know the purpose is being met? (What are the outcomes?)*	*Who is the program/process intended to serve?*	*Who is being served? Who is not being served?*	*What would it look like when the program/process is fully implemented?*	*How is implementation being measured? (Should it be measured differently?)*	*What are the results?*
The intent of RtI at Marylin Avenue is to: Implement, in every classroom, quality, research-based instruction and assessment strategies that address students' needs and differences, and are based on essential learning standards. Maximize *all* students' learning. Reduce behavior problems. Ensure that *all* students are primarily educated in the general education environment, with access to the general education content, materials, and expectations. Ensure the appropriate identification of students with special needs.	When RtI is implemented as intended, instructional coherence and a continuum of learning that makes sense for all students will be evident. What students learn in one grade level will build on what they learned in the previous grade level: Individual student achievement results will improve each year. All students will be proficient in all areas. No students will need to be retained. Progress monitoring and common formative assessments, conducted within the classroom setting, during the school day, will be utilized to identify struggling students and why they are struggling. Interventions matched to student needs will result in student learning increases for all students. Number of office referrals will be minimal. Students will not be placed in special education for the wrong reasons, such as teachers wanting students out of the classroom because of behavior or lack of learning response, poor test-taking skills, second language learning/ English language proficiency levels not having received high-quality instruction or adequate interventions. Attendance will improve.	RtI is intended to serve all students within the general education environment. When a student has difficulty mastering specific skills, the classroom teacher will adjust instruction in order to assist that child's learning. Classroom teachers, with support from others, will provide additional intensive instruction in small groups for a specified period of time, and then one-on-one.	The California Standards Test (CST) will show which students are proficient and which students are not proficient. Progress monitoring will show which students are and are not making progress, before, during, and after interventions.	When all teachers at Marylin Avenue are implementing RtI as designed by staff, they will: Identify essential student learning standards, in their grade level teams. Create/adopt assessments of the standards, in their grade level teams. Administer agreed-upon assessments in their classrooms to understand what students know and do not know in order to focus their instructional strategies to meet the needs of all students. Provide instruction adjusted to student needs. Assess students every three weeks. Review assessment results with grade level team members. Provide additional instruction and interventions for the students who are not proficient. Provide regular grade level instruction to all students. Only identify students for special education when insufficient progress has been demonstrated. Ensure that students who are proficient continue to grow.	The degree to which teachers are implementing RtI is being measured through the classroom observation tool, and through the results of common formative assessments. These measures are discussed in grade level meetings. Classroom observations show that teachers are implementing the components of RtI. Data are used with the RtI flowcharts to understand if the system is working as intended.	CST results show there is instructional coherence in the school in some subjects. Most students are making the equivalent of one year's growth, or better, on state proficiency tests. There is a reduction of retentions. The percentage of the school population identified for special education services has decreased and does not exceed state or national averages. Students, teachers, and parents feel that students can do the work and that they are learning at adequate rates to prepare them for the future. Student absences were down this year. Teacher morale is good, but lower in 2010. Staff and parents feel the school has a good public image. Teachers are better at meeting needs of the lowest performing students, as measured by progress monitoring assessments.

Appendix I

FLOWCHARTING SCHOOL PROCESSES ACTIVITY

School processes data are important for continuous improvement because they are what produce school and classroom results. If different results are desired, processes must be changed. To change processes, staffs must—

- Be clear on what is being implemented.
- Study the results of these processes over time.
- Understand the relationship among processes, results, mission, vision, and actions.
- Study the research on effective processes.
- Create plans to achieve different results.

Purpose	The goal of this activity is to clarify what is being done now, so that all staff can understand how they are getting current results, and to determine what needs to change to get different results. A flowchart allows everyone to see the major steps in a process, in sequence, and then evaluate the difference between the theoretical and actual, or actual and desired.
Target Audience	School staff.
Time	Usually less than one hour (set aside enough time with staff to do this well and to share).
Materials	Copies of the flowcharting symbols, paper, and pencils for everyone; chart pad paper, masking tape, tacks, markers. Student achievement data if staff are not already aware of achievement strengths and weaknesses.

Process Protocol	1. Ask staff to choose a process that needs to improve.
	2. Direct them to build "the flow" of how they are teaching students now, using the flowcharting tools.
	3. Ask staff to: ♦ Define the beginning of the process being charted. ♦ Decide on the level of detail to be used. ♦ Determine the major steps in the process and their sequence. ♦ Label each step in the process. ♦ Verify the flowchart. Is it clear?
	4. Evaluate. Compare the charted version of the process to the "desired" flow.
	5. Create the desired flow after reviewing *What do we want out of this process?*
Comments to the Facilitator	There are variations of this activity that give staff a visual pathway for understanding current processes. The first is to show the flow for staff. The second is to show the work process flow for students. Let staff determine which will work best for them.
	Remember, if you want different results, you must change the processes that create the results. One approach to assessing the impact of school processes is to study the resulting flowcharts and note the discrepancies between currently implemented processes and desired processes. (Three examples, in Figures I1 through I3, follow to help participants see the possibilities.)

Figure I1

EXAMPLE GRADE 3 READING RESPONSE TO INTERVENTION (RtI)

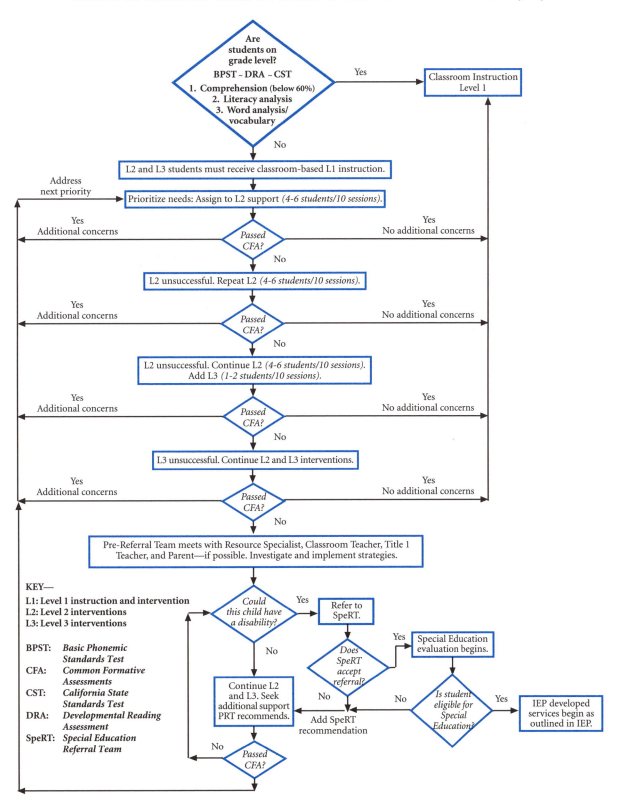

Figure 12
EXAMPLE HIGH SCHOOL PROCESS FLOWCHART

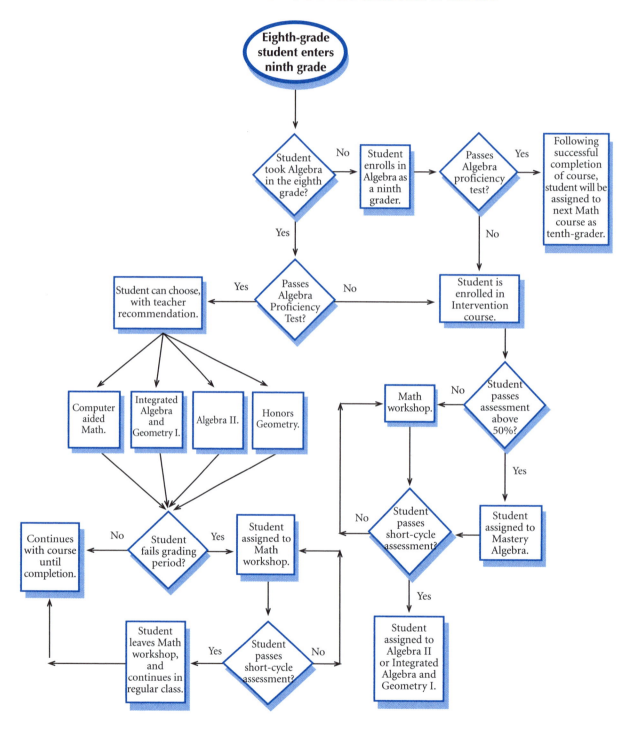

Figure 13
THE PROCESS OF USING DATA IN
PROFESSIONAL LEARNING COMMUNITIES

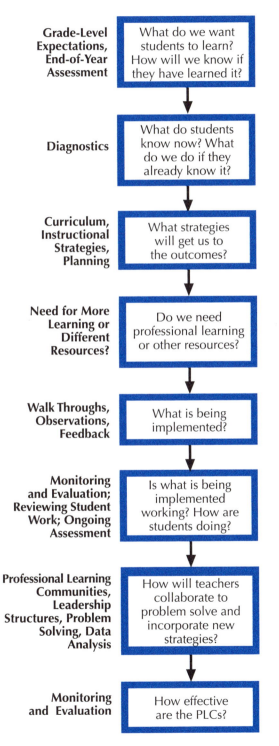

Grade-Level Expectations, End-of-Year Assessment — What do we want students to learn? How will we know if they have learned it?

Diagnostics — What do students know now? What do we do if they already know it?

Curriculum, Instructional Strategies, Planning — What strategies will get us to the outcomes?

Need for More Learning or Different Resources? — Do we need professional learning or other resources?

Walk Throughs, Observations, Feedback — What is being implemented?

Monitoring and Evaluation; Reviewing Student Work; Ongoing Assessment — Is what is being implemented working? How are students doing?

Professional Learning Communities, Leadership Structures, Problem Solving, Data Analysis — How will teachers collaborate to problem solve and incorporate new strategies?

Monitoring and Evaluation — How effective are the PLCs?

In this PLC structure, the learning community teams—

1. Review what they want students to know and be able to do, and how they will know when the students have learned it.

2. Assess what students know now.

3. Determine the best strategies to help students reach those end-of-course/end of-year expectations.

4. Given #2 and #3 above, identify professional learning and other resources that will help teachers ensure all students' learning.

5. Observe each other and provide feedback, knowing that they can only improve with practice and feedback.

6. Review teaching observation feedback with the student assessment results.

7. Collaborate to determine what needs to change to get different results through problem-solving strategies and deeper analysis.

8. Finally, evaluate the PLC structure to ensure that its intention of improving teaching and learning is achieved.

REFERENCES AND RESOURCES

Ainsworth, L. (2006). *Common formative assessments: How to connect standards-based instruction and assessment.* Englewood, CO: Advanced Learning Press.

Ainsworth, L. (2003). *Power standards: Identifying the standards that matter the most.* Englewood, CO: Advanced Learning Press.

Ainsworth, L. (2003). *Unwrapping the standards: A simple process to make standards manageable.* Englewood, CO: Advanced Learning Press.

Allington, R. L. (2009). *What really matters in response to intervention: Research-based designs.* Boston, MA: Allyn & Bacon.

Allington, R. L. (2006). Research and the three tier model. *Reading Today,* 23(5), 20.

Allington, R. L. (2002). Research on reading/learning disability interventions. In A. E. Farstrup & S. Samuels (Eds.), *What research says about reading instruction* (3rd ed., pp. 261-290).

American Evaluation Association. *http://www.eval.org*

Beginning Phonic Skills Test (BPST). *http://www.sjcoertac.org/docs/BPST*

Bender, W. N. (2009). *Beyond the RtI pyramid: Solutions for the first years of implementation.* Bloomington, IN: Solution Tree Press.

Bernhardt, V. L. (2009). *Data, data everywhere: Bringing all the data together for continuous school improvement.* Larchmont, NY: Eye on Education.

Bernhardt, V. L., & Geise, B. J. (2009). *From questions to actions: Using questionnaire data for continuous school improvement.* Larchmont, NY: Eye on Education.

Bernhardt, V. L. (2006). *Using data to improve student learning in school districts.* Larchmont, NY: Eye on Education.

Bernhardt, V. L. (2005). *Using data to improve student learning in high schools.* Larchmont, NY: Eye on Education.

Bernhardt, V. L. (2004). *Data analysis for continuous school improvement* (2nd Ed.). Larchmont, NY: Eye on Education.

Bernhardt, V. L. (2004). *Using data to improve student learning in middle schools.* Larchmont, NY: Eye on Education.

Bernhardt, V. L. (2003). *Using data to improve student learning in elementary schools.* Larchmont, NY: Eye on Education.

Bernhardt, V. L. (2001). *The school portfolio toolkit: A planning, implementation, and evaluation guide for continuous school improvement.* Larchmont, NY: Eye on Education.

Black, P. J., & Wiliam, D. (1998). *Inside the black box: Raising standards through classroom assessment.* Phi Delta Kappan, 80(2), 139-148. Available from: *http://www.pdkintl.org/kappan/kbla9810.htm.*

Bransford, J. D., & Stein, B. S. (1993). *The IDEAL problem solver* (2nd Ed.). New York, NY: Freeman.

Brown-Chidsey, R., & Steege, M. W. (2005). *Response to intervention: Principles and strategies for effective practice.* New York, NY: The Guilford Press.

Buffman, A., Mattos, M., & Weber, C. (2008). *Pyramid response to intervention: RTI, professional learning communities, and how to respond when kids don't learn.* Bloomington, IN: Solution Tree Press.

Calkins, L. M. (2000). *The art of teaching reading.* Boston, MA: Allyn & Bacon.

Calkins, L. M. (1994). *The art of teaching writing.* Portsmouth, NH: Heinemann.

Christ, T. J., Burns, M. K., & Ysseldyke, J. E. (November 2005). Conceptual confusion within response-to-intervention vernacular: Clarifying meaningful differences. *NASP Communiqué,* 34(3).

Christenson, S. L. (2001). *Schools and families: Creating essential connections for learning.* New York, NY: Guilford Press.

Comprehension, Accuracy, Fluency, and Expanding Vocabulary (CAFÉ). *http://www.thedailycafe.com*

Cooperative Learning. *http://edtech.kennesaw.edu/intech/cooperativelearning.htm*

Council for Exceptional Children. *http://www.cec.org*

Coyne, M. D., Kame'enui, E. J., & Simmons, D. C. (May/June 2004). Improving beginning reading instruction and intervention for students with LD: Reconciling "all" with "each." *Journal of Learning Disabilities,* 37(3), pp. 231-239.

Cummings, K. D., Atkins, T., Allison, R., & Cole, C. (March/April 2008) Response to intervention: Investigating the new role of special educators. *Teaching Exceptional Children,* 40(4), pp. 24-31.

Cunningham, P., & Cunningham, J. (2010). *What really matters in writing: Research-based practices across the elementary curriculum.* Boston, MA: Allyn & Bacon.

Data Director. *http://www.riversidepublishing.com/datadirector*

Designing schoolwide programs. (March 2006). Non-regulatory Guidance, U.S. Dept. of Education. Retrieved from *http://www.ed.gov/policy/elsec/guid/designingswpguid.doc*

Denton, C. A., Fletcher, J. M., Anthony, J. L., & Francis, D. J. (2006). An evaluation of intensive intervention for students with persistent reading difficulties. *Journal of Learning Disabilities,* 39, 447-466.

Developmental Reading Assessment (DRA). *http://www.pearsonschool.com*

Dorn, L. J., and Henderson, S. C. (2010). A Comprehensive Intervention Model: A Systems Approach to Response to Intervention (Chapter 4). *Successful approaches to RtI: Collaborative practices for improving K-12 literacy.* Newark, DE: International Reading Association.

DuFour, R., DuFour, R., Eaker, R., & Many, T. (2006). *Learning by doing: A handbook for professional learning communities at work.* Bloomington, IN: Solution Tree Press.

DuFour, R., DuFord, R., & Eaker, R. (2004). *Whatever it takes: How professional learning communities respond with kids don't learn.* Bloomington, IN: Solution Tree Press.

Education for the Future parent questionnaire. Retrieved from *http://eff.csuchico.edu*

Education for the Future staff questionnaire. Retrieved from *http://eff.csuchico.edu*

Education for the Future student questionnaire. Retreived from *http://eff.csuchico.edu*

Explicit Direct Instruction (EDI). *http://www.dataworks.ed-com*

Fisher, D., & Frey, N. (2010). *Enhancing RtI: How to ensure success with effective classroom instruction and intervention.* Alexandria, VA: Association for Supervision and Curriculum Development (ASCD).

Fuchs, D., & Deshler, D. D. (2007). What we need to know about responsiveness to intervention (and shouldn't be afraid to ask). *Learning Disabilities Research & Practice,* 22(2), pp. 129–136.

Fuchs, D., Devery, M., Morgan, P. L., & Young, C. L. (2003). Responsiveness to intervention: Definitions, evidence, and implications for the learning disabilities construct. *Learning Disabilities Research & Practice,* 18(3), pp. 157–171.

Fuchs, D., & Fuchs, L. S. (November 2009). Responsiveness to intervention: Multilevel assessment and instruction as early intervention and disability identification. *The Reading Teacher,* 63(3), pp. 250–252.

Fuchs, D., & Fuchs, L. S. (May/June 2007). A model for implementing responsiveness to intervention. *Teaching Exceptional Children.* Arlington, VA: Council for Exceptional Children.

Fuchs, D., & Fuchs, L. S. (2006). A framework for building capacity for responsiveness to intervention. *School Psychology Review,* 35(4), pp. 621-626.

Fuchs, D., & Fuchs, L. S. (January/February/March 2006). Introduction to response to intervention: What, why, and how valid is it? *The Reading Teacher,* 63(3), pp. 250–252.

Fuchs, D., & Fuchs, L. S. (2006). Introduction to response to intervention: What, why, and how valid is it? *Reading Research Quarterly,* 41(1), 93-99.

Fullan, M. (2010). *All systems go: The change imperative for whole system reform.* Thousand Oaks, CA: Corwin Press.

Fullan, M. (2009). *Motion leadership: The skinny on becoming change savvy.* Thousand Oaks, CA: Corwin Press.

Fullan, M. (2007). *The new meaning of educational change* (4th Ed.). New York, NY: Teachers College Press.

Grigorenko, E. L. (March/April 2009). Dynamic assessment and response to intervention: Two sides of one coin. *Journal of Learning Disabilities,* 42(2), pp. 111-132.

Grigorenko, E. L., & Hollenbeck, A. F. (2007). From IDEA to implementation: A discussion of foundational and future responsiveness-to-intervention research. *Learning Disabilities Research & Practice,* 22(2), pp. 137–146.

Guided Language Acquisition Design (GLAD). *http://www.projectglad.com*

Guskey, T. R. (1999). *Evaluating professional development.* Thousand Oaks, CA: Corwin Press.

Hall, S. L. (2008). *Implementing response to intervention.* Thousand Oaks, CA: Corwin Press.

Hargreaves, A., & Shirley, D. L. (2009). *The fourth way: The inspiring future for educational change.* Thousand Oaks, CA: Corwin Press.

Hattie, J., & Timperley, H. (2007). The power of feedback. *Review of Education Research,* 77, pp. 81-112.

Heads Together. *http://www.teachervision.fen.com/group-work/cooperative-learning/48538.html*

Hill, P., & Crévola, C. (1998). Evaluation of a whole school approach to prevention and early intervention in literacy. *Journal of Education for Students Placed at Risk,* 3(2), 133-157. Lawrence Erlbaum Associates, Inc.

Howard, M. (2009). *RtI from all sides: What every teacher needs to know.* Portsmouth, NH: Heinemann.

Jennings, M. J. (2008). *Before the special education referral: Leading intervention teams.* Thousand Oaks, CA: Corwin Press.

Jenson, E. (2009). *Teaching with poverty in mind: What being poor does to kids' brains and what schools can do about it.* Alexandria, VA: Association for Supervision and Curriculum Development (ASCD).

Jimerson, S. R., Burns, M. K., & VanDerHeyden, A. M. (2007). *Response to intervention: The science and practice of assessment and intervention.* New York, NY: Springer Science+Business Media.

Johnson, E., Mellard, D. F., Fuchs, D., & McKnight, M. A. (2006). *Responsiveness to intervention (RTI): How to do it.* Lawrence, KS: National Research Center on Learning Disabilities.

Johnson, R. S., & LaSalle, R. A. (2010). *Data strategies to uncover and eliminate hidden inequities: The wallpaper effect.* Thousand Oaks, CA: Corwin Press.

Kaufman, M. J., & Lewis, L. M. Confusing each with all: A policy warning. In R. Gallimore, L. P. Bernheimer, D. L. MacMillan, D. L. Speece, & S. Vaughn (Eds.), (1999). *Developmental perspectives on children with high-incidence disabilities,* pp. 223–244. Mahwah, NJ: Lawrence Erlbaum Associates.

Killion, J. (2008). Assessing impact: *Evaluating staff development* (2nd Ed.). Thousand Oaks, CA: Corwin Press.

Literacy Studio. *http://library.uwf.edu/About/.../DigitalLiteracyStudioProposal.pdf*

Marsh, J. A., Pane, J. F., & Hamilton, L. S. (2006). Making sense of data-driven decision making in education. Evidence from Recent RAND Research. *RAND Occasional Papers.* Retreived from: *http://www.rand.org/pubs/occasional_papers/2006/RAND_OP170.pdf*

Marzano, R. J. (August 2004). *Building background knowledge for academic achievement: Research on what works in schools.* Alexandria, VA: Association for Supervision and Curriculum Development (ASCD).

Marzano, R., McNulty, B., & Waters, T. (2005). *School leadership that works: From research to results.* Alexandria, VA: Association for Supervision and Curriculum Development (ASCD).

Marzano, R., Pickering, D., & Pollock, J. (2001). *Classroom instruction that works: Researched-based strategies for increasing student achievement.* Alexandria, VA: Association for Supervision and Curriculum Development (ASCD).

Mastropieri, M., & Scruggs, T. (2005). *Effective instruction for special education* (3rd Ed.). Upper Saddle River, NJ: Pearson Allyn & Bacon.

McCarney, S. B., & Wunderlich, K. C. (2006). *Pre-referral intervention manual* (PRIM) (3rd Ed.). Houten, Netherlands: HES.

Mellard, D. F., & Johnson, E. S. (2007). *RTI: A practioner's guide to implementing response to intervention.* Thousand Oaks, CA: Corwin Press.

Miller, D. (2008). *Teaching with intention: Defining beliefs, aligning practice, taking action.* Portland, ME: Stenhouse Publishers.

Moss, C. M., & Brookhart, S. M. (2009). *Advancing formative assessment in every classroom: A guide for instructional leaders.* Alexandria, VA: Association for Supervision and Curriculum Development (ASCD).

National Association of State Directors of Special Education. (2006) *Response to intervention: NASDSE and CASE white paper on RtI.* Alexandria: VA: NASDSE, Inc. Retrieved from *http://www.nasdse.org*

National Association of State Directors of Special Education. Publications include *RtI Blueprints for Implementation for district and school.* Retrieved from *http://www.nasdse.org*

National Center for Learning Disabilities. *http://www.ncld.org*

National Center on Response to Intervention (several documents and information). *http://www.rti4success.org*

National Research Center on Learning Disabilities. *http://www.nrcld.org*

Northouse, P. G. (2009). *Leadership: Theory and practice.* Thousand Oaks, CA: Sage Publications.

Open Court Reading. *http://www.opencourtresources.com/*

Popham, W. J. (2010). *Everything school leaders need to know about assessment.* Thousand Oaks, CA: Corwin Press.

Popham, W. J. (2008). *Transformative assessment.* Thousand Oaks, CA: Corwin Press.

Promoting Instructional Coherence (from research conducted by SEDL under a contract with *Regional Education Laboratory*). Retrieved from *http://www.sedl.org/expertise/historical/pic.html*

Read Naturally. *http://www.readnaturally.com*

Reeves, D. (2006). *The learning leader: How to focus school improvement for better results.* Englewood, CO: Advanced Learning Press.

Reeves, D. (2002). *The daily disciplines of leadership.* San Francisco, CA: Jossey-Bass.

RtI Action Network, a program of the National Center for Learning Disabilities (resources and information). *http://www.rtinetwork.org*

Searchable bibliography database for resources on *Educational Reform, Coherent Teaching Practices, and Improved Student Learning.* Retrieved from *http://www.sedl.org/pubs/pic02/bibintro.html*

Searle, M. (2010). *What Every School Leader Needs to Know About RtI.* Alexandria, VA: Association for Supervision and Curriculum Development (ASCD).

Senge, P. M. (2006). *The fifth discipline: The art & practice of the learning organization.* New York, NY: The Crown Publishing Group.

Shinn, M. R. (2007). Identifying students at risk, monitoring performance, and determining eligibility within response to intervention: Research on educational need and benefit from academic intervention. *School Psychology Review, 36*(4).

Shores, C. (2009). *A comprehensive RtI model: Integrating behavioral and academic interventions.* Thousand Oaks, CA: Corwin Press.

Shores, C, & Chester, K. (2009). *Using RtI for school improvement: Raising every student's achievement scores.* Council for Exceptional Children. Thousand Oaks, CA: Corwin Press.

Simmons, D. C., & Kameenui, E. J. (March 1996). A focus on curriculum design: When children fail. *Focus on Exceptional Children,* 28(7).

Simmons, D. C., Kuykendall, K., King, K., Cornachione, C., & Kameenui, E. J. (March 2000). Implementation of a schoolwide reading improvement model: No one ever told us it would be this hard! *Learning Disabilities Research and Practice,* 15(2), pp.92-100.

Smith-Mercier, J. L., Fien, H., Basaraba, D., & Travers, P. (May/June 2009). Planning, evaluating, and improving tiers of support in beginning reading. *Teaching Exceptional Children,* pp. 16-22.

Step Up to Writing. *http://www.cambiumlearning.com*

Stiggins, R. J. (2007). *An introduction to student-involved assessment for learning* (5th Ed.). Upper Saddle River, NJ: Prentice Hall.

Stiggins, R. J., Arter, J. A., Chappuis, J., & Chappuis, S. (2009). *Classroom assessment for student learning: Doing it right—using it well.* Boston, MA: Allyn & Bacon.

Strickland, C. A. (2009). *Professional development for differentiating instruction: An ASCD action tool.* Alexandria, VA: Association for Supervision and Curriculum Development (ASCD).

Systematic Instruction in Phoneme Awareness, Phonics, and Sight Words (SIPPS). *http://www.devstu.org/sipps*

Tomlinson, C. (2004). *How to differentiate instruction in mixed ability classrooms* (2nd Ed.). Alexandria, VA: Association for Supervision and Curriculum Development (ASCD).

Wright, J. (2007). *RTI toolkit: A practical guide for schools.* Port Chester, NY: National Professional Resources; Dude Publishing.

INDEX